A Howlin' Wind

First published in Great Britain in 2011 by Soundcheck Books LLP, 88 Northchurch Road, London, N1 3NY

Copyright John Blaney ©2011

This edition published by Paper Jukebox © 2023

All rights reserved. No part of this book may be reproduced or transmitted in any form or by any means, electronic or mechanical, including photocopying, recording, or any information storage and retrieval system without permission in writing from the publisher.

This book is sold subject to the condition that it shall not, by way of trade or otherwise, be lent, resold, hired out or otherwise circulated without the publisher's prior consent in any form of binding or cover other than that in which it is published and without a similar condition being imposed on the subsequent purchaser.

We've made every effort to fulfil requirements regarding the reproduction of copyright material. The authors and publishers will happily rectify any omissions at the earliest opportunity.

A Howlin' Wind
Pub Rock and the Birth of New Wave

John Blaney

Paper Jukebox

Contents

VI	Acknowledgements
X	Introduction
13	Chapter 1 Amphetamines, Jean-Paul Sartre And John Lee Hooker
21	Chapter 2 Spotty Mods
30	Chapter 3 The Shape Of Things To Come
38	Chapter 4 The Buddhas Of Suburbia
43	Chapter 5 Shorter, Sharper And More Interesting
51	Chapter 6 It All Depends Which Side Of The Bar You're On
56	Chapter 7 Putting The Bomp In
63	Chapter 8 Nervous On The Road
68	Chapter 9 Leery, Beery, Gruff and Sneery
76	Chapter 10 If It's Clean ... It's Not Laundry
86	Chapter 11 Glimpse Number Two For The Reader
92	Chapter 12 Too Much Monkee Business
97	Chapter 13 A Present ... For The Future
103	Chapter 14 It's Hello From Us ... And Goodbye From Them
109	Chapter 15 Naughty Rhythms
113	Chapter 16 Taxi To The Terminal Zone
117	Chapter 17 Teenage Depression
122	Chapter 18 A Howlin' Wind
133	Chapter 19 There's A Riot Going On
137	Chapter 20 Something's Going To Happen In The Winter
141	Chapter 21 Letsgetabitarockin'
146	Chapter 22 If It Ain't Stiff
152	Chapter 23 Here Comes The Weekend
158	Chapter 24 I'm Not Interested That You're Interested
164	Chapter 25 Surfing On A New Wave
167	Chapter 26 Sneakin' Suspicion
171	Chapter 27 Cider Bottles At Dawn
180	Chapter 28 Old Wave, New Wave, No Wave
187	Chapter 29 The Tommy Cooper Dialectic
195	Chapter 30 Crawling To The USA
204	Chapter 31 If We Make It, You've Got It Made
218	Where Are They Now?
224	Discography
233	Sources
241	Index

Acknowledgements

My sincere thanks go to Jon 'Mojo' Mills for getting the ball rolling by publishing my article about Brinsley Schwarz in *Shindig!* magazine, Ian Gomm for his help, generosity and good humour, for putting me in touch with 'the boys' and providing photos from his personal archive. Thanks to Mark Wirtz, Martin Belmont, Dave Robinson, Brinsley Schwarz, Billy Rankin, Bob Andrews and John Steele for consenting to being interviewed, their time and help. Thanks to Ian Whiteman for helping with The Action timeline, Will Birch for his tips, pointers and kind permission to cite from his book *No Sleep Till Canvey Island*. Thanks to Pete Frame, Paul Kendall and Andy Childs for their permission to cite from articles published in *ZigZag*. Thanks to Mark Sanders and Matt Hemmingsen for the Brinsley Schwarz cuttings, photos and memorabilia. Sincere thanks to Kris Needs and Mike O'Connor for permission to use photos and material from the Friars Official website http://www.aylesburyfriars.co.uk/. Thanks to Mike Halpern for his contacts. Stuart Shea and Ian Mundwyler get a round of applause for their proofreading skills. And last but not least, thanks to Mitch Cantor.

For Charlie Gillett, Lee Brilleaux, John Mellor, Sean Tyla, Barrie Masters, Martin Stone and Wilko Johnson.

Introduction

It's mid-1970s London. The sound of a band at full throttle spills enticingly from the inside of an imposing Victorian pub and onto an anonymous north London street. Stepping inside, you're hit by a blast of hot air and loud music, and the combined scents of stale tobacco, smelly overflowing toilets and beer-saturated carpets that the soles of your shoes stick to. As you make your way through the packed bar for a pint of warm, flat Watney's Red Barrel you pause to notice that the orange and chocolate decor has been enhanced with a few gig posters in an attempt to make it look more like a music venue than the back room of a pub. At one end of the large, square room, on what passes for a stage, there's an anonymous looking five-piece beat group decked out in the kind of checked shirts and drainpipe jeans that went out of fashion when the Who began writing rock operas. They're pounding out a mix of original songs and cover versions derived from the same R&B building blocks that inspired the beat boomers a decade earlier. There's room enough in front of the low stage to dance, or seating at the side if you prefer to finish your pint, which cost you all of 20p (they always stick a couple of pence on a pint when there's a band on). In keeping with the bleak economic climate of the time, everything from the venue to the band has been stripped down to its basic elements. This is pure, good-time music. This is Pub Rock!

Based in London, with significant input from Southend-on-Sea (just down the A13 as Billy Bragg was to observe in the '80s), pub rock was a geographical circuit of boozers that provided a training ground for newcomers looking for a break and a means of employment, or for old hands trying to avoid a day job. An American group, Eggs Over Easy, got the ball rolling at the Tally Ho in Kentish Town. Then former Jimi Hendrix road manager, Dave Robinson, ran with the idea and began booking groups into other London pubs. Pretty soon he'd built a live circuit that included the Lord Nelson, the Kensington, the Windsor Castle, the Cock Tavern, the Hope and Anchor, and the Nashville. This was a 'north of Regent's Park' movement as the late Roy Carr noted in the *NME*. In one of life's little ironies, the best pub rock nowadays can be found south of the river at the Half Moon in Putney or the Windmill in Brixton.

On most nights of the week you could experience an eclectic mix of music ranging from hard-nosed R&B (Dr Feelgood, Kilburn and The High Roads, Ducks Deluxe, Bees Make Honey) to Soul/Funk (Ace and Kokomo) and Country Rock (Brinsley Schwarz, Kursaal Flyers, Chilli Willi and the Red Hot Peppers). As stylistically diverse as the music was, those working the circuit had a shared sense of purpose and a common goal. It wasn't so much what these groups liked that bound them together as what they didn't like. And what they didn't like was the mainstream music business.

Brinsley Schwarz were the victims of one of the most disastrous attempts to hype a group in rock history. Totally disillusioned by the experience, Brinsley Schwarz and their manager, Dave Robinson, began rebuilding their career in the only way they knew - their way. Inspired by Eggs Over Easy, they went back to basics and into the pubs. Out went the Marshall stacks and big PA and in came small Fender combos and a custom made PA hand-built by the group themselves. Lengthy songs about mayflies and beauty queens were ditched in favour of short, sharp, perfectly constructed songs that drew on Country Rock, R&B and Sixties Pop. Moving into a large communal house in north London with their wives, girlfriends, children and trailblazing manager they got their act together and emerged with a sound and attitude that defined the scene.

Forty miles along the river Thames in the seaside resort of Southend, another cabal of like-minded musicians were desperate to quit their day jobs and turn pro. Dr Feelgood, the Kursaal Flyers and Eddie and the Hot Rods all headed to London and the pub rock circuit in search of regular gigs and recording contracts. Like their London-based counterparts, they connected with audiences looking for something other than the lightweight fluff of Gary Glitter's glam movement or the heavyweight ponderings of Emerson, Lake and Palmer and other purveyors of stodgy prog rock. Dr Feelgood quickly established its commercial potential but managed to keep its outsider edge while playing footsie with the mainstream. It did something few other pub rock groups managed; it crossed over and appealed to an emergent generation of disaffected teens and teenybopper queens. Dr Feelgood was the first sign that something significant was stirring on the streets; an indicator of the changes to come. The Feelgoods were at the head of a symbolic generational conflict that, a year after their *Stupidity* album topped the album charts, would explode across the country.

Even with a hangover there were those who could see something was happening. But what? Eddie and the Hot Rods took what Dr Feelgood had started and moved it up a gear. Playing faster, harder and with a ferocity as yet unseen, they were punk with a small 'p' but were often confused with groups with a claim to be Punk with a capital 'P'. This was simply because no one had a handle on what 'Punk' was or where to position the Hot Rods. Until the music press began to wrestle with its taxonomy, punk was as fluid as the gob running down Johnny Rotten's face.

Initially, punk and new wave were interchangeable terms that described a kind of attitudinal music that emerged during 1976. Punk was a subculture, of which music and fashion played an important part. New wave was always a more nebulous term that could describe everyone from Graham Parker to the Sex Pistols. For the purposes of this book, I'm using new wave to describe groups that emerged from the pub rock scene alongside the punk upstarts. Graham Parker and the Rumour, Elvis Costello and the Attractions and Ian Dury and the Blockheads shared an outsider attitude, but framed it in more melodic and forward-looking terms than their punk counterparts. New wave tended toward lyrical complexity, had a more polished production and delighted in playing stylistic games. To be new wave was to be modern, perhaps post-modern; it stood apart from the mainstream, it was to be different but not in a threatening way that might limit its commercial appeal.

British new wave might have disappeared without trace had it not been for two rock 'n' roll pirates who delighted in surfing its rocky waters. Dave Robinson and Jake Riviera both managed pub rock groups before setting their sights on reshaping the music business in their own image. Drawing on a pool of pub rock failures, they formed a management company (Advancedale) and an independent record label (Stiff Records) that would shake the very foundations of the rock establishment and more than any other define new wave.

Stiff Records' co-founders had been instrumental in developing the pub rock circuit, managing groups and venues and defining its ethos. They were ideally placed to sign up anybody with a happening song and a fire in their belly. Using little more than their wits and contacts, they built a roster of oddball artists that would challenge orthodoxy and change the musical landscape forever. Stiff Records was irreverent, hip and, above all, happening. Unlike major record companies, it valued its artists and treated them as musicians, not mere product to be sold like so much soap powder. It didn't pay big advances, because it couldn't afford to, and in some instances didn't even have its acts under contract. Because it could move faster than the lumbering dinosaurs that dominated the music business, it could sign a happening group, get them in the studio and have a record out in the blink of an eye. Its marketing and advertising was often provocative and witty. Billing itself as "The World's Most Flexible Record Label", it undertook a series of unusual but highly effective promotional campaigns that broke acts as diverse as Elvis Costello, Ian Dury, Lene Lovich and Jona Lewie and broke the hearts of others. In a little over three years it went from selling records from the back of a car to an American distribution deal with the most powerful record company in the world, Columbia Records.

It wasn't quite a case of David beating Goliath, because the mighty monsters that ruled the music business always had the upper hand, but for a while a bunch of losers, oddballs and mavericks, who'd been written off more times than they cared to remember, did revitalise music and revolutionise the business of music for the better. This book is for them and their legacy.

1
Amphetamines, Jean-Paul Sartre And John Lee Hooker

When The Beatles unleashed 'Love Me Do' onto an unsuspecting public at the tail end of 1962, rock 'n' roll was less than eight years old. In the years following its arrival little of interest happened. Johnnie Kidd, Vince Taylor and Cliff Richard all cut some classic British rock 'n' roll records, but they were imitators rather than innovators. For too long rock 'n' roll had been treading water, it had become fat, lazy and dominated by pretty boy vocalists, novelty songs and soppy ballads. In short, it had become as dull and boring as the quicksteps and foxtrots it had replaced a few years earlier. 'Something Better Change', as The Stranglers' observed twenty-five years later, but what?

If Bill Haley was the fuse and Elvis Presley the dynamite, The Beatles were the explosion that shook the world. The Beatles weren't mere copyists; they possessed a cool, knowing detachment that marked them as originators. Their uncanny knack of capturing the zeitgeist ushered in a new era of pop music that was instinctively contemporary and perceptive. The Beatles were something special, as Nick Lowe explains: "The Shadows, even though I liked them, were a bit before my time, but when The Beatles came along I got interested in groups." Jesse Hector of the Hammersmith Gorillas puts it more forcefully: for him The Beatles were an epiphany. "The Beatles were the first loud heavy rock 'n' roll band. The music was very loud and aggressive, it was different. Although Johnny Kidd and The Pirates had already been playing wild R&B they were still stuck in the '50s, style-wise.

The Beatles were totally new! The Beatles changed everything and gave British musicians the courage to be themselves rather than adopt fake Americanisms. By far the most creative group to emerge from the Mersey Beat boom, The Beatles didn't copy slavishly; they threw their influences into a melting pot and made music that, while influenced by the originals, was different. By the time The Beatles appeared on *Thank Your Lucky Stars* as fully formed avatars of cool, beat music had developed into a stylistic hodgepodge that Brian Wilson described as "synthetic and composed of earlier styles all worked in together".

Not everybody was as enamoured with this new approach to pop music. In a July '63 issue of *Melody Maker*; Bob Dawbarn noted rather disparagingly: "Beat, rock, skiffle - they are all just ways of lousing up the blues." However one approached it, beat music took its inspiration from artists like Little Richard, Howlin' Wolf and James Brown, and according to Dawbarn the kids weren't alright and were doing a pretty good job of messing it up. What he failed to notice, like those who criticised skiffle, was that they weren't messing it up as much as appropriating it and making it their own. The shift wasn't so much what was played, but how it was played. It didn't matter that The Beatles had limited vocal and instrumental skills. Like Lonnie Donegan before them, they resisted the idea that musicality was a gift or that talent could only be perfected with years of study at the Royal College of Music. The need to play louder had an impact on the sound beat groups made, too. A four-piece beat combo couldn't produce nearly the same volume as a 20-piece dance band. All that most beat groups had by way of amplification were puny 15-watt amplifiers with homemade speaker cabinets. Consequently, guitarists and bassists kept things simple and cranked up the volume. Drummers played louder and adopted a simplified technique - no subtle stick control or clever paradiddles for them. But while the music was kept simple, vocals and harmonies became more expressive and important to the overall sound.

Someone had to define this stylistic shift, and naturally it fell to journalists. The phrase "beat boom" was used to describe everything from rock 'n' roll to jazz and R&B. Hardly surprising considering that beat groups were performing seemingly everything, including original compositions, covers of obscure but contemporary R&B songs and classic show tunes. For example, the Gerry and the Pacemakers anthem 'You'll Never Walk Alone', adopted by Liverpool football fans, came from the Rodgers and Hammerstein Broadway hit musical Carousel. The strict genre divisions we suffer today were unknown - in fact, barely imaginable - back in the early '60s. As loose as classifications were, the thread that wove everything together was R&B. Having said that, important stylistic differences existed almost along the lines of a North/South divide. The Mersey Beat groups that cut their teeth in the Cavern Club and Hamburg's Reeperbahn grew out of the skiffle boom. They mainly ignored the blues; rock 'n' roll, R&B and country influenced their distinctive sound. In London, 'beat' groups like The Rolling Stones and The Yardbirds were more likely to have developed from blues groups and were more inclined to musical purism, or snobbishness, than were their Scouse cousins.

London's answer to the Cavern Club was the Marquee in Wardour Street. Originally a trad jazz club, it began to cater to blues fans and, later, gave Mod godfathers The Who their big break. For those whose taste ran to soul-influenced blues, there was the Flamingo, originally a modern jazz club favoured by London's Afro-Caribbean community and later where Georgie Fame came to prominence. Speaking in the late '70s, Lee Brilleaux, vocalist with ace R&B revivalists Dr Feelgood attempted to define what R&B had come to mean for a British audience. "I think in England the word R&B has come to mean something different [to what it means in America]. I think it's come to mean a small band, two guitars, bass, drums and possibly keyboards playing pretty upfront music based on John Lee Hooker and Muddy Waters, rather than the modern slick style that is current today."

Whatever form R&B took, it did more than influence styles of music. Media theorist and sociologist Dick Hebdige suggests that Afro-American artists became symbolic of an alternative lifestyle, "where another order was disclosed: a beautifully intricate system in which values, norms and conventions of the 'straight' world were inverted". Music let them step beyond the conventions imposed by straight society. They couldn't break the rules, but they could bend them. Their smart suits and sharp haircuts made them look respectable, but their articulation of a set of secret codes - language, fashion and music - let them operate as both insiders and outsiders.

R&B based beat music wasn't simply for the feet; it was for the head, too. Who cared if teenage pop princess Helen Shapiro was 'Walking Back To Happiness'? Beat music cut through the flab of Tin Pan Alley pop and connected with a generation of teenagers who looked to music to help them work through the problems of the day and give them a sense of belonging. As reassuring as she was, Miss Shapiro didn't do that. The Mod world did. Like many who owed their careers to the Pub Rock era, Graham Parker had been a Mod and told *Rolling Stone* magazine that it had been similar to the punk rock scene in as much as it gave people an identity.

Like anything new it was criticised - demonised, even. For the most part, those who put it down were the same purists and guardians of taste who found Haley and Donegan shocking. Ted Heath (the band leader not the Tory organ playing Prime Minister), was one of them. That he'd probably condescended to feature some 'rock 'n' roll' in his act made no difference, he still held the opinion that beat music was "strictly adolescent". Micky Ashman, another bandleader, railed against the new beat music: "It's nothing but rock'n'roll without the movements! Real rhythm-and-blues, as I know it, is done by people like Louis Jordan and Fats Domino." Guitarist Diz Disley wasn't as dismissive, he cited the same influences, but was more open to new ideas. "British beat music is just as much authentic R&B as Chris Barber is real authentic jazz!" The late Mr Disley was obviously down there with the kids, because he hit the nail firmly on the head. British beat music was unique and therefore as 'authentic' as the original American model. It wasn't a slavish copy; it was the articulation of a set of values, beliefs and attitudes exclusive to Britain in the early '60s.

Reg King, lead singer with The Action, explains: "A lot of bands in this country were taking good American soul songs and simply copying them. That's never been good enough for me or any of the lads, because we weren't copyists. We'd take an influence and use it. To a certain degree you are copying, because you're playing the same song after all, but what we'd always do was to take a song and add to it. We'd play around with the song and do our own arrangements so by the time it hit the stage it was worth playing."

Formed in 1963 as The Boys, they backed Sandra Barry on the single 'Really Gonna Shake' before cutting their teeth in Germany. King recalls: "Around this time we'd met this great guy called Ziggy Jackson. He said he could get us work in Europe, said we were a good band and should do what The Beatles did and exercise ourselves over there. He said an English band could go over there and give crap to the Germans and they'd love it. By the time we'd get back, we'd be an excellent band. Over there, we didn't do half hour spots, we'd do six or seven slots per night." Germany made men of The Boys, who on their return were snapped up by Kenny Lynch for Pye Records. "We went along to the studios and he asked us to play a couple of our own songs," recalls King. "We took along 'It Ain't Fair' and 'I Want You'. Kenny liked the songs, said they sounded good and they came out on Pye."

The original Mod scene comprised elite sharp-dressing, existential-reading, modern jazz-and-blues fans. "Amphetamine, Jean-Paul Sartre and John Lee Hooker. That was being a Mod," recalls Steve Sparks. These Mods were new bohemians whose rigorous sense of individualism distinguished them from previous generations and the false prophets of pop. Based in London, Mod prefigured Pub Rock in as much as it was spread through a circuit of clubs that included the Goldhawk Social Club (Shepherd's Bush), the Noriek (Tottenham) and the Crawdaddy (Richmond). These Mod hangouts operated outside of the mainstream club circuit and played a mix of what the music papers would describe as beat music, but with the emphasis placed on less commercial, and therefore more authentic, R&B. In fact, the more obscure the R&B the better. Such was the demand that Pye Records started to re-issue its newly acquired Chess-Checker catalogue with the zeal of a neophyte.

While America was being charmed by British beat groups, British Mod audiences came under the spell of American R&B. This was underground music that took the tenacity of a zealot to track down. "My records were being beamed in from the pirate ships - at that time the BBC was not playing our records," recalled head of Motown Records, Berry Gordy. Luckily, Gordy had some influential fans who helped spread the R&B gospel. The Beatles did their best to promote the sound of young Detroit whenever they got the chance; The Rolling Stones did the same for Chicago's elder statesmen, and *Ready Steady Go!* disseminated fashion tips and the latest dance steps via the small screen. But it was the club scene that supplied the hard-core Mod with a weekly fix of hot wax.

The Scene Club was a prime Mod hangout whose disc-jockey, Guy Stevens, played the hottest sounds in town. Norman Jopling, a journalist with the *Melody Maker*, described the club as, "really seedy but in retrospect really hip. Anybody who was in on the rock 'n' roll end of the R&B spectrum hung out there - musicians, managers, publicists, girls, fans - Guy knew everybody - and the place was still half empty!" Half empty or not, Stevens' choice of records impressed The Boys who had recently adopted the edgy Mod moniker, The Action. "That's where we picked up a lot of our influences," explains King. "All black music. I don't think The Action ever played any songs by white artists." Guy Stevens was the driving force behind some of the best R&B platters issued in Britain. In 1964, he joined Sue Records, licensed to Chris Blackwell's recently formed Island Records, and began to promote R&B with a passion. Initially, the label issued masters from Juggy Murray's US family of Sue Records. But with Stevens in control it began to license from a number of different sources. Stevens wanted the music he loved to reach as wide an audience as possible, not just the hard-core Mods he played to at the Scene club. "The main thing about Guy is that he proselytized about music," recalls Cliff White. "It was the total opposite of the later Northern Soul scene which tended towards secrecy as to the identity of certain records and led to the so-called 'cover ups'."

With a record - albeit a flop - under its collective belts, The Action acquired a manager, Rikki Farr, and a residency at the Marquee Club supporting The Who. The long hours spent performing in Europe paid off, and they began attracting a large and loyal following. With one of the hottest bands in the country on his books, Farr set about acquiring a new recording contract for his boys. King remembers that Farr, "went screaming round" to see George Martin, who was then setting up his independent production company. "He told us to go round to Abbey Road studios and he'd see what we were like, whether we were worth recording. Rikki told us this and we went 'Wow!!' But we didn't really know what songs to play him. Rikki said that he thought George wanted to hear any creations of our own but also to have a couple of covers as stand-bys for B-sides or whatever. We went there and it was like 'Hello George.' It was like meeting the Prime Minister of Rock. We were nervous but he put us at ease. It was, 'Come on boys relax, you won't put anything down well on tape unless you relax. Don't let me worry you, just do it your normal way.' So that afternoon we recorded 'Land Of Thousand'-1000 Dances' and, I think, 'Since I Lost My Baby'."

The Action released a further two Mod anthems in 1966, 'I'll Keep Holding On' and 'Baby, You've Got It', but neither were hits. As '66 turned into '67 George Martin was occupied with The Beatles' *Sgt Peppers* album which meant there was little time for other artists. The Action were also beginning to drift musically and were struggling to maintain a cohesive musical direction. Nevertheless, they managed to squeeze another two singles out of Martin, but as King recalls: "George told us that he was going to make 'Shadows and Reflections' our last single. If it didn't make it big he was going to have to say goodbye. And as much as it may have deserved to be a hit, it just wasn't. It sold pretty well, got to about the Top 50 or something, but it didn't go that high. So that, unfortunately, was that."

Around this time the group suffered its first casualty when guitarist Peter Watson left. Accounts of his departure differ. Mike Evans recalled: "It was to do with the group changing and being caught in an identity crisis a lot of the time. We wanted to do something else and it really didn't work with him. He was a good player, but not a wild bluesman, and we were getting more into experimentation." King remembers it differently. "He didn't leave - we sacked him. We got fed up with two things. His musical ability was good but he wasn't getting any better. We were getting more progressive and developing and he wasn't really up to it." The experimentation was attributed to Ian Whiteman. Joining the band in late '66, Whiteman had moved to London to join a jazz group but through a karmic twist of fate found himself ensconced in a group of hardened Mods. His infatuation with Bill Evans rubbed off on the others and affected their playing. Song structures became more flexible as they began to stretch out, interact and improvise. The music developed layers and textures that drew on R&B, jazz and psychedelic rock; forcing them to abandon the three-minute pop song for something more liberating, lengthy and spiritual.

Having been dropped by Parlophone, and with little in the way of live work, the group found itself in financial dire straits. This it appeared was due to their manager lining his pockets at their expense. "We were working for him in the end without realising it," explains King. "We just didn't have time to think about all the details of how much tax we should be paying, all that rigmarole. He was busy collecting on our behalf and in the end we had lots of bills that were just not paid. We had writs and all kinds of things out on us. So, we went back and had a meeting between us and Rikki and said enough's enough and we left him."

The Action found themselves adrift in changeable waters which over the next 18 months would test their endurance to the limit. Working without a manager they recorded some demos for a proposed album, but although Polydor Records showed some interest in the tapes, it decided against signing the group. Undeterred they recorded more demos for the legendary producer and impresario Giorgio Gomelsky who had half an idea to sign them to his Marmalade label. These demos also came to nothing because as King explains Gomelsky wanted "a smash hit single, which [they] finally got with Julie Driscoll and Brian Auger's 'This Wheel's On Fire'. But from the material that we did he couldn't see one."

By now Whiteman was dominating the song writing, but according to his replacement, Martin Stone, he decided to take a temporary break from the group. "Basically, he came into music from a different angle," says Stone. "He came at it from a jazz point of view, very much different from the other lads who were pill popping ... club, working-class trip in a way. I think there was some kind of explosion from different points. Ian felt he was too delicate to handle that sort of thing, and he was asked to leave. So we did gigs together just to work me in and then that was it." Only a few years earlier Stone would have been laughed out of this pill popping, working-class group of Modernists. But times and attitudes were changing and so were The Action. Dropping Carnaby Street chic for Ladbroke Grove clobber they too were beginning to resemble their hippie guitarist. "He had a woolly hat with long hair and a long beard," explains King. "We were getting a bit 'iffy' looking ourselves but he was way ahead of us. We liked him and he was just what we were looking for. He played great bluesy, rock and roll guitar."

Stone was a blues boom veteran who'd played with Juniors Blues Band, the Rockhouse Band and his own Stone's Masonry, who cut a single, 'Flapjacks', for the Purdah label in 1966. (A second incarnation of Stone's Masonry turned up on the Stiff Records compilation, *A Bunch of Stiff Records*.) When Stone's Masonry crumbled to rubble he joined label mates Savoy Brown. "When I joined them it was made very clear to me that I was a rhythm guitar player, but I didn't particularly get off on Savoy Brown," he recalls. "They were a joke ... a kind of synonym for a good, honky imitation. But on the other hand I'd had enough of a taste of being on the road to jump at it, and they were playing Chicago stuff, so it wasn't too much of a compromise." With Stone on board, The Action changed beyond recognition. "The clincher came when Martin Stone joined us and we discovered drugs!" Evans says. "Our entire ideas about music changed at that stage, it was the period of re-awakening and we started doing long, freaky numbers which just didn't appeal to the audience that we'd had before." Because they'd stopped playing snappy R&B-based pop songs, King found himself sidelined. With little to do during the long improvisations other than shake a tambourine, he decided he too should jump ship. "Reggie found that he was playing a less important part in the music," recalled Evans. "He just had to stand there whilst everyone was into playing long instrumental passages."

Without a manager or lead singer most groups would have considered calling it a day. Not The Action, they weren't finished yet and had secured the services of Blackhill Enterprises. The company was founded by the four original members of Pink Floyd with Peter Jenner and Andrew King and had offices at 32 Alexander Street, later the spiritual home of Stiff Records. Although Blackhill Enterprises would go on to manage several big names, including The Clash and Ian Dury, by the late '60s it had lost all its big acts. By this time Whiteman had re-joined and he recalls: "We moved to Blackhill just after the Floyd and T. Rex had left them and in some ways we were their biggest name group at the time, which might sound like a joke!"

The joke turned out to be Blackhill Enterprises, which treated the group appallingly. Work remained thin on the ground and the group desperately needed new equipment, neither of which was forthcoming. "One gig we did for Blackhill shows the difficulty we were up against," explained Whiteman. "We played some hall above a pub in Wolverhampton and the sound was atrocious, our gear was falling to bits and we didn't have the bread to replace it. The promoter came up afterwards and said, Finders Keepers, (a local group who'd come along to watch the famous Action 'pop' group. It included Glenn Hughes who went on to found Trapeze and Deep Purple, so they were entitled to their opinion) think you're fucking terrible." It wasn't that the disintegrating equipment made them necessarily sound "fucking terrible"; they'd changed and so had their fans. "We were too clever dick for our own audience," Stone admitted later. "Those poor little Mods in their fur-trimmed Parkas were not expecting The Action to tell them the world was going to end when a rogue asteroid hit the Earth in a couple of weeks because we didn't love each other. Or they didn't want to hear a forty minute version of John Coltrane's 'India'.

They wanted 'Land Of A Thousand Dances', or 'Baby You've Got It'." Stone's 'poor little Mods' had changed, but not in a good way. While The Action were searching for spiritual enlightenment, a section of the original Mod subculture had mutated into Skinheads. Mods always had a reputation for random acts of violence, and by the late '60s the word 'Mod' was a synonym for hostility. According to Chris Welch they were a new breed without "roots, tradition, or culture". Their musical tastes were, "blue beat, reggae, rocksteady and ska - the kind of beats best to be seen clomping boots to." The Action weren't about making boot clomping music, Slade was carving a niche for itself in that particular musical sub-genre. The Action wanted to fly by the seats of their pants. They wanted their songs to evolve as the mood and inspiration took them, so they could soar to new musical heights. The group fed off its audience, even if they insisted on sitting crossed legged on the floor, and if that reciprocity wasn't there they were more likely to sink than soar. But on the rare occasions that rock group and audience did become one, the experience was indeed magical. In an attempt to distance themselves from the Mods and Skinheads that occasionally turned up at gigs, The Action briefly became rock 'n' roll alchemists and renamed themselves Azoth.

2
Spotty Mods

In August 1966, Brinsley Schwarz joined Dave Cottam and Pete Wale to form Three's A Crowd. Inspired by the Mod sounds they heard in club land, Schwarz recalls the group played "the kind of harmony pop stuff that was the order of the day". Gravitating toward the popular end of the Mod scene, Three's A Crowd soon realised that a three-piece line-up had its limitations. If they were to develop musically they'd need another instrumentalist. Schwarz knew the ideal person: his old school friend and organist, Barry Landeman. Now that they were four, they needed a new name. As they were rehearsing at the Schwarz family home in Kippington Road, Sevenoaks, Kent, they decided to name the group after the house, and Kippington Lodge was born.

Phase two of the plan was to secure a manager. This they found in Irving Press, a local optician with cash to invest in an up-and-coming pop combo. While Press supplied the cash, his cousin, Malcolm Glazier, would deal with the group's day-to-day management. Glazier's first priority was to secure a recording contract for the group. Speaking to *Melody Maker* in 1974 Schwarz recalled, "Our manager at the time went 'round to talk to the record producers in companies and Mark Wirtz said he'd like to listen to us." According to Keith West, lead singer with psychedelic darlings Tomorrow, Mark Wirtz was "mainly a pop writer who was into all sorts of things like classical music as well. I think he was trying to be like Tony Hatch, actually." Like any producer worth his salt, Wirtz didn't sit around and wait for the hits to roll in. "Very often artists would come to the studio and say, 'Can I see Mark Wirtz?' And I was very open to that," he explains. "I actually signed several artists that way." Wirtz booked the group into EMI studios, Abbey Road, on 8 September 1967 for a test session. Wirtz liked what he heard and signed Kippington Lodge at a time when record companies were snapping up groups at the drop of a kaftan. Record sales were booming and nobody wanted to miss the next Beatles. In a 1971 interview with *ZigZag*, Schwarz said: "It seems they signed us at a time when they were signing up lots of small groups, but we weren't bothered - we were with EMI... a big company had shown interest in us."

Presented with a demo of 'Shy Boy', written by Keith West, Kippington Lodge spent two weeks learning it in readiness for their next session. "So we rolled up, set up the gear, and waited for Wirtz, who eventually turned up with the engineers, and said, 'Okay, would you like to go and put the voice on now?' He had the backing done already by his session men, and he even got the Ivy League in to put on the vocal harmonies. So all that went on the record was my vocals," recalls Schwarz." Wirtz had his reasons for not using Kippington Lodge on the A-side of their first record. "Back then it was typical to have session players for one simple reason," he explains. "Musicians back then were nowhere near as skilled as they are these days. But the main thing was not because of what they could do or their ability; it was simply because their instruments were not geared to the studio. And we were on a very tight time schedule. We couldn't spend an hour [trying to] get a drum sound so I used studio musicians. And they were okay with that. In Kippington Lodge's case I did actually record them as a band as well because if it was their material it was fine. They were great musicians. But if it was my material it saved a lot of time."

While Wirtz was happy to spend hours perfecting his own material, when it came to recording Schwarz's compositions the tables were turned. Schwarz recalls, "a guy came in and put up the mikes, before retiring back into his box. He then got the drummer to play his bit, and the guitarist did the same and the drummer does a little bit. 'Thank you.' A quick run on the guitar. 'Thank you.' And then he says, 'take one' and we run through it very nervous and he says, 'Right, thank you, that's your lot', and that was it, whereas they took three hours to do the backing track with session musicians on the A-side." In the weeks that followed, Kippington Lodge did get to record several Schwarz compositions including 'Fugue', 'And She Cried' and 'Land Of Sea'. But according to Schwarz their fate was sealed from the beginning. "It was preordained what we would do," he says. "I think Keith West, who was part of the 'Teenage Opera', had some songs and they'd decided to try to release them."

While Schwarz suggests that Wirtz had a master plan, the producer claims otherwise. "We didn't know until the [songs] were recorded what might be a single. When the [songs] were finished, then we would decide which was going to be a single. And when I say 'we,' that was not necessarily a decision with the artist; that would be myself with EMI. And so, frankly, it was not predictable which songs from any session would be the single. With some of my other productions I did go in with the idea of it being a single because the cost factor might have been so significant. However, in the case of Tomorrow or Kippington Lodge, we recorded tracks and then we decided what was going to be the single and then it was up to the fates and the BBC to go from there."

Even with 'Shy Boy' riding on the back of Keith West's remarkable success with 'Excerpt From A Teenage Opera', the single flopped. Publicity was practically non-existent. As far as EMI was concerned, Kippington Lodge was just another group, 'Shy Boy' just another single. According to Schwarz, EMI had a policy where "they release fifty singles a week on the assumption that one of them is going to make a large amount of money." EMI weren't wholly responsible for the record's lack of success. Although pirate radio did its bit to promote up and coming groups, it was the BBC that could make or break a record. Mark Wirtz explains: "What used to happen was that EMI used to decide how many records to ship and they could somewhat influence the charts. That didn't allow for returns, but then they changed their policies and they only shipped records that were ordered. Nobody would order the records unless they were on the air so the BBC was pretty much the boss. If the BBC didn't play it, that was it. EMI would have been happy to promote if they could get anybody to play it."

While Keith West could be part of an alternative scene and top the pop charts, Kippington Lodge were struggling to make any kind of impact on what was a rapidly changing music scene. The musical melting pot was getting very mixed up indeed. As far as Schwarz was concerned Kippington Lodge was part and parcel of a musical confection that blasted from the radio every time he switched it on. "There wasn't a real distinction; it was just what you heard on the radio, on pirate radio," he says. "You heard early Cream, The Beatles, The Hollies, The Stones and The Supremes. There really wasn't a distinction; it was just young people's music. And it was called pop music."

The rock 'n' roll project had always been about the shock of the new. But a lot had happened in the ten years since rock'n'roll smashed its way into the public consciousness. By the mid-'60s musicians could mix and match from any number of styles. The Beatles recorded entire songs with Indian classical performers. Brian Jones was making field recordings of the Master Musicians of Joujouka. The only limits on those intent on making music were their imaginations and the technology that could help them realise their dreams. As part of the cultural machine that was driving change, musicians engaged in the kind of free play that previously had been unthinkable. This extended to more than making music. Initially rock'n'roll offered little more than a change of fashion and the prospect of a good time, but ten years in, the project had evolved to encompass social, cultural and moral change.

Kippington Lodge, however, were minor players in the new global multi-media exchange network. The records they made, particularly those with Wirtz, displayed an individual Britishness that masked their interest in American R&B and Jamaican Ska. While the big players wore their influences on their sleeves, Kippington Lodge, while under Wirtz's direction, made music that could only have originated from provincial, suburban England. If England really was swinging, it wasn't swinging to records like 'Shy Boy' or 'Lady On A Bicycle'. Kippington Lodge simply weren't interested in entering into any kind of dialogue other than musical. They were happy to sing about girls with mousey hair and cups of tea, leaving the revolutionary stuff to others. All they wanted was to be a top notch pop group. Lowe explains: "What we wanted to do was be like the Herd. They were a pop group, but they were a really good pop group, and they really stood out. The Move had a similar sort of thing, and Yes."

On 3 November 1967, Kippington Lodge auditioned for BBC Radio. Described by the review panel as "tone deaf" and "amateurish", they were not added to the BBC's list of artists available for airtime. BBC session recordings were broadcast whenever possible to save on costly needletime (the number of hours the Corporation could play records each day). In 1967 Radios 1 and

2 shared seven hours' needletime each day. With this kind of rationing, the chance of getting an unknown act broadcast on national radio was almost impossible. "We only had the BBC and for the most part they only dedicated several hours a week to pop music," explains Wirtz. "It was almost like a lottery. You'd make a single with somebody and if it made some noise you made another single, and if that took off then you would continue making singles."

Although 'Shy Boy' made no real impact on the chart, Wirtz was convinced he could make a hit record with the group and offered them a dog's chance. On 15 December they returned to EMI Studios and cut another Schwarz song, 'Seventeen Heaven', and remade 'And She Cried', issued as the B-side of their next single. But Schwarz was already disillusioned with the music business and Cottam disenchanted with their musical direction. Schwarz wasn't happy at being told to sing along to another pre-recorded backing track. "I wasn't going to do it," he says, "but you get persuaded round, you know - someone else in the band says, 'Come on, you've got to do it', you just have an argument within the band really. We did it in the end, and then we did the next one which was even more stupid, they did the backing track and then found out that it was too high for me to sing the song in, so they had to slow down the tape so it got lower. It was like Pinky and Perky or something."

Dave Cottam was even less happy with the direction Wirtz was taking the group and wanted to lead them towards the kind of R&B that The Action had mastered. The rest of the group, however, wanted to stick with pop. "There was a difference of musical direction between Dave and Pete," explains Schwarz. "Dave was interested in Motown and wanted to go that way rather than stay with the poppy stuff." Unhappy with the direction the group were headed, Cottam packed his bass and left. With Cottam gone, Schwarz called Nick Lowe and asked if he'd like the job. "I got a call one day from Brinsley Schwarz, who I'd been at boarding school with, and he had this group, Kippington Lodge, who had a record deal with Parlophone - I'd heard them on the radio. Their bass player was leaving and he asked me to join. I just had to do it. God knows what my folks thought, especially my old man. But in those days there was no unemployment so no fear of that; my old man pressed a tenner into my hand and off I went on the back of a bloke's scooter, giving me a lift all the way to Kippington outside Tunbridge Wells."

Lowe thinks he joined Kippington Lodge on 11 February 1968, but he might have joined sometime earlier because their next single, 'Rumours', was cut at EMI Studios on 5 February along with 'Barefoot And Tiptoe' and 'Come Tomorrow'. Lowe may have joined the group as early as October 1967 because a BBC 'application for a light entertainment (sound) audition' form signed by Schwarz on 19 October 1967 has Cottam's name crossed out and replaced by Lowe's. Whenever he got the call from Brinsley he didn't need much persuading. His career as a journalist wasn't all he'd hoped for and rock 'n' roll was much more exciting. "I wanted to be a journalist, a war correspondent, but I ended up reporting on flower shows. I soon realised I didn't have what it took," he says.

As with the previous single, 'Rumours' was recorded by session musicians. "We practiced it all, got it all right, went up to the studio and said, 'Right, where do we put the gear then?'; and they said they only want Brinsley," explained Lowe. The records Wirtz made with Kippington Lodge were little gems, but 'Rumours' didn't fare any better than the previous single. "I was very disappointed that things didn't go the way I'd hoped," says Wirtz. "We never really got a shot of going where we wanted to go, because there was some good writing going on. The band were good musicians, and Brinsley had that slight jazz tinge to his song-writing."

In April 1968, Kippington Lodge got a second chance to audition for BBC Radio. Performing Marmalade's 'I See the Rain' and two songs by Cream, 'Swlabr' and 'I'm So Glad', they passed with flying colours. Their change in direction was put down to their new bassist, Nick Lowe. "I turned up and was the Mod who thought I knew the lot and started rearranging things. I said, 'We can't have this bubblegum nonsense.' But when we had our go it all went downhill rapidly and EMI dropped us very soon after I joined". Lowe's influence may have led to them eventually being dropped by EMI, but the group's change in direction paid dividends with the BBC audition panel. Described as a "sharp end pop group" their choice of material says much about the way they and popular music was heading at the time. Marmalade's 'I See The Rain' highlights their continued interest in harmony pop, but the material from Cream's first two albums suggests a move towards more progressive sounds. But even with the corporation's blessing it made little difference to the success of their next single. 'Tell Me A Story', produced by Mike Collier, was issued in August 1968. Less polished than Wirtz's earlier productions, it was another slice of radio-friendly pop that failed to hit with the record buying public.

While Kippington Lodge were busy promoting their new single, their future manager, Dave Robinson, was on a tour of America with the Jimi Hendrix Experience. The previous year, Robinson had secured the Dublin based group, The People, a couple of prestigious gigs at UFO and the Speakeasy. UFO was the alternative night out. "Suddenly there was somewhere to go on a Friday night," recalls Mick Farren, "This old Irish showband ballroom with a revolving mirror ball and stuff."

With their Dublin background, The People must have felt right at home. The gig brought them to the attention of Mike Jeffery, who co-managed Jimi Hendrix and The Soft Machine with Chas Chandler (Ex-bassist with The Animals, Chandler produced Eggs Over Easy's debut album and supported them during their stay in Britain. But more of that later). Meanwhile, Jeffery offered The People a contract to support Hendrix in America because being Irish, they were outside the Musicians' Union 'exchange' programme, which meant that he didn't have the bother of booking an American group to play

Britain. With an American tour booked, the group was re-named Eire Apparent by Jeffery's wife and Robinson was engaged as their road manager. "Jeffery suggested we need someone in charge on a personal level," explains Ernie Graham, "and we thought it might as well be Dave. So Dave was basically brought in as personal manager. For a while it worked really well- he was never tight with money - he would never see a trip suffer because there wasn't bread."

Kippington Lodge, however, were suffering. Like their previous singles, 'Tomorrow Today' had flopped and Landeman had had enough and quit to join Vanity Fare. An advert in the *Melody Maker* brought a new keyboardist, Bob Andrews. He'd taken piano lessons at the age of seven, but turned to the guitar when rock 'n' roll hit. "The first ever record I bought was Chuck Berry," he recalls. "That influenced me a lot because it made me want to learn to play the guitar." It was his talents as a pianist, however, which got him into his first group. "When I was about sixteen a friend of mine was looking for somebody to play in his band, and they were looking for a keyboard player, and I said, 'Well, I can do that', and my father helped me get a Farfisa keyboard and I suddenly discovered the organ. It was like a whole new world." Andrews headed for Germany and the American air force bases where he got into playing everything from Booker T. to Larry Young and Al Kooper. "I used to play seven nights a week, 12 hours a night, it was unbelievable. But it was such a learning ground. I learned how to play everything from that time. How to play, how to gig, how to do the whole thing," he laughs. Returning to England, he got a gig with P. P. Arnold for a few months before looking for work elsewhere.

Andrews joined Kippington Lodge just in time for a tour of northern England backing J. J. Jackson. Their agent had an unusual motivational style when it came to ensuring the band gave of their best. "We got recruited to play with J. J. Jackson by our agent," recalls Schwarz, "who threatened us with never being able to play again. I laughed at him and said, 'Well there are loads of other agents.' And he said, 'No, I think you miss understand me. You won't be capable of playing again.'" Packing their bags, Kippington Lodge headed north and despite their reluctance discovered that playing with a soul legend was fun, even if it wasn't where they were heading musically. Schwarz explains: "By then we'd headed off to a more progressive side. Brian Auger and that kind of thing, a bit more than straight-up pop. That's where we were endeavouring to go." One group that made a big impression was Yes. On 15 July 1969, Kippington Lodge opened for the up-and-coming prog rockers at the Marquee Club. "They were so incredibly tight and dynamic that I stood with my mouth open," reveals Schwarz. Kippington Lodge's last Parlophone single, a cover of The Beatles' 'In My Life' with Andrews on vocals, was clearly influenced by the prog rockers. "That's what Kippington Lodge was kind of like," says Andrews. "Yes was one of the strong influences. At the time we thought ['In My Life'] was brilliant with all the modulations and that kind of stuff going on. I remember trying to get the organ to scream as loud as I could without [the engineer] going, 'It's distorting', and us saying, 'We like it like that."

Despite the best efforts of the big hitters like The Beatles to shake things up, the music business still had a long way to go to catch up with musicians themselves, and Kippington Lodge were rapidly losing patience with the business side of things. If it wasn't agents threatening violence or engineers telling them to turn it down, it was producers trying to manipulate their image. Not content with just producing the group, Roger Easterby had strong ideas about how they should look. "Roger Easterby came along to groom us; black polo necks, black trousers and scarves were what he wanted us to wear," recalls Schwarz. However, Kippington Lodge didn't want to make it as some gimmicky boy band, it had to be on their own terms or not at all. "We always wanted to be successful, and we still do, we want to have hits," explained Lowe. "But we want to make it because we're so bloody good." To be "bloody good" meant a commitment to musical authenticity. So far that had proved unsuccessful. That is, for Kippington Lodge. Other groups like Led Zeppelin, Yes and Cream proved that anti-commercialism could be very profitable indeed. Their determination to be different, to exist outside of the pop mainstream, was what excited their fans. Kippington Lodge were still too mainstream to benefit in the way these groups had. They were good, but they didn't have a Page, Howe or Clapton, nor did they fully engage with the alternative music scene in the way that the Deviants, Pink Fairies or Hawkwind did. They weren't that kind of group and never would be.

With a new single to promote, the group should have focused on British appearances. But with little in the way of work on their home turf, they headed for the bright lights of Munich. Booked into the PN Hit House, they were expected to 'mach schau' under the club owner's watchful eye for hours on end. "You'd play all night, and on the weekends you'd play all day and all night, and for hardly any money," recalls Lowe. "I'd led a very sheltered life up till that time, and I had eyes like saucers over what I saw and experienced. It was also great training musically. You had to expand your repertoire. Our little two hours we could scrape up before we went to Germany didn't get us anywhere. You'd try to eke it out with drum solos and guitar solos, all that business, and you got fed up with that very quickly. So, we had to get into the DJ's booth when the club was closed and listen to what everyone was dancing to between the live music, which was nearly all soul and R&B stuff back then. Europe was really into it in a big way. So, it was a fantastic training ground."

Billy Rankin also happened to be in town and re-acquainted himself with the group. He'd met them when they shared a Boxing Day bill with his group The Martin James Expression in Tunbridge Wells. An American by birth, Rankin started playing drums when he was eleven. "I used to play with this little Shadows [type] group; I can't even remember what they were called. And then I progressed to a band called Friskers Rex, which was a soul/R&B band, and then I was with a proper soul band called Luther Morgan Relationship." Rankin turned professional at seventeen. Packing his drum kit and a suitcase, he persuaded his brother to drive him to Folkestone, from where he made his way to Munich. "The lead singer and sax player from the Luther Morgan Relationship [had] formed this James Brown tribute band. We used to play the American bases out in Germany, and we used to do a complete James Brown show with an eleven-piece soul band and the girls dragging him off. I think I was on £20 a week and we had to live in a hovel in Munich and drive around in a Transit van." Rankin became firm friends with Kippington Lodge and a fan of the group. "They were fantastic musicians; [they] were brilliant compared to whom I'd been playing with. I thought Bob Andrews was an astounding organist, and Brinsley's a very good guitar player. Nick I always thought was a great bass player as well. I always rated his bass playing and he's a good songwriter." Tired of living out of a battered van, he decided to return to England. Kippington Lodge followed him and took up a residency at the seaside resort of Margate.

Unknown to their drummer, Pete Wale, the rest of the group were planning his departure. According to Lowe there were personality differences: "We were doing 'naughty things' [drugs]. The drummer, when he started doing 'naughty things' and he started sussing it all out, he somehow thought that he'd had some kind of revelation that only he could see. He started to think, er ... well, he started to think that he was God, really." Whether or not Wale thought he was God, Andrews recalls that he simply didn't fit in any longer. "He just wasn't the right kind of guy for where we wanted to go," he explains. All good things come to an end, and Wale was sacked at the end of the residency.

At around the same time Rankin landed a job in Leicester Square in a nightclub called The Wunderbar. "You'd start about 6 p.m. in the evening and go right the way through until 2 a.m. in the morning. It was an incredible apprenticeship," he recalled. "Then I went back to Tunbridge Wells and I got into Kippington Lodge." Rankin's timing wasn't great, by now Kippington Lodge had hit rock bottom. "[It] just went sort of downhill really. The records didn't get off and we got very tired of doing what managers told us to do," explains Schwarz. More importantly, live work, their main source of income, was drying up. "We were getting less and less gigs because we were getting more and more prissy," explains Lowe. "It was always, 'Can you sit down on the floor please, we're about to begin.'"

Money was so tight that Rankin would take Lowe and Andrews round to his mum's house to feed them. But they were young, and money wasn't everything. "Nick and Bob were [...] so into the music. That's all they lived for," recalls Rankin. "As long as they could get a coupla quid at the weekend for, you know, coupla quid deal, they'd just play all day." Drugs had already played a part in the departure of Pete Wale and would affect the music they made, but as Lowe recalls it was a general disillusionment with what passed for the music business that depressed them most. "Meanwhile me and one of the other blokes in the group had started smoking pot quite enthusiastically and grew increasingly dissatisfied with our lot. It was the end of the era for that pop thing. There wasn't really a music business back then. Our first agent had comedians, strong men and plate-spinners on his books - we were his pop group. The college scene looked much more fun; the girls were prettier. We wanted some of that." But the college circuit was a way off, and if Kippington Lodge wanted to play to pretty girls instead of spotty Mods they'd need a plan, something they didn't have.

3
The Shape Of Things To Come

Teenburger Designs, a "creative commune" situated in London's Portobello Road, opened for business in 1969. Founded, funded and functioning under the auspices of a young graphic artist, Colin Fulcher, known to his friends as Barney Bubbles, it would provide graphic inspiration for every self-respecting underground group and publication working out of this part of London. Bubbles epitomised the kind of far-out creative types that had made Ladbroke Grove their home. Here he'd rub shoulders with the likes of Hawkwind, The Deviants and Mighty Baby, most of whom lived nearby. "Bam [King] and I lived in Tavistock Road for a while", recalls Mike Evans. Ian [Whiteman] lived off St Luke's Mews off Westbourne Park Road and Martin [Stone] lived in Westbourne Park Road just past Portobello Road ..."

A talented artist but poor businessman, Bubbles desperately needed somebody to take care of his finances while he concentrated on being arty. By chance he met businessman Edward Molton who offered his services as agent-cum-debt collector. Besides realising a reasonable profit of 10% from putting the squeeze on Bubble's debtors, Molton saw the agreement as his way into London's alternative culture which he'd now be ideally placed to exploit. At roughly the same time, Molton met Stephen Warwick, an assistant film sound editor with a harebrained plan to develop a 'Pleasuredome' - a kind of hippie Butlins for freaks - but not the wherewithal to finance it. Once again, Molton suggested a partnership and together they set about building a shaky business empire. Molton looked kosher but was no more than a cheap huckster. Mark Williams, then music editor of *International Times*, claimed the music business was full of them. "The rock business was full of the same sharks as it always had been full of except they were wearing kaftans and smoking dope instead of sinking pints of beer and wearing suits." With both feet planted firmly in London's alternative business community, Molton opened for business. Renting space at 307 Portobello Road he launched 'Motherburger', the first of several dodgy companies. A company called Seatribe Ltd that was intended to transform the sea forts once used by Radio 390 into a vast hippie entertainments centre followed. Next they formed Grandslam Ltd to handle television productions; Message Makers was an information company; T. F. Murch Ltd. published *Friends* magazine; JPM & W Ltd. traded in film titles and special effects. There was also an antiques business called Forbidden Fruit.

Forming the companies was easy; the difficult part was financing them. Molton, however, knew a way round the problem - kite flying. The practice of moving money from one account to another to raise cash or credit over and above one's real worth, kite flying wasn't illegal but it was sharp practice.

"They had their fingers in all sorts of pies, but films were their main thing," recalls Nick Lowe. "What they used to do was, as soon as one of their companies made any money, they'd sign a cheque for that amount to all the other companies; so for three days the other companies could get on with it. They could make it look as though they had thousands of pounds when they had next to nothing."

While Warwick was trying to get his 'Pleasuredome' up and running, his former partner, John Eichler, had ambitions of his own. A colour matcher at Strand Cosmetics, Eichler spent his time daydreaming about managing a rock band. So strong was his desire that when recruiting staff for the company his job ad read: "Wanted: Process Workers with Musical Ability". Along with his wife and daughter, he shared a house in Barnes with Dorothy Burn-Forti, a secretary with the Bryan Morrison Agency. Working at the agency, Dot, as she was known to her friends, came into contact with Dave Robinson, Eire Apparent being one of the groups on the agency's books. It wasn't long before Dot fell for Dave's Gaelic charm and they became an item. Moving in with Dot, Robinson hit it off with Eichler and together they began planning a future together in the music business. Several ideas were mooted, but they settled on a management company - Famepushers.

The problem was they didn't have any groups to represent; neither did they have any money. However, Stephen Warwick and Edward Molton had money or, at least thanks to Molton's kite flying, looked flush. In late 1969, Eichler met with Warwick and told him of his plans for Famepushers. Warwick suggested both parties should meet at the Red Lion pub in Mortlake to discuss the matter. Robinson impressed Molton and Warwick with tales of road managing Jimi Hendrix to such an extent that they agreed to fund Famepushers there and then. Molton set them up with offices at 305 Portobello Road, and on 16 October he bought an off-the-shelf company, Wornet Ltd, which was renamed Famepushers. Robinson was appointed managing director and they opened for business. Touting for acts, Famepushers placed an advertisement in the *Melody Maker* for a "Young song writing group with own equipment". Inundated with scores of uninspiring tapes, Robinson finally found something he thought he could work with when a demo tape by a Tunbridge Wells based beat group dropped through his letter box.

Kippington Lodge were kicking their heels and about to call it a day when new boy Billy Rankin saw Famepushers' advert in *Melody Maker*. "I was a bit pushy," he confessed. "Brinsley was a very sensible married man with young kids. Bob and Nick lived in a flat with a guy call J.C. who was a chef and they liked to party a bit. I saw the advert in *Melody Maker* and I went round and saw Brinsley and said, 'look at this, they want a band'. So anyway we rang them up and did an audition for Dave and his girlfriend Dotty." Although they told Robinson they owned their own equipment, he soon discovered that the van was hired and the amps were on hire purchase and being paid for by Irving Press. Their only asset was Nick Lowe's blossoming talent as a songwriter. "I thought Nick had a little something," says Robinson, "so I talked to him about the songs and suddenly he'd written two more, which I thought was very quick for those days. I had in the back of my mind that if you're going to sign a group, and it's one of the things I said to Molton, you should try and sign somebody who writes because the idea of finding songs and going through that kind of poppish bit was painful."

Kippington Lodge had nothing to lose and everything to gain. With Robinson's knowledge of "what musicians were all about" and Lowe's burgeoning talent as a tunesmith they'd soon be out of their dispiriting rut and into a new groove. Their only problem was that they couldn't decide what kind of music they wanted to groove on. "By the time the winter of '69 came along we were changing radically," explains Andrews. "Along came things like *Astral Weeks* and Crosby, Stills & Nash. We got into singing harmonies, and we got into doing a whole different kind of thing. And we decided that we're going to change." As far as Kippington Lodge were concerned, Crosby, Stills & Nash were the bee's knees. Exiles from some of the most successful and influential groups of the day, together they made music that some considered as fresh and new as The Beatles. Along with groups like The Flying Burrito Brothers, The Band and the Roger McGuinn-led Byrds, Crosby, Stills & Nash showed that there was life outside mainstream pop. For Lowe, applying the CSN template to Kippington Lodge was the only way to stay ahead of the game and keep some credibility. "We thought it was the only way we could play the way we wanted to and stay in the progressive stream, not be sort of popsy-wopsy." Kippington Lodge were transforming themselves from a provincial pop group into something altogether more impressive. With a new drummer, management contract and musical direction it was time to wipe the slate clean, and the best way to do that was to give the group a new name. Once again, their guitarist and singer provided the inspiration. Despite his opposing the idea, the group insisted it be re-christened Brinsley Schwarz.

By January 1970, Famepushers had two groups on its books and was considering how best to launch them. Help Yourself were put on a retainer and left to get on with it. "The early days seemed magical, making tapes in the basement," recalls the group's guitarist Richard Treece. "Malcolm [Morley] would start playing and singing and somehow we'd have a song." Robinson kept a watchful eye on them and asked Ernie Graham to help out where he could. "When Dave Robinson finally split from Eire Apparent one of the first people he teamed up with was Malcolm Morley and he got me to go over a couple of evenings to Malcolm's flat and help work out a couple of Malcolm's ideas," he recalled. "And I'd met the Brinsleys because Dave had asked us to do them a few favours when he was first trying to get them off the ground, like borrowing our PA, and things." All Famepushers had to do was nurture both groups and hope that everything would go to plan. However, Brinsley Schwarz were far from a bankable commodity, as Robinson was to discover. "It was very difficult to get the band off the ground, to get a good record deal, the album publicised and so on - I mean, I remember offering people the band for nothing ... I even offered to pay them money, but they'd just say 'Brinsley Schwarz?' Bollocks!" Various ideas were mooted to kick-start the group's career, Nick Lowe recalls: "They couldn't get us any gigs, though, so they thought up these big publicity stunts. I'd written this number called 'Ballad of a Has-Been Beauty Queen' and they were going to get all these old beauty queens at the Festival Hall for some complicated extravaganza. Then someone came up with the idea of getting a gig in America and flying all the press over for it. It was psychologically good, because nobody's going to be impressed with a new band at the Speakeasy, but they would be with a weekend in America."

The Brinsleys ill-fated showcase in New York City has been well documented, particularly by Will Birch in his excellent book *No Sleep Till Canvey Island*, and in the sleeve notes for the *Surrender to the Rhythm* CD, but it's worth re-telling again, briefly. Molton and Warwick desperately needed money to finance a film they were making with Omar Sharif. They reasoned, correctly, that the music business was awash with money. "The music business was the engine of the underground, the source of finance," says former music business insider Steve Sparks. "The great thing about the music business was that there was always some cash floating about." All Molton and Warwick had to do was find a way into the music business, turn on the financial tap and watch the money pour in. When they heard the demo tapes Robinson had recorded with Brinsley Schwarz they were convinced they'd hit pay dirt. Speaking to *ZigZag* in late 1970, Dave Robinson opined: "Before that American trip last April, Famepushers had £100 in the bank; then Eddie and Steve heard the tapes we'd made and got terribly impressed ... they thought they were the biggest thing to hit the Klondyke, and everybody got carried away."

The Klondyke gold rush had started with a trickle that grew into a stampede. The problem Robinson faced was how to get the trickle going. He wasn't helped by the Byzantine nature of the music business. "The reason why we went [to New York] was because we couldn't get an agency to get us gigs, and we couldn't get a record company because we didn't have an agency. It's hard to get people to pay attention to your music and your band and give you a shot, so then we decided we'll do something really unusual because playing down the local pub and trying to get people to see you and make some kind of decisions was as bad then as it is today," Robinson stated. A scheme was hatched to 'hype' Brinsley Schwarz by organising an all-expenses-paid beano for the British press to see them in New York City. The plan was to launch Brinsley Schwarz on the back of the publicity they'd receive, and secure them an agency and a record contract with a fat advance. Molton and Warwick loved the idea, in their minds the bigger they could make it the better. All that remained was for Robinson to use all his perspicacity and tenacity to pull off the stunt. Against all odds, he secured a meeting with uber promoter Bill

Graham and persuaded him to book Brinsley Schwarz at union rates plus rehearsal time at $7 an hour - not that they would ever have the chance to rehearse - to play the Fillmore East.

Brinsley Schwarz would open for Van Morrison and Quicksilver Messenger Service in New York on 3 and 4 April 1970. With the gig in the bag, Robinson's next priority was to find them a recording contract. Robinson used the old trick of playing two companies (RAK and United Artists) off against each other. But as Mickie Most (RAK) had already tried his hand at producing the group without success, it was unlikely that he'd sign them. Everything relied on Andrew Lauder at United Artists. With what sounded like a well-planned publicity campaign and a strong debut album ready to roll, Lauder agreed to sign the group for £22,000. Robinson also secured contracts for Help Yourself and Ernie Graham to record for United Artists. Unlike most A&R managers, Lauder wasn't interested in instant hits, he was of the opinion that groups should be allowed to develop. "Andrew Lauder was a different kettle of fish," recalls Robinson. "He was an A&R man signing bands that he liked that he thought were musical and letting them get on with it. That's not to say that United Artists [didn't have] huge records in the charts, but there was support from your record company which was because of him really, and that we were able to [apply] to various musical events."

With freshly signed management and recording contracts under their belt, Brinsley Schwarz moved into the Red Lion pub in Barnes. "We used to practice and do gigs from there," recalls Rankin. "It was a funny little old hotel. It had an Irish manager and Dave and Dotty lived round the corner. We had the time and used to rehearse a lot. Nick had a lot of songs and we learnt those and rehearsed them before we went to the studios." Recording sessions for their debut album began in earnest while Robinson worked to fine-tune the trip to New York City. Although Graham had booked Brinsley Schwarz, the Musicians' Union still insisted on upholding the Anglo-American exchange system that meant that if a British group wanted to play in America, it had to exchange with an American group to play in Britain. Arthur Lee's Love were booked to exchange with Brinsley Schwarz, but cancelled at the last minute. No exchange, no gig, insisted the Musicians' Union. Because Love had cancelled their visit to Britain, the American Embassy refused to issue visas or work permits for the trip. Matters weren't helped by Nick Lowe's minor conviction for possession of cannabis. Robinson decided that the best thing to do was to fly Andrews, Lowe and Schwarz to Toronto and re-apply for visas there. Rankin, being an American citizen, could fly directly to New York and await their arrival. After several days of frantic negotiations the group got its visas, but with hours to go before they were due onstage they were stranded due to a strike by air traffic controllers. There was no other option than to hire a small aeroplane to fly them to any airport that would take them. On arrival in New York, Andrews, Lowe and Schwarz made a mad dash through rush-hour traffic. Collecting Rankin on the way they made it to the venue with thirty minutes to spare. Unknown to Brinsley Schwarz, the journalists they'd invited to review their performance had suffered similar delays. The flight from London was postponed by four hours, its replacement was diverted to Ireland and what should have taken eight hours took eighteen. Like the group, the press made it to the Fillmore with minutes to spare.

Had Brinsley Schwarz shone they might have got away with it, but by their own admission they failed to impress. "The first two shows on the Friday night were very messy, because we'd only just landed from Toronto," Schwarz admitted. "I couldn't hear anything because my ears hadn't popped from flying in this little plane, and everyone was pretty freaked out." Despite this, not all of the reviews were negative. The *NME* was factual and fair: "They did well, got a good thing going to keep us awake, but only received lukewarm applause." Contemporary reports also suggested that the audience was "staid, slow and relatively unappreciative". Once they'd overcome their initial nervousness, on the second night they were pretty good. But it was too late. Press reaction to the New York trip was mixed. Practically every review featured the verb 'hype', questioned the validity of the enterprise, and spent more time discussing the trip than the Brinsleys' performance. Famepushers and Brinsley Schwarz had done the unthinkable, they'd broken the unwritten rule that said 'thou shall not hype'. As far as most of the press were concerned, Brinsley Schwarz were no better than The Monkees. How could the press take them seriously after such shameless and unjustifiable publicity? The one thing that Robinson had wanted to establish through extensive gigging and musicianship - credibility - was lost to a wave of indifference.

The British press may have considered the whole enterprise a disaster, but the group secured a lot of well-paid work off the back of it. But more importantly the experience galvanised their attitude to the music business and influenced everything they did subsequent to it. Dave Robinson is clear that his and the group's attitude was informed by their attempts to play the major record companies game and the press reaction to it. "It was an attitude we all got. We got fed up with the idea. You'd go along with what people think you should do, something special, something unusual, and then they'd turn on you. A lot of those people didn't even see the gig that wrote those bad comments. They didn't get in because everything was delayed. The plane was delayed and crash landed at Shannon Airport, so by the time people got there, 'A' they were drunk and 'B' they didn't want to go to a gig, they wanted to go to a hotel. They treated it like a jolly rather than paying attention and seeing what the band were like."

This understandably had a negative effect on the band. When interviewed for *Melody Maker* not long after the Fillmore trip, an unnamed member of the group said: "You imagine what it's like to be famous ... but when that fame comes, it's completely the opposite of what you expect, and it utterly smashes you." The Brinsleys forgot all about being famous. It was a world they knew nothing about and wanted nothing to do with. As far as Lowe was concerned the Fillmore fiasco was a blessing in disguise. "Since then I have had occasion to fall to my knees to give thanks since it put paid to any thoughts I might have entertained of being a household name. Since then I've thought it a lot cooler to be a little quieter; anyone standing on a carpet surrounded by flashbulbs, unless they were Cary Grant or Stewart Granger, looked ridiculous. 'Never again,' I thought."

If nothing else they'd gained some real insights into the way the music business worked and, despite the press backlash, some much needed publicity. "We got a lot of front pages out of it," says Andrews, "we got a lot of publicity out of it and whether it was bad or good, that's immaterial really." Rankin agrees: "We [had been] sort of stuck poking around doing local gigs. We were on the dole and it was all pretty seedy. [Gigs] were slowing down, we were stuck in Tunbridge Wells and whatever anyone can say about it, it turned us from a pro local band into a nationally known band. It got us on the front page of the *Financial Times*. Suddenly we went from a £60 band in Tunbridge Wells to getting £200 a night." As Robinson notes, it lit a slow burning fuse on a musical time bomb: "It was a huge success," he says. "Here was a little band from Tunbridge Wells that were going nowhere. They say any publicity is good publicity, but that's not always strictly true, but we did a lot of things off the back of that. And eventually the attitude of turning your back a little bit on the major record companies caused us to start the pubs and start that whole thing going. It had an effect."

With record company and publishing advances in the bank, and with plenty of well paid gigs coming in, the group appeared financially secure. However, Molton's kite flying was getting seriously out of hand. Robinson discovered that he'd been dipping into the Brinsley Schwarz account without his knowledge. Somehow Molton had managed to move money from their account, despite withdrawals requiring his and Robinson's signature. Robinson decided to investigate Molton and didn't like what he found. Confronting Molton with evidence of his deceit, Robinson left Famepushers taking his acts with him. With his empire crashing around him, Molton did what any self-respecting huckster would do in his situation and faked an illness. Barney Bubbles friend, John Muggeridge, says: "The crunch came when Molton arrived at Teenburger and announced his doctor had told him he was suffering from a severe heart condition which meant he had six months to live. Of course it was pure hype. He had spent all the money we had earned. Soon after he disappeared and that was it."

Released to capitalise on the acres of press coverage they experienced post Fillmore hype, Brinsley Schwarz's eponymous debut album was issued on 17 April 1970. An uneven affair, it caught them in a musical no man's land unsure of where they were going. "It was a mish-mash of songs left over from the Kippington Lodge era and [new] songs that were coming up," Andrews notes. "Nick's writing was still maturing and we were going from this Yes-type progressive rock band to something that was much more American influenced," Rankin explained. The transition would take another year or so before Brinsley Schwarz achieved their potential. "The music wasn't ready," says Andrews. "It wasn't until August of that year (1970) that we [got close] to what we wanted to do." United Artists did their best to promote the album and Brinsley Schwarz plugged it on a couple of TV shows, but their hearts weren't in it. "We think it's terrible because before it the only studio experience we'd had was making a few chirpy sing-along singles as Kippington Lodge," they told the *Melody Maker*.

With Molton and Warwick out of the picture, John Eichler and Dave Robinson set up a new management company, Down Home Productions. At roughly the same time, Brinsley Schwarz moved out of the Red Lion pub and into a large house in Northwood, Middlesex. According to Schwarz, the group were "freaked out" by playing the kind of well paying gigs it had taken them so long to secure. They were obviously under a lot of pressure and in need of some time out to get it together. The house in Northwood gave them that opportunity. Speaking to the British music weekly, *Sounds*, Schwarz said: "We just freaked out altogether. It was the end of the line. So we stopped, got this house, moved in, and started over again."

4
The Buddhas Of Suburbia

By the summer of 1969, The Action had finally emerged from their Mod pupae and re-emerged as brightly coloured hippie butterflies. Ian Whiteman's jazz sensibility had influenced the group's approach, but the transformation was placed firmly on the shoulders of Martin Stone, who introduced them to the delights of marijuana. From the moment Stone shared his first reefer with the group their ideas about music changed. Gone were the Mod anthems that got the Marquee regulars dancing and in came long, improvised numbers that their original audience found downright perplexing.

Having ditched their original manager, they signed with Blackhill Enterprises. However, they were far from happy hippies with the new arrangement and when their former roadie, John Curd, stepped in with an offer to manage them, and issue an album on his newly formed Head Records, they jumped at the chance. "John's like us you see," said Roger Powell. "He's a bit of a looner but he's got a serious side as well. He's worked so hard to get the company off the ground and he's always been very fair with us. It was him who re-christened us Mighty Baby." Produced by their Mod mentor, Guy Stevens, the album mixed an Eastern vibe with acid-rock and country influences. The years of constant gigging, recording and refining of ideas ensured that when they entered the studio the music flowed effortlessly. Inevitably heavy rock overtones crept into the group's sonic palette, but this was less music for head bangers than it was music for the head.

Re-christened Mighty Baby by Curd, the new name couldn't have been more appropriate. They were a band reborn; full of life and with a rare gift of esprit. Unfortunately the band was dogged by bad karma. Because four of the group were still signed to Blackhill it threatened to place an injunction on the album, ensuring its delay by several months. Curd was forced to payoff Blackhill to liberate the foursome from its clutches before he could finally get the record into the shops. But no sooner was the album issued than disaster struck, again. Curd was busted for possession of marijuana and sentenced to three years at Her Majesty's Pleasure. Forced to return to self-management, the group spent much of 1970 gigging and looking for a new recording contract. Stone finally secured the group a deal with Mike Vernon's Blue Horizon label which issued their second album *A Jug Of Love* in 1971. Reflecting their continued interest in jazz, it also revealed Stone's growing interest in country music. The guitarist had developed a crisp country tone and Gene Parsons influenced phrasing after seeing The Byrds at Middle Earth. "I was hooked," said Stone. "I wanted to be a country and western musician. Fuck pop music! Eventually we turned country rock, although not really enough for my tastes." Stone's playing certainly hints at the full-on country styling he'd perfect with Chilli Willi and the Red Hot Peppers. But *Jug Of Love* isn't a country rock album, it has a baroque, meditative feel that points to a growing interest in the spiritual rather than the material. It's music made by sensitive types searching for something deep within them that could only be expressed through music.

They may have developed a taste for country music, but that didn't stop them performing long improvised pieces whenever the mood took them. When they appeared at the Glastonbury Fayre in June '71 they played for three hours and finished with a 16-minute song 'A Blanket In My Muesli' that had developed from jamming on John Coltrane's 'India'. Issued on the Glastonbury Fayre triple album, the sleeve of which was designed by Barney Bubbles, it was a country mile from the down home rootsy country-blues that Stone would record with Phil Litham. Song titles like 'A Blanket In My Muesli' suggest that the group hadn't lost its sense of humour. But with Stone taking a more active role in directing the group both musically and spiritually, things got a little more serious when, with the exception of Bam King, they developed an interest in Sufism and joined the Dervish order. Their devotion to Islam was the beginning of the end. "That killed Mighty Baby really," Stone said. "We couldn't just turn up at a gig where everyone's swigging Newcastle Brown. We weren't saying 'You're going to Hell ... or anything: it just seemed like a world that was not relative to what we decided we were interested in, and so hence the end of Mighty Baby." The end came after a particularly fraught tour of Holland that coincided with the festival of Ramadan, which meant that with the exception of King none of the group could eat during daylight hours. Inevitably tempers frayed and by the time they arrived back in Britain it was all but over.

While Mighty Baby were busy getting religion, Brinsley Schwarz discovered that instant fame, like instant karma, wasn't all it was cracked up to be. Thoroughly disillusioned by the New York episode, they nevertheless drew strength from it. Despite being ripped off by Molton they still had enough money to take time out to consider their future and do their own thing. Speaking to the *Melody Maker* an anonymous group member said: "Of course due to the pressures early on, we weren't able to play what we want to play. But now that the heat's off we can." Brinsley Schwarz had survived the hype and if anything come through it stronger. Having dilly-dallied with whimsical pop and dangled their toes in the prog pool, they were still searching for a sound they could call their own. They eventually found what they were looking for in The Band. A musical antidote to the synthetic commercialism and self-indulgent excesses that was beginning to dominate much of what passed for music at the time; there was something about The Band.

One look at the sepia toned photograph of a bedraggled, wind-swept group of hard working musicians on the cover of their eponymous album said it all. The Band oozed an indefatigable tenacity and rootsy musicality that excited the Brinsleys. "It wasn't that we wanted to sound like them," explains Gomm, "it was just that we liked what they were going for."

Fired up by The Band, they decided to go for it too and had another crack at auditioning for BBC Radio. By now even staid Auntie Beeb realised it was time to restructure her network. Radio 1 would feature mainly progressive music, with Radio 2 given over to pop. With Radio London's emphasis on new music, the Brinsleys were well placed to win over the newly enlightened audition panel. It was indeed a case of third time lucky and on this occasion they were described as, "an interesting harmony styled group with a slight Crosby, Stills and Nash approach". Paul Williams was less enthusiastic with his appraisal of their audition: "The material is not particularly outstanding," he said, "but they are certainly musically competent and worth booking for radio shows if something different is required." Even before the bureaucratic BBC had processed the audition panel's recommendations, Brinsley Schwarz recorded a session for the Hairy Cornflake himself, Dave Lee Travis, followed by appearances on *Disco 2*, *Top Of The Pops* and *Top Gear*.

With their debut album selling well in America, the time had come to record the difficult second album. Not that it was too difficult because Lowe was rapidly becoming a songwriter of note. With enough tunes for an album, Brinsley Schwarz returned to Olympic Studios to record what became *Despite It All*. Once again, Robinson co-produced and got them swinging with a little weed. "I remember recording 'Country Girl'," recalled Rankin. "Dave Robinson produced a joint of Acapulco gold and [when] we played it was just amazing, absolutely fantastic! We were so stoned but it swung like an elephant's dick as they say." When issued as a single, Tony Blackburn made 'Country Girl' his record of the week and Brinsley Schwarz was offered an appearance on BBC Television's flagship pop show *Top Of The Pops*, but decided against it. "What a ghastly record to have been labelled with," said Lowe. "Straw in our hair. Soon as summer was over we'd have been dead."

Nevertheless, *Despite It All* was a turning point and 'Country Girl' a better indication of where they were heading musically than their previous records. "That's when we started to get reasonably good," recalls Rankin. "We started to play some really solid three minute songs. We went more country-rock, whereas the first album was definitely heavy-duty hippy stuff." All the same the album still contained more than its fair share of songs that predated their conversion. 'Piece Of Home' clocked in at over six minutes and 'Old Jarrow' found the group grooving for well over seven. "As fast as we found one little niche we'd be off somewhere else. And we were also internally tugging around in doing it," recalls Andrews. "But mostly we followed where Nick Lowe's writing went, because he was the one who drove the engine."

The Brinsleys were heading in the right musical direction, but they now faced the age-old problem of reproducing what they did in a recording studio on stage. Oddly they initially considered recruiting a new keyboard player, but decided that with two keyboardists in the group already, what they really needed was a second guitarist. An advert placed in the musicians wanted section of the *Melody Maker* brought them Ian Gomm. "I answered this advert and me and my girlfriend went to this house in Carew Road, Northwood. So I turned up, not knowing they were all tripping, and I went in and jammed with them for about 20 minutes and Nick said, 'He's great, you're in man!' Then I sat out in the garden for a little bit and they played a couple of songs in the rehearsal room, and I was saying to my girlfriend, 'They're bloody great'. Dave Robinson turned up and Nick said, 'We've got somebody, this ginger headed guy, he's fantastic!' Dave said, 'But you're all tripping!' And I had to go and do another audition when Dave Robinson was there and they were all straight. And I still got it."

Speaking not long after Gomm joined, Lowe reflected why he instinctively knew Gomm was the right man for the job: "We wanted a simple good guitarist, who can also sing and not the usual Les Paul, hair and passport type of guitarist." Gomm was as far from a hair and passport guitarist as you could get. He'd spent his formative years playing in Tamla-styled trios at Mod hang-outs in the Shepherd's Bush area. He had the right attitude, the right guitar (a Fender Telecaster, the choice of many country axemen) and the right haircut, even if it was ginger. The Brinsleys had already devoted themselves to music, now it was Gomm's turn. Offered a place in the group, he decided to leave home, quit his job and move himself and his girlfriend into the Brinsleys' pad in Northwood.

While Brinsley Schwarz were getting it together and writing what would become their *Silver Pistol* album, Mighty Baby had abandoned music and Martin Stone found himself painting houses to help support the community of Sufis he was living with. House painting brought in some much needed money, but it wasn't reward enough for somebody as creative as Stone, and before long his thoughts turned once again to music. Stone fired off a letter to his friend Phil Lithman who was working with the mysterious Residents in America. Like Stone, Lithman was interested in American roots music and had been drawn to The Residents' collective because they were supposed to have a huge collection of Cajun records. "When he [Lithman] went to America for that period of time we lost touch a little bit, but I used to get letters from him. So after a while of doing next to nothing, I bought a guitar again, wrote Phil a letter and said 'come back'," Stone recalled.

Northwood was home to upper middle-class types who'd moved up from semi-detached suburbia to something a little better. Its quiet streets were only disturbed by women pushing prams on their way to the shops and the station car park was packed with Rovers and Triumph 2000s. The Brinsleys lived in one of the quieter streets past two private tennis courts and an old people's home. A ten bedroom house with large garden, it was originally an annexe to a girls' school. The house at Northwood turned them into a band of brothers, but also isolated them from the outside world. "We used to practise all the time, and get very stoned," says Lowe. "Every time we went out of the house it seemed weird. The only normal thing in the world was what was happening in that house, because we knew what we'd been through. Nobody else understood at all. We were getting very tight together. It was like a strong discipline, in a way. We were going to show these bastards we could do it; and we sussed it all out and thought everybody else was against us."

Lithman hurried back to Blighty and moved into a house with Stone's brother. It wasn't long before Stone started sneaking over to escape the Sufis and have some fun playing old country songs and smoking dope. "He [Lithman] came over to the Muslim commune where I was living and we'd rehearse and play Hank Williams songs all night." recalled Stone. "Before long I decided that this is really what I wanted to do. Originally we didn't think about a band really, because Phil had gone through a personal musical fad - he'd gone back into straight bluegrass music. So we didn't contemplate a band as such as it seemed easier to make a record. I met the people from Revelation and they liked us, so we made an album. So one day, fed up with being a hypocrite, I said I'm quitting all this: let's start a group. That was the start of Chilli Willi and the Red Hot Peppers".

No sooner had Stone started working with Lithman than he was temporarily side-tracked. He couldn't resist the thought of playing in a group again and, when asked if he'd like to join Uncle Dog, jumped at the chance. "At the point where my heart turned back to music I bumped into George Butler who was playing drums with Uncle Dog at the time," he recalled. "He'd been an old friend from Head Records days, and he asked me down to their rehearsals. I still hadn't got an electric guitar but they had lots of them, so I sat in with them on a couple of rehearsals, and they asked me to join. So I did, although by this time I was working with Phil on the Willis thing, rehearsing for the album."

5

Shorter, Sharper And More Interesting

Two years after Dave Robinson tour-managed Jimi Hendrix, a trio of American musicians made their way to London to make a record with the now late guitarist's former manager and producer, Chas Chandler. Eggs Over Easy had its roots in a duo formed by Austin De Lone and Jack O'Hara. O'Hara told the *NME*: "We met Brien Hopkins in the fall of '69 in New York and we worked there for two months." Spotted by Peter Kauff at a club date in Greenwich Village they were signed to Cannon Films to spearhead its new music division. Kauff knew Chandler from his days with The Animals and sent him a demo tape of the group with the idea that he might produce the Eggs' debut album.

Back in London, Chandler began to solicit opinions about the group from friends and colleagues. "Sometime in 1970, Chas played me this tape and said 'What do you think of this?'" recalled John Steel, "It was a song called 'I'm Going To Canada', written by Austin De Lone. The song was very good. It was about ducking over the border into Canada to avoid the Vietnam draft, which was a reality at the time for young Americans at the age of these guys. They were all shit scared of being drafted and being sent out to Vietnam." Steel had played drums with The Animals and remained friends with Chandler before joining his production company in '69. He loved the Eggs' laidback approach and convinced Chandler to produce the New York based trio.

Eggs Over Easy travelled to London in late '70 and were met at Heathrow Airport by Steel whose job it was to drive them to and from the studio each day. Booked into Olympic Studios, Eggs Over Easy discovered that Chandler wanted to record them with a drummer. This was a radical departure because up until then they hadn't bothered with drums. "The history of the band has been really quiet and we don't want to have a drummer just for the sake of it," O'Hara told the *NME*. Chandler, however, had hired a part-time plumber, Les Sampson, to sit in on drums. "Chas had got a recommendation from Noel Redding, a young guy called Les," recalled Steel. "He was discovered by Noel Redding when he came to unplug Noel's sink. Noel got him some work and Chas got him in to do the sessions with Eggs at Olympic Studios." At some point in the sessions Steel had to visit the studio to get Chandler to sign some papers. That day the session had ground to a halt because Sampson was struggling with a light, swingy O'Hara song called 'III Avenue C'. A rock drummer, he simply couldn't 'swing' the way Chandler wanted. Steel, however, could. Chandler told him to jump on the drums and see what he could do. Steel's jazz background saved the day and he had the group swinging quicker than they could say 'Count Basie'. "Their jaws dropped," he says, "because it was sort of a one take thing. The next thing I knew, it seemed to happen almost immediately, Les was dumped and I was in the band."

Returning to America for the Christmas holidays, Eggs Over Easy arrived back in England in early '71 and moved into a three bedroom house in Alma Street in Kentish Town. Cannon Films was still paying them a retainer but, because of contractual problems, money was tight. According to Dave Robinson, Cannon Films all but abandoned Eggs Over Easy, who had no other option than to look for work. "They came to England with some kind of record deal that went sour. It didn't happen, they had no money, the record [company] people brought them over when they didn't want to make a record, they didn't even want to think about the band. The band had to make some money and they did what it seems American bands have always done, they go down the nearest pub or bar and try and get some work."

The Eggs scored some gigs at the American Embassy and a few college dates outside London which brought them to the attention of the national music press. But regular work eluded them until O'Hara walked into the Tally Ho in Kentish Town and simply asked if the Eggs could play there. A typical red brick Victorian pub [now sadly demolished and replaced by a block of flats called Tally Ho Apartments], it showcased small, un-amplified jazz combos but was struggling to attract either jazz fans or drinkers. "It was going down the pan as a jazz venue," recalled Steel, "it just wasn't doing anything. So the landlord and landlady, Jim and Lillian, decided to give us a Monday or Tuesday night or whatever was their worst night and half a dozen people were there just because it was a pub."

Eggs Over Easy soon won over their small audience with a mix of originals and a vast repertoire of cover versions. Strongly influenced by The Band they produced a funky, folk-rock vibe that infused everything from their original material to covers like The Band's 'The Night They Drove Old Dixie Down'. Such was their confidence that they'd sometimes improvise songs as the mood took them. "We would start off the second or third set in that way, with an impromptu song (complete with lyrics), or just a spur of the moment instrumental jam," remembered O'Hara.

News of this remarkable group spread like wildfire. "It started out with just a handful of squatters and Canadian ex-patriots on a Monday night and just turned into a great party three nights a week - very casual, no pretence - nothing to do with the music business, just living," O'Hara recalled. Without any publicity or record company backing, Eggs Over Easy built a reputation as one of the capital's hottest attractions. "We did the Tally Ho and built it up into a phenomenal success at that level," recalled Steel, "it was simply word of mouth that built up from a handful of people to jammed out every time we played, which was several times a week."

The small stage and intimate setting suited Eggs Over Easy perfectly.

Everything was stripped down and their small amps meant that they could all hear one another and really rock or swing as the fancy took them. Barry Richardson of Bees Make Honey, who followed Eggs Over Easy into the Tally Ho, thought their success was down to the fact that they "were able to play loose enough music to appeal to the old jazz crowd, whilst still drawing in a younger rock crowd". Eggs Over Easy achieved a perfect union of jazz and rock sensibilities. Mighty Baby had been attempting something similar, but what they took from jazz was a love of improvisation that produced long, mellifluous compositions that were the very opposite of the swinging good time music being made by the Eggs. What Eggs Over Easy appropriated from jazz was an ability to swing which they applied to perfectly tailored country-tinged songs that instinctively tapped into a juke-joint vibe that got people dancing and drinking.

Eggs Over Easy quickly outgrew their one night at the Tally Ho and were given a second and a fee of £25 a night. "We also got to pass the hat around as well," recalled Steel. They weren't going to get rich playing the Tally Ho, but as their reputation grew they secured bookings in pubs across the capital. Nevertheless, everything remained on a more or less semi-professional basis. "I was doing it on a kind of after hours level," suggests Steel, "working at the office and things. But things got so busy, the number of sessions at the Tally Ho and other places started to build quite dramatically. It began to be a bit of a strain, so Chas very generously let me more or less drop the office side of things and I became the drummer with Eggs Over Easy for a while."

The Eggs soon attracted the kind of media types who could make or break a group. But as Steel explains, the Eggs had an in-built self-destruct mechanism. "They had this will to fail." he says. "John Peel turned up one night, completely unsolicited. I spotted him straight away. But somehow Brien managed to screw the night up by being too stoned and Peel was underwhelmed and went off and nothing more happened." Dave Robinson chanced upon the three-piece Eggs line-up (Steel's time with the group was drawing to a close and for a while he stopped playing with them) at the Marquee Club and was immediately smitten. "The penny just dropped," he says, "it was one of those things. Bands in those days did very long [sets] because that's what was required to be able to play the universities, and everyone was smoking an awful lot of dope so their music was a bit boring and long. Here was a band playing three-minute numbers, some of them covers, but with a certain kind of attitude which I had thought all along was how it should be, so here was somebody who could demonstrate that it was a worker, that it sounded great." Robinson made his way backstage to meet the Eggs and insisted they return to the Brinsleys' house in Northwood. Their combination of down-home musicianship and do-it-yourself attitude was the final piece of the jigsaw the Brinsleys had been looking for. More important was the revelation that Eggs Over Easy could make a living from playing pubs.

The club scene provided most groups with a livelihood, but was in decline.

The very groups that had sustained the club scene, The Who, Taste and Led Zeppelin, had priced themselves out of the market. As Brinsley Schwarz had discovered to their cost, rock music had become big business. Universities, however, could pay over the odds for groups and add to club promoters' woes. The band Yes were regulars on the university circuit and Jon Anderson explained how it worked. "The students running the gigs were putting on a couple of hundred quid over the top just to make sure they got the bands." Because of the way universities were funded, student unions were awash with cash which they could spend pretty much as they pleased. How times have changed! Michael Alfandary explained the system to the *Melody Maker*: "Every time a chap goes to college his local authority pays him a grant. And about £6 of that grant goes direct to the student union." So, the larger the college, the larger the grant and the more they could spend on attracting top drawer bands.

Clubs couldn't afford to subsidise rock groups in the way that universities could. There was no way the Cavern Club or the Twisted Wheel could afford The Who, but Leeds University could. This was another contributing factor to the decline in medium-sized music venues. But when the Conservative Party came to power in 1970, rock groups experienced a double whammy. The Conservatives inherited a weakened economy and poor industrial relations that got worse as their term in office progressed. One way they could save money was to cut university funding. This was also partly politically motivated because some student unions were using government funding to subsidise radical political causes that the Conservatives opposed. Something had to give because as Alfandary noted: "... some of the money ... was going to some funny destinations so there was a clamp-down. The effect of that was that every expenditure had to be justified." Bad luck Yes!

It wasn't only the super groups that were struggling; every group in the country found it difficult to find gigs that made a profit. "You could never turn down work because we had to eat," Gomm explains. "They'd say, 'we've got you a gig', but it was up in Glasgow." Because they were on such a tight budget the Brinsleys frequently had to resort to chicanery to make ends meet. "We'd rent a Transit van then we'd take the speedo cable off because it was the first 50 miles free and then so much per mile afterwards," explained Gomm. "We set off first thing in the morning and drove to Glasgow, but we didn't have enough money for bed and breakfast so we drove back the same night. Around Lockerbie this terrible noise came out of the front wheel, and it was the front bearing. We got the AA out, who got a bearing from Carlisle. When we got back to London, knowing that the AA had been called out in Lockerbie, which is 500 miles [from London] we had to try and work out how to spin it [the odometer] on."

Making 1000 mile round trips to play one-off gigs wasn't cost effective, but they had no other option because as Dave Robinson explains: "There were no venues, you could not be in London and make a living. You had to go out.

You had to get an agency, you had to go round the country, you had to do various things. I couldn't see why music wasn't a more functional item, why it wasn't a little bit more a part of things and didn't need major record companies and major stupidity. Most of the music put out by the major record companies was crap, so your only chance of a career was to join that band. I didn't really fancy it and the band didn't really fancy it, because they saw the error of that particular kind of movement."

Profit and loss wasn't the only concern. Robinson told *Rolling Stone* magazine that every time Brinsley Schwarz played a university they had to compromise because they were expected to follow conventions they considered cliched. Robinson claimed that bands were forced to follow a formula that left the music devoid of feeling. Rock shows had become predictable and that meant that the only way for a band to progress was to play to bigger and bigger audiences, rather than focusing on the emotional content of their music. Brinsley Schwarz didn't want to play bigger and bigger halls, they'd had their fill of that scene, what they wanted was to become better and better musicians and they discovered that they could do just that by playing smaller and smaller venues.

For middle tier groups like Brinsley Schwarz, playing pubs opened up another important income stream and meant they could avoid having to rely on hackneyed rock 'n' roll cliches. Even if clubs were closing down left, right and centre there were still plenty of venues in London to play. Hobbit's Garden, Sisters Club and the Country Club all booked groups comparable to Brinsley Schwarz. Public Houses like the Red Lion in Leytonstone, the Green Man in the Euston Road and the Wake Arms in Epping also offered rock music on a regular basis. But what Robinson and the Brinsleys wanted was to create a scene they could call their own. The pub rock circuit would belong to those who created it, and Brinsley Schwarz would play an important part in giving it credibility. "We had to create that because there's nowhere else to go, right?" Barry Richardson of Bees Make Honey told *Melody Maker*. "We found places to play. Shortly afterwards the Brinsleys, who were having a hard time of it on the road, came into the Tally Ho. I mean we were doing pretty well, but the fact [is] that an established band came in made the Tally Ho an important gig in London."

The Brinsleys weren't doing pretty well. Their advance from United Artists and Capitol was long spent and a long line of creditors were still snapping at their heels. Ian Gomm donated his life savings to the group simply to keep it going until Robinson could find them steady work. Pubs offered a ready source of income, but as far as Nick Lowe was concerned also the perfect place from where to exact revenge on the music business. "In our outsider state, we felt at perfect liberty to snipe at mainstream pop and rock, these really hopeless blues-boogie groups like Ten Years After who were going to America and making scads of money," he says. "At the time we thought, 'These people are awful and Something Should Be Done.' Then we ran into this American group,

Eggs Over Easy, playing a pub in north London, and got friendly, and saw an opportunity to create a scene that would be so jumping that people wouldn't dream of going to see ELP because it would be such a drag."

Eggs Over Easy, Bees Make Honey and Brinsley Schwarz were leaders of the pub rock pack. They were also at the forefront of a broader cultural shift being played out across the pages of the music press and 'serious' television programmes like *The Old Grey Whistle Test*. Writing in *ZigZag* magazine, Andy Childs reported on a discussion on *Whistle Test* between Dave Dee (A&R manager for Atlantic), Geoff Brown (journalist), Richard Williams (journalist) and Ray Davies (pop star) on the merits of pub rock. "The actual discussion was so inept", he wrote, "as to be hardly worth recording, but they all came to the conclusion that pub rock bands (a generalisation that is ridiculously misleading) lack the image, youthful exuberance and fresh ideas to provide the basis of a 'new scene.'" He continued, "If image is that important, more important than the music itself, then the British rock scene must be a disaster area."

British mainstream music was in a mess. But there were always alternatives, and thankfully journalists like Childs, managers like Robinson and groups like Brinsley Schwarz were shaping that alternative. In fact, the Brinsleys were already part of an alternative live circuit that included benefit gigs and the developing festival scene. "Our philosophy was to play to anybody and everybody," says Andrews. "We did a lot of benefit gigs because we could. And our philosophy was that we should be playing music for everybody." Ian Gomm concurs: "We were so fair we'd do charity gigs for free, but if we played for the Black Panthers we'd go out of our way to play for the White Panthers to try and even it up." [The White Panther Party were formed as a sympathetic response to The Black Panther Party whose founder Huey P. Newton, when asked what white people could do to aid the Black Panthers, told them to form the White Panthers].

As far as Robinson was concerned it was all work and playing festivals was just another way of keeping them razor-sharp. As honed as they were, Robinson thought they could be sharper. "So we played all the festivals and we did all that thing and at the back of it we thought music could be shorter, sharper and more interesting. And there seemed to be a lot of bands hanging around in London with the same kind of attitude," he says. "In those days you kind of had alcoholic jazz going on where people were asleep, you know, 15 people asleep in the back room of a pub with the band kind of drinking their way through the set. Boring!"

By rescuing pubs from death by jazz, Eggs Over Easy paved the way for an explosion of small rock venues that operated outside a mainstream circuit still dominated by dodgy showbiz agents and monolithic record companies. Robinson could see the possibilities and opportunities an alternative live circuit offered and grabbed the chance with both hands. "There was no circuit," he says, "so we thought let's make a circuit. Because the Brinsleys had a name we were able to spearhead that circuit, because people would come to the opening night if Brinsley Schwarz played."

By opening up the pubs and peppering their set with off-kilter cover versions, Eggs Over Easy influenced not only where music was made but what was played. "When we started playing the Tally Ho, the audience was quite cosmopolitan, quite diverse," recalls Gomm. "The idea was that you had to play for three hours. The first week you'd play your usual set, but if you came back the next week, playing the same thing, they'd suss it out. That's why a change was necessary. In the beginning we started with a rush of our own songs - but later that mellowed out a bit. After you get over the initial urge of writing your own songs, you begin comparing them to others. Obviously you tend to think that yours are better - but after a while you get bored and you are aware that there are other songs. At that point we began learning other songs as well as our own for the stage act."

Playing cover versions meant they had to think about what they played as well as how they played. The focus was on the music rather than the image. "They had to really think about their music," says Robinson. "Every week they were going to play the same place so they had to do a bit of rehearsal and learn a few more songs. You couldn't play the same three sets every week. So people had to pay attention to their music a little bit. The music roots of it all." The first group in a long time to give the cover version credibility, Eggs Over Easy, had shown that there was nothing wrong in performing other folks' material. When Lennon and McCartney kicked the hack song writers out of Tin Pan Alley in the early '60s they effectively devalued the cover version; that is unless it was one of theirs. Almost overnight it became essential that groups write their own material. It was one measure of how successful a group was.

Martin Belmont was among the first to see the group at the Tally Ho and was bowled over by their choice of cover versions. "Suddenly this whole new approach opened up of playing in pubs and they were doing things that would have been deemed extremely un-cool just a few months before," he recalled. "They would play their own stuff and they would play some great covers, but then they would do 'Brown Sugar' or something which you wouldn't have dreamt of doing normally just because it wasn't esoteric enough and they just made a complete nonsense of that whole thing. You can play anything so long as you do it well and with the right vibe and attitude and the punters like it."

The perfect antidote to the self-indulgent rock operas and progressive symphonic bombast being performed by the likes of The Who, Genesis and Yes, performing cover versions with a twist showed you had attitude. Not only was it anti-prog, it was fun. The Brinsleys and their contemporaries discovered that there was no need to make any comparison with the original, playing a cover version could be just as creative as writing their own songs. Because they were making something new and original they could make it their own. "We started mixing it up with more R&B stuff we liked as well, and eventually it got to the stage where we'd play whatever was in the charts that week," recalls Lowe. It didn't matter who wrote the song as long as it showed you were taking a stand. "I can remember believing for ages that The Beatles wrote 'Roll Over Beethoven'," said Lowe. That they didn't made little difference, they'd made it their own, and with a little detective work it was relatively simple to track down the original by Chuck Berry.

The Brinsleys began doing what every British group had done since American rock 'n' roll came blasting out of the nation's wireless sets - they began blending it with their own unique sensibility. When it came to making great music, two cultures really were better than one. "When British bands do that whole American thing it comes out as a very effective blend," Lowe told the *NME*.

Besides getting back to rock's roots, it made music fun again and got people dancing. All you could do at a Genesis gig was sit in awe at the musical virtuosity and react accordingly as the carefully planned set progressed to its inevitable climax. Playing pokey three-minute songs put out a lot of energy and created the kind of reciprocity between group and audience that Pete Townshend had wanted for The Who when he wrote 'Join Together'. But when The Who played some enormous stadium they were so distant, and their show so contrived, that the audience could no more empathise with them than it could join them for a drink at the bar. It was much easier to develop reciprocity with an audience if it was crammed into a sweaty basement or back room with a few drinks to liven things up.

Pub venues were small, 250 capacity on average, and according to Charlie Gillett the average audience wasn't particularly hip or young either. "It was people just going out for a night's drinking, mostly in their late twenties and mid-thirties and some of the same people who might have gone to a jazz gig. It was never hip, it was teachers, college students, whatever. With clubs these days, it is what you are wearing which dictates whether you get in the door or not, but it was not remotely like that. Everybody was pretty scruffy looking. There was a bit of dancing in front of the stage and basically it was a beer drinking, cigarette smoking scene, no drugs, just a pub scene."

Building on Eggs Over Easy's groundwork wasn't going to be simple. But Robinson wasn't the kind of person to let that stop him. If he could stage something as audacious as flying an aeroplane full of journalists to New York to see an unknown band, then creating a new music scene from nothing was child's play. Just as the pub circuit began to take off Eggs Over Easy were forced to return to America. The deal with Cannon Films having collapsed, the album they recorded with Chandler went unreleased. Signed to A&M the group re-recorded the album with Link Wray producing and issued it as *Good 'n' Cheap* in 1972.

6
It All Depends Which Side Of The Bar You're On

On 2 February 1972, Brinsley Schwarz began a twelve-week residency at the Tally Ho that coincided with the release of their new album, *Silver Pistol*. The gigs were as low-key as the promotion given to their album. As modest as these gigs were, they were no less demanding than college or theatre dates. Because they'd be playing to a regular audience each week they needed to expand their repertoire and fast. "Part of our plan [is] to learn up loads and loads and loads of numbers so that you won't get bored with doing the same thing every night," Lowe told *Sounds*. (Some of the new songs given an airing in early '72 included Smokey Robinson's 'She's Got To Be Real', Otis Rush's 'Home Work', the traditional 'Midnight Train' and Allen Toussaint's 'Wonder Woman').

Eleven days after beginning their residency at the Tally Ho, Brinsley Schwarz appeared alongside label mates and staunch free festival favourites Hawkwind at the Greasy Truckers Party, with Welsh rockers Man (another United Artists act) also on the bill. Brinsley Schwarz were no strangers to the festival circuit themselves, as Dave Robinson explains: "The year after the Fillmore we played pretty much every free festival in England. John Peel and us were the ones you could count on at every festival in the country." Inspired by a bunch of San Franciscan hippies calling themselves the Diggers, Dave Robinson and Doug Smith, proprietor of management company Clearwater Productions, formed The Greasy Truckers, an organisation that helped fund various underground causes. In this case the money was to provide an alternative rock venue in Notting Hill.

As the music business was the engine that drove the underground, what better than to relieve it of excess cash than by organising a festival at the hippest venue in the country, the Roundhouse. Musically Brinsley Schwarz stuck out like a sore thumb. While Hawkwind and Man belted out long improvisations at deafening volume, or what passed for deafening volume in those days, the Brinsleys triumphed with their low-volume set of snappy country-rock and R&B. Comprising a mix of covers and original material drawn from *Despite It All* and their recently released *Silver Pistol* album, they won over the audience of freaks who were more tolerant than many of today's gig goers.

Silver Pistol had been recorded the previous summer. In keeping with their reaction to the Fillmore fiasco, the Brinsleys recorded what Robinson described as "an anti-album, with none of the things you normally expect". He continued: "A live album now might be groovy but the whole thing is geared towards the gig and the recording is a secondary effect." Indeed, who needed an album when all you had to do was pop down your local boozer, club or university and see the real thing being performed before your very eyes.

Albums were becoming pretentious, turgid affairs. The Brinsleys weren't interested in making huge artistic statements, they weren't even going to record in a proper studio. Rather, they arranged for some eight-track recording equipment to be set up in their front room which they'd sound-proofed with old mattresses. One reason the group decided to record at home was because it was cheap. "We got so much per album, and it was cheaper for us to hire a mobile studio and do it in the house," explains Rankin. Recording at home also mirrored the way The Band had made their eponymous album. Renting a large house from Sammy Davis Jr, The Band turned the pool house into a recording studio by nailing baffles to the outside wall. Replicating the set up in London, Brinsley Schwarz aped their heroes and ensured the project stayed real. "It was like something we had to do," said Schwarz. "If we had gone into the studio to record this album, it would have been a lie."

It wasn't the first time musicians had recorded at home, nor would it be the last; Les Paul developed the idea in the 1950s. Pete Townshend had a passion for home recording, and Paul McCartney had recorded the bulk of his debut album at home. But unlike Les Paul, the American guitar wizard who'd pioneered multi-track recording, or McCartney, who overdubbed all the instruments himself, the Brinsleys were determined to keep overdubs to a minimum. "We did *Silver Pistol* which was the opposite of *Despite It All* - no over-dubbing at all except the accordion which we had to do because it made so much noise," Schwarz recalled.

Bob Andrews recorded his accordion part in the conservatory, but the Brinsleys were prepared to go even further in their pursuit of aural perfection. When playing at outdoor festivals they'd noticed that they got a very dry, clean sound. With no walls for the music to bounce off, there was no echo or reverb to 'colour' their sound. It made perfect sense to set up their gear in the garden and record outdoors. 'Egypt' and 'Silver Pistol' were the result. 'I remember Brinsley had a wasp on his finger while he was playing," Rankin amusingly recalls. "He kept his nerve all the way through it." Despite the threat of being stung by pesky insects and Lowe's pedigree Labrador, Poacher, barking through the back garden fence at the neighbour's cat, it gave them precisely the sound they were searching for.

While the Brinsleys took recording to extremes, they weren't alone in wanting to side-step what had become an expensive and contrived practice. Writing in the October '72 issue of *Let It Rock* magazine, Gary Herman suggested that there had been "a reaction against what seems to be unnecessary sophistication turning a craft object - the record - into an art object." Herman claimed there was a vogue towards returning to simpler recording techniques in an attempt to capture the immediacy and exuberance of live rock 'n' roll that opposed the intricate stereo and quadraphonic recordings also being produced at the time. Of course, one didn't need expensive studios to record sophisticated sounding records. John Lennon recorded his *Imagine* album at his house in Berkshire on the same kind of eight-track equipment used by the Brinsleys. The difference, as Herman noted, was attitude and objectives: "The choices should be made according to the mutual aims of producer and performer in the communication of their art." Nowhere can that be more clearly heard than on the Brinsleys' *Silver Pistol* album, which communicated the Brinsleys' attitude to music making in the clearest way possible. In other hands it would have been commercial suicide. But the Brinsleys couldn't have cared less. Everything about the record, from the way it was recorded to the washed out colours used for the cover, was as opposed to mainstream music as it was possible to be in a climate dominated by the guile of glam and the pretentiousness of prog.

Although they were living the dream, not all was well with the group. According to Rankin they were all struggling to keep it together. "Nick was a bit depressed when we did that. We all got into the lysergic acid a bit and lots of dope. It changed me completely as a person. It was a depressing time and it's quite a depressing album really. 'Silver Pistol' is about committing suicide. Nick was in that sort of state. We were skint, [it was] the 3-day week, there was no petrol and you couldn't drive anywhere. We were just surviving really." Isn't the rock 'n' roll lifestyle glamorous! Like Rankin, Lowe was changed by taking too much acid. "I finally lost my mind through taking LSD. I had to be literally led around for nine months. I was also in a terrible state. I was covered in lice and I had gonorrhoea. I was a horrible hippie case and my mind had really gone. I certainly thought I was never going to be mentally well again, and as a matter of fact, I don't think I'll ever recover from it." The situation affected everyone, regardless of their chemical intake. Ian Gomm, who was more familiar with battery acid than the hallucinogenic variety, says: "We lived it. It was like all for one and one for all. That's what a commune is. I wouldn't say we were exactly hippies, but everybody else thought we were down that street. But I was suffering their pain. When you're all living together you do."

In April, Brinsley Schwarz decamped to Rockfield Studios in Wales to record their next album, *Nervous On The Road*. This time they were going to record in a proper studio, albeit an affordable one. Rockfield was the brainchild of Charles and Kingsley Ward, whose father owned the farm on which they set up the facility. Inspired by Joe Meek's quirky studio set up, Kingsley decided to build his own version in the country as an affordable alternative that would let musicians record at a more leisurely pace. "We recorded *Nervous On The Road* at Rockfield because it was cheap and [it gave us] plenty of time to do it," Rankin recounts.

Initially, the studio was little more than two Revox tape machines in the potato loft. Over several years of steady growth it developed into a 16-track state of the art facility, but kept its down home feel with old mattresses used to line the drum booth and mud and straw trodden into the mixing room floor. By the early '70s, Rockfield had been redesigned with a large, rectangular live room that meant groups could record together rather than being stuck in isolation booths. "We'd set up live in the studio, wait until we got a decent backing track and then overdub on that," explains Rankin. "We'd play it like we'd play it live and basically try to get the rhythm section sorted."

As accommodating as the studio was, its reputation was due in no small part to the music Dave Edmunds had made there. In 1970, Edmunds used it to record his transatlantic smash 'I Hear You Knocking'. Besides launching Rockfield, the single made Edmunds an overnight star and producer of note. A studio junkie who disliked touring, he found his instant fame as difficult to deal with as had the Brinsleys. Like them he had previous form, having issued records with the Human Beans and Love Sculpture. His frantic reading of 'Sabre Dance' helped secure a place in the pantheon of guitar legends, but like the Brinsleys he found it difficult to find a style he could call his own. "Really we [Love Sculpture] were a happy group but musically it just didn't work. We didn't know what we wanted to do. We didn't have any direction," he told the *NME*.

Edmunds lived close to the studio and was in effect the house producer who defined its sound. Speaking to *Let It Rock* he explained how he did it. "When I'm recording with a band I put the sound in completely flat; no tricks. Then the band comes in the control room and listens. And I do things with the tapes that I think they might like. It's all done in the mixing. And I never do anything the band doesn't like." Edmunds was an elusive figure in the habit of recording late at night after Brinsley Schwarz had called it a day. But one night he turned up early and asked if he could have a go at mixing the song they'd recorded earlier. "Edmunds listened to one of our recordings and asked us if he could have a tinker with it," recalls Lowe. Dave Robinson, who was our producer, looked a bit tense, but we all thought it was a good idea. Our recording was very tiresome, but Edmunds got a few Revoxes going, patched in some echo effects and suddenly the thing was jumping. In next to no time, he had transformed our leaden sound into an all-singing, all-dancing groove. We were a bit slack-jawed and saucer-eyed at this, although Dave Robinson got a bit cross. After Edmunds and Kingsley Ward left the room, Robbo said, 'You can't have that, it's not real!' 'Real' was the word we bandied about! But I'm not blaming Robbo; we were all learning."

Time spent in the studio with Edmunds was time well spent, sitting at the feet of the master. A few years later it gave Lowe the confidence to do for Stiff Records what Edmunds had done for Rockfield Studios. And it wasn't only Lowe who learnt from Edmunds, for Schwarz the experience taught him a lot. "He involved us in lots of things. In those days you did what is now known as chorusing or automatic double-tracking by recording a track onto a Revox two-track machine and playing it back simultaneously while altering the speed of the Revox so it would fluctuate and go in and out of tune very slightly. I remember spending hours standing by this thing twiddling this knob. It was an eye opener for us as far as record production was concerned."

The Edmunds mix wasn't used because the group's credo of keeping it 'real' didn't allow for such production conceits. But attitudes within the band were changing, if slowly. The Brinsleys were constantly reinventing themselves in subtle ways, but never with an eye on the charts. That would change when Edmunds was given his head as producer of their swansong, *New Favourites*, but by then it was way too late. For the moment, at least, what you saw or heard was what you got. The Brinsleys were indefatigably themselves, even if it meant being needlessly self-defeating. It wasn't that they didn't want success, but it had to be on their terms.

7
Putting The Bomp In

Robinson and Eichler's merry band of musicians did more than open up a new circuit of venues; they became the unwitting parents to the first new group to emerge from the scene they'd helped create. Ducks Deluxe were the progeny of Brinsley Schwarz and Help Yourself with the Flamin' Groovies as Godparents. Each group harboured a frustrated roadie with dreams of making it in the music business, and with a little help from their friends their dreams soon became a reality.

Martin Belmont left college in 1970 and found himself in London where he met up with an old friend, Chris Gabrin, who introduced him to the Brinsleys. The group was looking for a roadie and, as no experience was required, Belmont got the job. "I moved into the house in Northwood, where they were living at that time. That would have been about 1971, I think. It was great for me because I was fresh out of college, I was 21, and it was great. I won't say being a roadie was particularly great, but it was great seeing a band work. It kind of opened my eyes to what you needed to do."

While Robinson was working hard to break the Brinsleys, Eichler was doing his best to make things happen for Help Yourself. A regular visitor to United Artists' offices, he encountered budding bar-room bully Sean Tyla during one of his visits. Tyla was working at United Artists on various projects and going slowly "round the twist". If first impressions count for anything, Tyla wasn't impressed by what he saw. "John Eichler, the manager, looked like an overweight troll and when Richard Treece appeared I was convinced they were on day release from the funny farm! Joking aside, they helped me enormously and I tried to help them, but they did little to help themselves." Ironic really for a band called Help Yourself.

Despite reservations, Tyla moved in with the Helps who were living at Down Home Productions headquarters at Headley Grange, Hampshire. An old Victorian poorhouse, it was a rundown three storey building with little in the way of home comforts. Its one advantage was that they could make as much noise as they liked without annoying the neighbours. If Tyla's first impressions weren't favourable, he soon changed his mind. "Living with the Helps really helped me find myself after years of following the middle-class' code'. I'd married too young and I was lost in time. Later on, because of Malcolm Morley's illness I got a chance to do my stuff and I liked it. I never really knew what they thought of me but I cared for them a lot. They were all extremely talented but they didn't have a plan. If we hadn't met I wouldn't have had a career at all - I'm convinced of that."

Belmont busied himself working for the Brinsleys, acquired a modified guitar, the Gommcaster, from Ian Gomm and got to know their publicist, Dai Davies. Hatching plans to launch himself as a manager, Davies introduced Belmont to Tyla. "We met each other and shared mutual musical tastes," explains Belmont. "But then I got really ill and I ended up in hospital with meningitis and everything was put back." While Belmont was recovering in hospital, Ken Whaley left Help Yourself and moved into a squat in Camden Town. He was joined by Tyla and, once he'd been discharged from hospital, Belmont. "It was great, we had this huge house with running water, electricity and no rent and a place to rehearse," says Belmont. Whaley joined the two guitarists on bass and they began informal rehearsals. "We just decided to have a blow together," explains Tyla. "And I can tell you the music was incredibly weird. It was very Dead-y, very Airplane-y in the beginning, which isn't Martin's kind of music at all, really. So Mart played his thing to it, while Ken was still doing the Jack Casady type of stuff. Then I think we broke it down to basics to make it work."

Tim Roper had no connection with the Brinsleys or Help Yourself and with the passing of time nobody seems to remember how he arrived on the scene. He could, however, hit the drums hard and keep time, so he got the gig as the Ducks drummer. With a handful of original compositions and cover versions in their back pocket, Ducks Deluxe followed Eggs Over Easy and Brinsley Schwarz into the Tally Ho. "At the time it was completely ridiculous to try and get anybody to get us any gigs," recalls Tyla. "The other thing was that we didn't want to start off in the usual way; you know - make an album, go out on an immediate college tour and wonder why the fuck everybody's going boo. That's a sharks' trip and we didn't want to do that. And basically, we weren't good enough to do that, and we thought the best way to get the band together was going and playing two-and-a-half hours in a pub, and that was why we did it. There was no other spectacular reason."

The pub circuit was to Ducks Deluxe what the Reeperbahn was to The Beatles. As far as Robinson was concerned pub rock was an egalitarian hotbed that would provide the music business with genuine, exciting talent. "It gives a guy the opportunity and the impetus to go out and see if he can do it on stage." he said. Ducks Deluxe didn't have flash gear but they knew how to rock an audience. From the moment they set foot on the Tally Ho's tiny stage they were a wind of change that vitalised the scene with a dose of loud, fast and dirty rock 'n' roll. If Eggs Over Easy grooved, Ducks Deluxe rocked. If Brinsley Schwarz turned the volume down, Ducks Deluxe cranked it up. If Bees Make Honey were the polite face of pub rock, Ducks Deluxe were snotty street urchins with attitude. It wasn't enough for Tyla to connect with his audience purely through music. Speaking to *Let It Rock* magazine in 1974, he said: "I write with the idea of communicating with people through a more physical vibe. I think we appeared as the first very rude band to play in a pub."

No sooner had Ducks Deluxe made in-roads onto the pub circuit than Whaley decided it wasn't for him and re-joined Help Yourself. "Ken must have been in [the band] for probably four, maybe five months. He left, he found it was not really his cup of tea or he didn't get on with Sean, I'm not sure exactly, but he left," explains Belmont. His replacement, Nick Garvey, had worked as a roadie for another United Artists' act, the Flamin' Groovies, and brought a pop sensibility with him. "I missed Ken but Nick made a huge difference straight away," says Tyla. "He had no predefined notions of how or what he should play. He had his own voice, he sang in tune, he took to the bass, although he could play just as well on the guitar and he fitted in immediately. He added a real melodic extension to the music overall but he rocked like a mother! His song writing was a real added bonus and I didn't feel so pressurised after 'Thick Gravy' arrived."

With Garvey in place, Ducks Deluxe soon progressed to larger venues and set their sights on out of town gigs. "It was just before Christmas '72, we'd done about sixteen gigs; and Dai comes round and says we're on at the [Edmonton] Sundown," recalls Tyla. "We were first on, and the bigness of the occasion was obvious to anyone who knew us. This enormous stage, tons of Marshall stacks everywhere, and we come on with two AC-30s and a T-60 and a beaten-up Premier kit. And we made a helluva row, I know that." On 19 December, Ducks Deluxe headed to Swansea to make a racket at Man's Christmas party. "That was through Dai Davis that we got on that bill," recalls Belmont. "That was the first thing that was ever recorded. They put out a double mini 10-inch album [that] we had one track on." Ducks Deluxe made their vinyl debut with 'Boogaloo Babe' on Man's *Christmas At The Patti*, but despite Tyla's connection with United Artists it declined to sign them.

At about the same time Ducks Deluxe secured the services of the Iron Horse agency, a subsidiary of United Artists, which signed the group partly because of Tyla's connection with its record division. Their residency at the Tally Ho brought in £30 a week which was just about enough to survive on, and Davies's position as David Bowie's publicist helped subsidise day-today running costs. Although the whole point of signing to an agency was to secure more work, the Ducks decided to continue honing their act on the pub circuit before launching themselves nationwide onto an unsuspecting public. Things were moving fast and the group were riding a pre-fame high. "I loved it! Then, when we had little money and before we signed a deal, I had never been happier in my life," explains Tyla. "I was churning the songs out daily. I'd be writing a 'newie' upstairs and Martin would be working the last one with Ken in the front room, Tim on the drums, windows wide open and nobody cared. Then, when *Time Out*'s ceaseless campaigning for us finally bore fruit it all got a little serious. It was a good time though."

Thanks to John Collis of *Time Out* magazine, Ducks Deluxe were being championed as the 'new Rolling Stones'. They were attracting a considerable following and gaining the attention of A&R managers from across London. Tamla Motown offered a derisory deal that was quickly dismissed as a joke by the Ducks and their manager. Signing with Motown would have been cool, but Davis used his connections to try and secure a contract with RCA. Although it showed considerable interest in the group, RCA wouldn't commit itself. Frustrated, Tyla claimed that the record companies "were just fucking about." "Their attitude was," he said, "'you do what you're told and you'll be all right.'" Ducks weren't the kind of group to be told what they should or shouldn't do. They'd seen what happened to groups that had followed that particular path. But like it or not there was no other choice. "There was no thought of signing to an indie label, there was no Stiff or anything," explains Belmont. "You signed to a major label. It was a whole different scene in those days. There were a lot of major record labels, it wasn't like today where there's two corporations that run everything."

The problem was that most of the major record companies didn't have the first idea how to deal with groups like Ducks Deluxe. RCA did eventually come up with an offer described by Tyla as "a real record contract, not a pretend one, and real interest and foresight." Although RCA had dithered it was something to get excited about. "We signed to fucking RCA for Christ's sake," Belmont exclaimed, "that's Elvis Presley's record label!" Signing with RCA did two things. It gave them credibility and transformed them from amateurs into professionals. "There was a big change in attitude," explained Tyla. "It became, 'We ain't no pissy little pub rock band, we're a fucking rock 'n' roll band, and one of the best there is.'"

Chilli Willi and the Red Hot Peppers weren't no pissy little pub rock band, but they weren't no rock 'n' roll band neither. Hell, they weren't even half a band. At this point in time Chilli Willi and the Red Hot Peppers were an acoustic country-blues duo formed by Martin Stone and Phil Lithman. Stone used his contacts to secure some support gigs on the embryonic pub circuit and a record deal with Revelation Records. (The label had been set up to offset the costs of the first Glastonbury Fayre and Mighty Baby had contributed a song to the resulting triple album.) Stone and Lithman looked like typical hippies but musically they had more in common with the Brinsleys than Pink Floyd or Soft Machine. Although they were content with their lo-fi, low-key approach to music making, when it came time to record their debut album they called on Nick Lowe, Bob Andrews and Billy Rankin to flesh out their sonic signature.

Issued in 1972, *Kings Of The Robot Rhythm* companioned the Brinsleys stripped-down aesthetic, right down to the washed out colours and textured card used for the Barney Bubbles designed sleeve. *Kings Of The Robot Rhythm* was the quintessence of the down home aesthetic. Described by Stone as an "extremely chaotic and under-produced" album, it sounded like an old Carter Family album recorded on wax cylinders. It reeked of utility and dusty Mullard valves. The look, feel and combined weight of the thick vinyl record and heavy-duty card sleeve reinforced the idea that it had somehow dropped through a hole in the space-time continuum and into the racks of your local record shop.

As wildly out of step as they were, Stone and Lithman were convinced the time was right to expand the duo and become a full-blown band. "The Brinsleys were on a couple of tracks, which gave it enough push to make us decide to go rock 'n' roll." says Stone. The process of acquiring musicians began with Stone and Lithman asking friends and acquaintances for recommendations. The late Jo Ann Kelly, who sang on the album, suggested a multi-instrumentalist called Keith who played banjo for Country Fever. "He came round and we realised straight away that he was too good for us," says Stone. "He was a bluegrass player, whereas we were old rock 'n' roll blues freaks who liked bluegrass music. We played some songs together and he seemed to enjoy himself, and when we said goodbye to him he said, 'See you again'. We then talked it over between ourselves and decided that we wouldn't be able to keep up with him. So we didn't contact him again and just thought, 'Well, who else can we get?'"

Stone remembered a banjo player called Paul Bailey from his days with The Action and set about tracking him down. "I didn't really know Paul," he recalls. "I just used to say hello to him ... I re-introduced myself to try and click everything into place for him, and then I asked him to join the group. He said, 'I'm sorry, I don't play banjo anymore'. So I said, 'OK, I'm just living round the corner, come by sometime'. I went back home and tried to think of who else we could try, but Paul came by and said, 'I had a go on the banjo last night and I can still do it'. So that was that, he joined on banjo." All that remained was to find a rhythm section. By chance Stone met fellow musician Robin Scott, who he'd played with a few years earlier, and who was looking for a record deal. Stone suggested he visit Revelation Records and see if they might be interested. Scott turned up with his bass player, Paul Riley, and Stone suggested they join forces. Scott's musical vision didn't dovetail with Stone's, but Riley's did and he signed up as the fourth member of the group. Scott went on to find success as M and scored a big chart hit with the catchy 'Pop Muzak' in 1979.

Chilli Willi and the Red Hot Peppers were still without a roadie or manager but once again Brinsley Schwarz saved the day. Andrew 'Jake' Jakeman was working as a roadie for Darryl Way's Wolf, but on the lookout for something more in line with his musical interests. He'd recently discovered the pub circuit and one night went to see Brinsley Schwarz at the Kensington, only to discover that their PA had developed a fault. Jakeman happened to have some equipment in the back of his van and offered it to the Brinsleys. Unfortunately for Jakeman his boss found out that he'd let another group use the PA without his permission, and what was worse he hadn't charged them for using it either. Jakeman's legendary temper got the better of him and he told him to stick his job and the PA where the sun don't shine. "That night I mentioned to the Brinsleys I had lost my job. They recommended me to Martin Stone and I threw my lot in with the guys from Chilli Willi," he explained.

Still without a drummer, the Willis had nevertheless acquired a roadie and a manager, John Coleman. The four-piece Chilli Willi debuted at the Roundhouse supporting either the Pink Fairies or Hawkwind, memories appear a little hazy (which may not be surprising given the reputations those two bands had for indulging in illegal substances). It wasn't long before they headed to the pub circuit and introduced London's drinking community to their unique brand of Western Swing. However, as Ducks Deluxe had also discovered, if you wanted to play the pubs you needed a PA, an expensive item then as now. Although they were receiving financial backing from Revelation Records, the group struggled with the debt incurred by purchasing the expensive but essential piece of kit. The only way to pay it off was by gigging and that's what they did, with a vengeance.

Although Lithman wanted to continue as an acoustic outfit, the rest of the group wanted to introduce amplification and that meant they needed a drummer. Paul Riley knew just the chap. He called up the drummer from Robin Scott's old group, Pete Thomas, and asked if he'd like to join the Willis. He did and with the addition of Thomas on drums the line-up was complete. All that remained was to head for the country to get their heads and act together. Jake's girlfriend had access to a farm in deepest Cornwall and it was here that they got a taste of the road manager's explosive temperament. "One evening, from amidst the braying and honking that accompanied a dispute amongst the group (instigated by some terrible rank pulling), he Jake rose up and gave Phil and Martin (its perpetrators) an almighty roasting, leaving them uncharacteristically lost for words," recalled Paul Riley. "He then proceeded to tell us all a few home-truths about our individual shortcomings, and rounded-off his performance with a stirring call-to-arms: it was a beautiful thing! The shift it caused in the balance of power marked a great change in the relations within the group - and with Jake. We returned to London a much fitter outfit, both musically and functionally."

Even though Jakeman was still officially their roadie, he'd shown remarkable managerial flair. By re-structuring the power base within the group, he'd transformed it from a collective of individuals into a band of brothers. He continued to inspire the group by persuading his girlfriend, who just happened to work at Revelation as a booking agent, to push the group in favour of the agency's other acts. Besides securing residencies at the Tally Ho and the Kensington, they were getting regular gigs outside of London. It was on the way back from one of these out of town engagements that Jakeman was promoted from roadie to manager. "One night we were leaving Southampton and a police car overtakes us. Jake throws a beer can bouncing off the police car's roof and the cops carry on as if nothing has happened. 'I say Jacko, d'you wanna be promoted to manager?' It was then that we started doing good - we didn't go straight to stadium level, or even ballroom level, but we played every pub in Britain a million times and the music press loved us," Stone recalled.

One reason the Willis were so popular, apart from being courted by the music press, was because Jakeman had a knack of thinking up snappy and memorable marketing campaigns. He'd had some experience of working in advertising and had an instinctive sense of how to advertise and market the group. Unlike major record companies that had fantastic budgets but no imagination, Jakeman was overflowing with ideas but had virtually no budget. His first act as manager was to instigate what overpaid advertising executives would today call a viral marketing campaign. Jakeman had Barney Bubbles design a striking two colour sticker that proclaimed Chilli Willi to be 'Real Sharp'. The budget only allowed for the production of 1,000 of the eye-catching stickers which were distributed by the group around London's telephone boxes and lampposts. "It was a bit like graffiti," he explained, "getting the band's name out there. In the end fans would ask for them at gigs."

Jakeman also suggested the band distribute its own free fanzine along the lines of the commercial examples that appeared in the '60s to capitalise on the success of beat groups like The Beatles and The Rolling Stones. To this extent he commissioned Bubbles to design a newsletter called *Up Periscope*. "We had everything ready to go, but I don't think it ever came out actually," says Stone. "I know it sounds like a Jake Riviera-type venture now, but it was a joint effort with the band. A lot of Jake-ish things derive from his time with us. We all had very similar senses of humour."

Employing Bubbles' remarkable artistic skills, Jakeman began developing an arsenal of marketing tools that would later define Stiff Records, new wave and his individual approach to management. Using the knowledge he'd acquired from the world of advertising, he developed a Chilli Willi brand that borrowed from a wide range of sources in the same way the Chilli Willis borrowed from any number of different musical styles. Jakeman was way ahead of the game. Major record companies simply didn't do this kind of marketing. The best they could come up with was 'Out Now!' which was hardly inspirational. Jakeman was tapping into the excitement the Willis created on stage and converting it into witty advertising copy that translated directly into punters going to gigs and buying records.

8
Nervous On The Road

On 18 March 1973, Paul McCartney and Wings played an unannounced show at the Hard Rock Cafe in London to raise funds for Release, a UK agency that provides legal advice for people charged with the possession of drugs. McCartney had recently had his collar felt by the cops in Sweden and Scotland for possession of cannabis, and may have benefited from the agency's advice. Besides sharing McCartney's enthusiasm for spliff, the Brinsleys were hot to play these kind of benefit gigs. Booked as the support group, the Brinsleys had no idea who the headline act was until they'd set up their equipment. "We opened at the Hard Rock Cafe and they said, 'Do you mind if the special guest uses your equipment' and we said, 'Well, who's that?', and they said, 'Paul McCartney'," recalls Andrews.

They were hardly going to turn down Macca's request, not that they would have anyway because they were too generous to do anything so mean spirited. The Brinsleys went down a storm and, as McCartney explained, they made him work that little bit harder. "Brinsley Schwarz were on before us and they kind of warmed it all up and they got a stand up," he said. "Once you've heard a band rock a bit you can't go on and not rock, you've got to play better. So we thought, 'Great', and we went on after Brinsley and that was the first night we thought we played at all well. We were all double made up with that night. We rocked a bit that night."

McCartney had been re-building his career and improving his group, Wings, just like Robinson had planned to do with the Brinsleys. McCartney's first move had been to take Wings on a short, unannounced tour of universities before playing larger venues as his confidence grew. With the new album *Red Rose Speedway* ready for release, he planned to promote it with a British tour. What better way to ensure that Wings worked hard every night than by inviting Brinsley Schwarz along as support act.

"So he said will you come and do [the tour]," recalls Andrews, "and we're not going to turn round and say no to him because there was a good feeling about it and that was always one of our things. If it felt right we'll do it." Actually, it wasn't quite as simple as Andrews suggests. McCartney's manager wanted the Brinsleys to pay to be on the tour. Most record companies would have paid to get one of their acts onto a high profile tour, but Robinson was adamant that they couldn't afford it. And anyway, why should they have to pay to play? Robinson pulled a few strings and got Wings' guitarist, Henry McCullough, who he'd managed when he was in Eire Apparent, to speak to McCartney about the group's predicament.

McCullough had a word with McCartney who arranged to meet Robinson and discuss the proposed 'buy on'. "Henry McCullough got it for us I think because we'd known him for ages since he was in Eire Apparent, and he and Dave did some talking," explained Lowe. Thanks to Robinson's tenacity, McCartney's manager agreed to book Brinsley Schwarz and pay them £125 a night. The Wings tour coincided with several gigs the Brinsleys had booked in advance which they insisted on playing even if it meant having to fly the length of the country to do it. Ian Gomm told the *NME*: "We'd go on at 7.30 before Wings, and then go to our own gig." Despite the Brinsleys apparent commitment to gigging, Robinson wasn't convinced that they shared his drive and determination. He was struggling to make the group understand that they'd have to work harder if the Wings tour was going to be a success. They wouldn't be playing to 150 people at the Tally Ho; this was something altogether more serious. The tour had the potential to help the Brinsleys break out of the pub rock scene and the limitations it placed on them. As far as Robinson was concerned, the Brinsleys weren't putting in the work and that was holding them back. "I was frustrated not at the lack of success but at the lack of work," says Robinson. "They could have worked harder and as a result they would have got further. That was my attitude and there was no point me killing myself if they weren't going to. I'd spent four years, being at every gig, getting up and being in the office every day trying to move the thing forward. There comes a point where you think, you know, if you're into it let's do it, if you're not into it ... The Wings tour was where I realised that Paul McCartney, who didn't need to, was still working very hard, and at sound checks trying to polish the music, trying to get it to be better, and my lot were in the pub."

It wasn't that the Brinsleys weren't working hard enough, what they lacked was discipline. While McCartney was honing his already considerable talent, some of the Brinsleys were cruising on auto-pilot. Speaking in 2009, Lowe admitted that he should have listened to what Robinson was saying. "I wish I had worked harder at being a good instrumentalist. If anything, I've worked on making my lack of dexterity a virtue," he said. It didn't matter how much Robinson nagged, Lowe's casual approach to his craft wasn't about to change overnight. On 18 May, the tour reached Liverpool - McCartney's hometown. While McCartney fretted over every aspect of Wings' performance, the same couldn't be said for the Brinsleys. Indeed, Lowe's attitude was so laidback that Ian Gomm recalls starting their set without him because he'd nipped out for a drink and hadn't got back from the pub. "I remember him walking on half way through the set at a gig at the Liverpool Empire on the Wings tour," he says.

Despite his lack of discipline, Lowe later suggested that the tour had been a real benefit in terms of learning: "They had a kind of poppy show which is something we like, we're all pop fans really, and they had this feel of being a very high class pop band." If only they'd put a little of what they'd learnt into practice. But typically, they continued to struggle against the music industry rather than attempt to work with it.

The first half of Wings' tour ended at the Hammersmith Odeon, and as they'd done throughout the tour the Brinsleys finished their set and headed down the road to play at the slightly smaller Kensington pub. Once they'd finished there, they headed to the end of tour party and an all star jam session. "By the end we had Elton John on piano, Denny Laine on bass, Henry McCullough on guitar, Keith Moon on drums. Bob Andrews - our keyboard player - was on guitar." Gomm recalled.

In July, Wings played four gigs in the north of England, again with the Brinsleys supporting. The tour ended on 10 July in Newcastle where the Brinsleys joined Wings for a blistering version of 'Long Tall Sally'. McCartney was obviously in high spirits because he joined them for a jam session back at their hotel. "We had two guitars and were singing and playing, and everyone obviously avoiding starting up any Beatles songs, until finally one of his crew said, 'Come on, enough beating around the bush, go on play a song'. So we started playing Beatles songs and that was quite amazing," remembers Schwarz.

If the Wings tour had felt right, the possibility of touring with Elton John felt very wrong. The bespectacled pianist was becoming very big news and was scheduled to play America from early August until October. The Brinsleys were asked if they'd like to support John on the American leg of an extensive tour that also took in Europe. The dates might have done wonders for the group's profile in America, but as far as they were concerned Elton John represented everything they were fighting against. "We turned down Elton John because we didn't want to play to Elton John's audience," explained Andrews. "Nobody in their right mind would do that, but that was part of our philosophy." The Brinsleys' decision seems to go against everything they stood for. Their attitude was to play for anyone regardless of colour, creed or political affiliation. "That's why we ended up doing gigs for the White Panthers because they were the public and we had to do it," says Andrews. "There was always a philosophical argument about anything we did. We went to Northern Ireland at a time when nobody was going to Northern Ireland. I remember sitting in Nick's bedroom with Dave Robinson and the whole band and we spent a great deal of time talking about it. There was a great deal of thinking going on. Too much thinking if anything."

Playing for the White Panthers was okay, but playing for Elton John's audience was too much to countenance. Billy Rankin suggests that sometimes they were a little too moral for their own good, "I think we were a little bit too righteous in some ways. We were going to do an Elton John tour of America, and because they were only going to let us play twenty minutes our manager said no." The Sutherland Brothers didn't have any misgivings about touring with Mr John and the exposure did them no harm whatsoever.

After three years managing the Brinsleys, Robinson decided to call it a day and quit in 1973. While Robinson headed for the Hope and Anchor, which he'd transform into the spiritual home of pub rock, the Brinsleys headed for

Jackson Studios to record their album, *Please Don't Ever Change*. "We ended up doing that ourselves," said Lowe, "because that was at the time that Robinson was not there anymore." If ever the group recorded a pub rock album it was this. Its mix of originals and covers reflected the group's eclectic repertoire and was both wildly out of step with contemporary musical trends and way ahead of them.

Please Don't Ever Change exudes images of Sunday afternoons sat in front of dusty valve wireless sets listening to *Two Way Family Favourites*. But then they throw in an instrumental version of Bob Marley's 'Hypocrite' - released earlier as a single under the pseudonym The Hitters. How many white pop groups at the time were covering songs by The Wailers? Few indeed. It didn't matter to the Brinsleys; it all went in their musical melting pot and came out sounding like they'd written it themselves. This odd juxtaposition of styles found favour with Lowe who loved the album. "I like it because that's the one we had most to do with making and I like a lot of the numbers on it as well," he stated. Schwarz, however, wasn't convinced. As far as he was concerned none of the albums they recorded captured the group at its best. "In retrospect, I don't think our records really showed what we were like. I don't think we managed to capture ourselves that well on record."

With Robinson out of the frame, for the moment at least, day-to-day management of the group was handed over to Schwarz. Earlier in the year, the Brinsleys had been offered, and refused, an appearance on the BBC television programme *The Old Grey Whistle Test*. Their reason for turning down the offer was because the programme's director insisted they mime. The group had made a few rules and were determined to stick to them. Miming on television wasn't what rock 'n' roll bands were about. Truth be told, Brinsley Schwarz did mime on television, several times, they just weren't any good at it. However, they were adamant that the only way they were going to appear on the '*Whisper Test*' was if they could perform live. Gomm told the *NME*: "They expect us to go on *Whistle Test* and play to a backing track that we've already recorded." That wasn't going to happen as far as they were concerned, even if it meant missing out on a major opportunity that most other groups would sell their souls for.

Being the Brinsleys they had to do it their way or not at all. "We refused to play on it unless we could play live," remembers Schwarz. As acting manager it fell on him to negotiate with the BBC. "After a couple of days of negotiations I eventually managed to speak to the producer, Mike Appleton," he says. "I managed to ask him in the end why it was that we couldn't do it live. It turned out that their mixer wasn't big enough and that's why we couldn't do it. We got a lot of hassle from our record company who thought we were crazy. But we were adamant that we were a live band and that's what we did."

However, because the Brinsleys had their own PA with a twenty-channel mixer they were able to resolve the problem of playing live in the *Whistle Test*'s tiny studio. Schwarz called Appleton and explained that they could take one feed for the backing and one for the vocals and mix the two together. Appleton agreed but only if the group's mixing desk and sound engineer were hidden from view. "We had a lot of PA cabinets, so I said it's all right, we'll build a little room out of PA cabinets and [the sound engineer] can stand in there." For once their bloody-mindedness paid dividends. Not only did they perform live on *Whistle Test* they changed the way the programme operated. "So we did it live and I think not long after that they thought it was so successful that they managed to persuade the powers to get a proper mixer so they could do it themselves."

It may have seemed like a minor victory but by insisting on playing live the Brinsleys changed the way 'serious' music was broadcast on British television. When the New York Dolls appeared on the show they may have looked dangerous, but it was obvious they were miming. How safe and predictable was that? Live performances introduced an element of uncertainty to the proceedings; anything could and sometimes did happen. Playing live gave bands the edge that was too often missing from pre-recorded studio performances. But more importantly it gave greater freedom to both artists and producers. Because the show was broadcast late at night, if a group wanted to extend its performance the producers had the flexibility to extend the show from its regular 25 minutes for as long as they liked.

When new wave broke in the late '70s, playing live on television became a badge of authenticity. By the time The Damned appeared on the *Whistle Test* in '79 it was unthinkable that they might mime. If they wanted to run riot in the studio and trash their equipment, providing they didn't damage any of the Beeb's, that was fine with the *Whistle Test* production team. The Clash resolutely refused to appear on television if it meant miming. When they made a rare live appearance on *Alright Now* in March '79, Joe Strummer said the only reason they agreed to appear was because they could 'plug in and play, just like doing a gig'. Without the bloody-mindedness of the Brinsleys that wouldn't have happened.

9
Leery, Beery, Gruff And Sneery

By early '73, London's pub rock circuit had blossomed. No longer an underground scene enjoyed by a select few, it had grown into a vibrant alternative music community. Championed by the music press, it attracted the kind of coverage that some of the original scene-setters had wanted to avoid. As national press coverage spread the word, similar scenes struggled to establish themselves in provincial hotspots. In Liverpool and Manchester the idea was formalised by the Music Liberation Front (MLF) and Music Force (MF). Both organisations wanted to develop live music in the north of England to benefit local musicians. The MLF in Liverpool found its own venues and arranged gigs outside those controlled by London agencies. The central difference between the London scene and that in the north was politics. Pub rock was never overtly political, but many of those active within the MLF and MF were. Politics may have played a part in the development of these organisations but it was music, and in particular live music, that was the driving force. What these organisations signalled was a growing dissatisfaction with the mainstream music business and a desire to create an alternative business model that wasn't controlled by a handful of London based agents.

While provincial cities did go on to foster vibrant music scenes, the truth of the matter remained that if you wanted to make it there was no alternative but to pack your bags and head for London. There were few provincial record companies at this time. All of the major record labels had their offices in London and when A&R managers did go scouting for new talent they weren't going to travel any further than they had to. The mountain really did have to go to Mohammed. As more pubs opened up their back rooms and began promoting live music, more groups moved in to meet demand. Most of them were as memorable as the flock wallpaper that adorned the walls of the pubs they played, but amongst the formula boogie bands and generic rock 'n' roll groups there was genuinely original and exciting talent. Kilburn and the High Roads were one such group. A dark, menacing, ramshackle collective, the Kilburns would make a gig down your local boozer a night to remember.

On 12 January 1973, Kilburn and the High Roads made their debut at the Tally Ho. A month later they appeared at the Hope and Anchor. Their distinctive appearance made them stand out from the other groups playing the pub circuit. If Brinsley Schwarz had the musicianship and Ducks Deluxe the raw power, the one thing Kilburn and the High Roads had was a touch of theatre. Frontman and leader of the pack, Ian Dury, was a cross between Gene

Vincent and Tommy Cooper. The group's pianist Russell Hardy recalled: "He [Dury] realised you didn't necessarily need to sing in tune, but providing you presented it right you could take it to an audience."

Ian Dury had harboured dreams of forming a group from the moment he discovered rock 'n' roll. He had the name - Kilburn and the High Roads - a full two years before he got round to forming the group in the winter of 1970. A talented artist and illustrator, Dury studied at Walthamstow College of Art, where he was taught by influential Pop artist Peter Blake, before gaining a place at the Royal College of Art. Although he was a successful painter and illustrator with work exhibited at the Institute of Contemporary Art and commissions from *London Life* and the *Sunday Times* magazine, he felt he could better express himself through music. "I didn't really think that I was doing something until I was doing something in music," Dury commented.

Dury was unlike most of the musicians that gravitated toward the pub rock circuit. He didn't have much time for American country-influenced groups like The Band, The Byrds and The Flying Burrito Brothers, much preferring jazz, rock 'n' roll and the Tin Pan Alley songs of his youth. Speaking to *Trouser Press*, he confessed to liking "Rosemary Clooney, stuff like that - absolutely unbesmirched songs. But you can't do a rock 'n' roll set like that all night, and so we started doing Chuck Berry tunes and Fats Domino ones, the usual, and then we got fed up with that and I started writing songs." His passion for rock 'n' roll was matched by his enthusiasm for jazz. Speaking to *Uncut* magazine he said: "When I first went to the Royal College of Art, there were four of us all sharing a flat, each of us had a different room for the particular style of jazz we liked."

As a student at the Royal College of Art, Dury got to hang out with all the right people and drink deep from a communal pool that influenced real social, cultural and political change. He later said he saw the "'60s from under art dealer Robert Fraser's kitchen table". Fraser was friends with both The Rolling Stones and The Beatles and held lavish parties for London's most beautiful people. Like the best musicians of the day, art students were at the cutting edge of a cultural revolution from which emerged a do-it-yourself Bohemian chic and the Beat Boom. Dury appropriated elements from both camps to create a unique style that, when fully matured, would appeal to disaffected punks and teeny boppers alike.

While at the Royal College of Art, Dury struck up a friendship with pianist Russell Hardy. The very opposite of the laddish Dury, Hardy was a quiet, retiring type with his own jazz trio. In 1960, Hardy formed the appropriately named Russell Hardy Trio with Terry Holman and Terry Day. Over a two-year period it developed into the Continuous Music Ensemble and finally The People Band. A free jazz ensemble, The People Band recorded a Charlie Watts produced album in 1968 that featured several musicians, including Hardy, Tony Edwards, Charlie Hart and George Khan. Dury would call on them to form Kilburn and the High Roads in the winter of 1970.

But before they fashioned themselves into a full-blown group, Dury and Hardy began making music with a mutual friend and guitarist Ted Speight. Dury had written to Chappell Music and blagged some free sheet music which the trio banged out round a piano. Dury was hooked and a few weeks later he assembled the first Kilburn and the High Roads line-up at a rehearsal studio in London's Covent Garden. "I used mates who were jazz musicians, like George Khan, who is now an actor," he told Chris Welch. "He played tenor sax and also managed the Jubilee rehearsal studio in Covent Garden, which we could use. We had Terry Day, who was a free-form jazz drummer and Charlie Hart on bass and my mate Russell Hardy from Dagenham on piano, with Ted Speight on guitar."

Despite populating the first line-up with jazz musicians, Dury had no intention of knocking out tired versions of Mingus or Coltrane. Rather he began shaping a set selected from his best-loved rock 'n' roll oldies and Tin Pan Alley favourites. In spite of Dury's obvious enthusiasm, the group fizzled out before it played a single gig. "We probably only [rehearsed] a handful of times because it wasn't really getting us anywhere," recalls Hardy. "There were some real clashes - particularly with Ian, who always has very positive views on how something should look, feel and sound."

For the next year Dury tried to concentrate on teaching art at Canterbury, but by late '71 he'd decided to re-awaken his group from its slumber and start again. Art colleges have long been breeding grounds for budding rock 'n' rollers, and he had no problem finding enough willing students to form his new band. Out went the seasoned professionals and in came a group of raw amateurs that Dury could mould into exactly the kind of rock 'n' roll unit he'd long dreamt of. Kilburn and the High Roads Mk2 comprised Dury, Russell Hardy, Keith Lucas, Chris Lucas, Ian Smith and Humphrey Butler-Bowden. Weekends were spent at Dury's family home in Wingrave where the group worked up a ramshackle set of rock 'n' roll standards. They debuted at Croydon School of Art on 5 December '71 and played a Christmas party at Canterbury College of Art the following week.

Rock 'n' roll was fun but it didn't pay the rent and Dury soon realised that if they were going to make any money from it they'd have to write songs of their own. "We wrote about 20 songs together, initially... I did the music and Ian did the lyrics," Hardy explained. "His words were always very funny ... we had a similar sense of humour - plus, I never used to argue with him!" With Hardy bashing out the tunes, Dury laboured over lyrics that defined his Mockney persona. Despite an instinct towards complicated melodies and improvisation, Hardy kept it simple so that Dury could follow the melody and stay more or less in tune. Hardy's jazz sensibility combined with Dury's talent as a wordsmith created a unique musical union that produced quirky but memorable songs like 'Upminster Kid', 'You're More Than Fair' and 'I Made Mary Cry'.

By early 1972, Kilburn and The High Road's line-up had already started to crack and shed personnel. Ian Smith lasted about a month before being replaced by Charlie Hart. Chris Lucas was replaced by Terry Day, who lasted until early '73, when he was replaced by the partially disabled David Newton-Rohoman. Several others drifted in and out of the group including Geoff Rigden, Paul Tonkin and Terry Edwards. They also acquired a saxophonist, Davey Payne. An ex-member of The People Band, he had a volatile personality but would become the longest serving member of Kilburn and the High Roads and reappear in The Blockheads.

For most of 1972 the group averaged no more than one gig a month, which was hardly enough to keep them in rolling tobacco and certainly not enough for them to turn professional. But Dury wasn't the kind of bandleader to sit around and wait for the gigs to roll in. A trip to Holland to drum up work came to nothing, but towards the end of the year Dury approached the manager of the Speakeasy, an exclusive London club that played host to the nation's rock elite, with the hope that he might book them to entertain his influential clientele. Beside securing the group some much needed work, Dury reasoned that playing in such a well patronised establishment would bring them to the attention of music business insiders and hopefully kick-start their career. "We were playing a gig at the Speakeasy in London," Dury recalled. "It's a horrible place, I never go there now. But we were there then, and so was Dave Robinson, looning about with Nick Lowe. Keith Moon and Pete Townshend were there, too - we had played on purpose, so all the tradey people would know about us."

The gambit worked. Dave Robinson was impressed and approached Dury after the gig to offer some advice. "Dave told us we ought to be working in the pubs," Dury recalled. "We said: 'Fuck that mate, we want the Royal Albert Hall.'" Although he was aiming for the stars, Dury didn't want to get there by hype alone, but neither, it appeared, did he want to wait. Although they didn't approach the group at the time, Townshend and Moon filed the name at the back of their booze-sodden minds for future reference.

Dury was determined to avoid playing the pub circuit and the kind of music its regulars expected. "I never subscribed to the so-called pub rock ethic," he said. "It always seemed like bland cowboy music. Every song sounded the same and they always did an encore of 'Brown Sugar'. Ducks Deluxe were quite lively and had a slight edge to them, and the Brinsleys were very mellow. It was nice to know all these people, but my policy was, I didn't want to play the same sort of numbers. If we played something vaguely country and western, then we'd add a calypso or a piece of reggae. It was just to keep the interest going, because I'd get very bored hearing the same tunes from these other bands. We'd try and be a bit unpredictable. We also came from art school and had a sartorial attitude that wasn't all tartan shirts and red neckerchiefs."

The theatricality Kilburn and the High Roads created wasn't the tawdry glam you'd find on *Top Of The Pops* or the kind of pompous affectations employed by the likes of Ten Years After and Emerson, Lake and Palmer. No Roxy

Music art school aesthetics or Wakeman-esque high camp for them. Theirs was a seedy, menacing presence that had Peter Erskine of the *NME* describe them as looking like, "demobbed cripples in chipstained Dannimacs and vulcanised slip-ons. They all had short hair - badly cut and partly grown out like ex-cons." Their shabby affectations weren't simply an antidote to the stultifying mainstream music being pumped out by the BBC, it was an honest expression of who they were and how they lived their lives. Like all groups at the start of their career, Kilburn and the High Roads weren't divorced from their environment, they were of it. They made no attempt to alter or distort their image to appeal to anyone. That's not to say that it wasn't considered and even contrived, but it reflected the reality of life rather than mask it behind a glamorous facade that was a shallow as it was cheap.

Kilburn and the High Roads were occupying so much of Dury's time that he was struggling to meet his commitments at Canterbury College of Art and was dismissed. "I got the sack for non-attendance, really, but the thing was I couldn't go there anymore cos at the time I was a rock 'n' roll singer." Like many at that time, Dury found himself unemployed. It was the kick up the arse he needed to take his role as leader seriously. Luckily for Dury and his fellow band mates, Robinson had mentioned them to broadcaster the late Charlie Gillett, who caught their act at the Tally Ho and became a fan. Intrigued by this motley crew of oddballs, and impressed by their music, he felt compelled to alert the capital to their existence. "I came back from the gig and on the radio show I said. 'There is this band that you have all got to go and see,'" he enthused. Thanks to Robinson's advice, which they eventually acted upon, they had regular work on the pub circuit and now, thanks to Gillett's plugging them on his radio show, free publicity.

In April '73, Stephen Nugent wrote about Kilburn and the High Roads in *Let It Rock* magazine. At this point, they were still managing themselves, but were on the lookout for a full-time manager. Dury must have made this known to Nugent, who wrote: "Although he [Dury] regards the problem of manipulation and hype as something of a necessary evil, Ian feels that they'd like to have their own villain to look after their interests. It's not a hard-nosed attitude but one which reflects the experience of members of the band and friends in other bands whose neglect of the unpleasant business of securing a decent relationship with the businessmen has resulted in need for either a battery of lawyers or unfortunate hyping and sudden (professional) death."

Dury had obviously listened to Robinson's words of wisdom and wasn't going to get his fingers burnt in the same way Brinsley Schwarz had. Although most of the group were unemployed they'd got to the point where they could no longer manage themselves and concentrate on the business side of the band. Having got wind of Gillett's interest, Dury approached the broadcaster after a gig at the Tally Ho and suggested he put his money where his mouth was. Gillett was somewhat surprised by Dury's suggestion, not least because he had no idea how to manage a rock group. "It had never crossed my mind to get involved in management," he recalled, "but I was sufficiently flattered and bemused and asked Gordon [Nelki] what he thought. For better or worse, we got involved in managing Kilburn and the High Roads."

Gillett and his business partner Gordon Nelki were planning to launch a record company, Oval Records, not manage a rock 'n' roll group. Had Gillett known what he was taking on he may have thought twice, but Dury couldn't have been happier with the deal and luckily for him Gillett and Nelki were anything but villains. "He was very honest and a gentleman," Dury said of Gillett. "I remember Rob Townsend, the drummer in Family told me, 'You are either managed by a crook, in which case you'll get a little bit of a huge amount, or by an honest person, which means you'll get a huge amount of fuck all!' It was absolutely true."

Fuck all of something was better than nothing and, besides being a gentleman, Gillett could promote the group on his Radio London show, *Honky Tonk*. At the time there were no commercial radio stations in Britain. The pirates had been banned or jammed by the government and such was the demand for 'free' or commercial radio stations that there had even been demonstrations and petitions to parliament. The BBC was in the process of developing a network of local radio stations, but its plans for 40 of these had been reduced to 20 by the government. Not that the BBC would have been particularly interested in a group like Kilburn and the High Roads. It would appear that the BBC wasn't interested in much at all apart from the top 20. The BBC dominated radio and television broadcasting and a lot of what was played on the radio was due to personal preferences. Rod Argent: "If someone like John Peel or Bob Harris doesn't like - say Emerson, Lake and Palmer then you won't hear them on the radio."

If the BBC weren't going to play records by the Groundhogs, Taste or The Edgar Broughton Band, then what hope was there for Kilburn and the High Roads or any of the other pub rock groups? As far as Argent was concerned the BBC lacked vision. "The whole attitude is a compromise all the time. You don't get one kind of music or the other. They don't even have a proper teenybopper programme." Fortunately, London did have a local BBC station with a presenter who had the kind of vision Argent was looking for. Charlie Gillett's radio show was focused and dared to be different. While Robinson got groups into pubs, it was Gillett who encouraged Londoners to get off their arses and go and check them out. London's *Time Out* magazine did a similar job promoting the pub circuit, but without Gillett's commitment the scene would have stagnated.

No sooner had Gillett signed the group than Dury instigated more changes to the line-up. His pedagogical instincts led to a power struggle within the group and the departure of Charlie Hart. "If musicians were too single-minded and not prepared to kow-tow to Ian, he found it hard to handle and he would rather not have them around," recalled Gillett. Hart wasn't the type to toe the line. He wanted to influence the group's musical direction as much as its self-appointed leader. That was too much for Dury, who decided it was time for the less demanding Humphrey Butler-Bowden to rejoin the group. The amiable Butler-Bowden had recently bought himself a bass guitar and was struggling to learn it, not that his musical limitations bothered Dury. After all, he'd already employed a disabled drummer who'd given the group its distinctive loose rhythmic groove. However, Gordon Nelki thought his slightly aristocratic, double-barrelled name didn't fit the group's street hardened image. Slipping into Larry Parnes mode, he re-christened the bassist Humphrey Ocean.

On 1 September '73, Kilburn and the High Roads played the 100 Club in London's Oxford Street. The engagement was reviewed by Nick Kent for the *NME*. His review paints a vivid picture of the capital's club scene at the time. Unlike some of London's hipper pubs, the 100 Club was still presenting old jazzers to a dwindling audience. Into these less than inspiring surroundings ambled Kilburn and the High Roads. Understandably, they made a big impression on Kent. Dury was described as, "simply the most charismatic figure I've ever seen on a small British stage" and that night's gig as "the most exciting performance I've yet witnessed". To say he liked them would be an understatement. Kent's delight at stumbling upon such a visually and musically stunning group in what was otherwise a musical wilderness leaps off the page. Unfortunately, it would take more than Kent's mythologizing to transform Kilburn and the High Roads' fortunes.

One way of breaking out of the pub circuit was to hitch a ride on the back of an already established and successful act. Brinsley Schwarz had supported several headline acts, but had yet to top the bill on a tour of their own. Now it was the turn of Kilburn and the High Roads to be invited by rock royalty to join them on the road. Since seeing Kilburn and the High Roads at the Speakeasy, Pete Townshend had been keeping tabs on their progress. Townshend seems to have cultivated quite an interest in music's more eccentric rock 'n' rollers. Besides producing the singular Arthur Brown and Thunderclap Newman, he'd also championed one of rock's finest oddballs, John Otway. An article in *Sounds* about The Who's guitarist claimed: "Pete Townshend has stayed involved, where a lot of big names get rather sniffy about newer pop groups." Townshend was about to do more than put in a good word for the Kilburns, he offered them the support slot on The Who's British tour. "We played eight gigs with them," Dury recalled, "and seven of our own, and then they said come and support us on our American tour-14 gigs."

The Who's British tour began at the Trentham Gardens in Stoke-on-Trent with the intention of promoting their recently issued sprawling concept album, *Quadrophenia*. But problems with backing tapes forced The Who to rethink their set and drop several songs for the duration of the tour. No such problems faced Kilburn and the High Roads, who simply carried on as normal, even to the extent of using their 100 watt PA on stage. But they did face their own set of unique challenges. Playing large venues made them realise that they still weren't ready for the Albert Hall. "It was a real culture shock ... we'd been playing in all these cramped pubs and clubs, where we were virtually having to stand on top of each other, and then there we were out on these massive stages, yards apart," recalled Hardy.

That didn't stop Townshend asking Kilburn and the High Roads to accompany The Who on their American tour. There was only one problem. None of the group had a passport. While they waited in London for the Home Office to issue some, Dury had another fit of pique and sacked violinist Paul Tonkin. Once again, it looked like they were on the verge of breaking up. While chaos reigned in London, Pete Rudge, The Who's tour manager, booked southern fried boogie merchants Lynyrd Skynyrd as tour support. It was probably just as well that Kilburn and the High Roads didn't tour America with The Who. Apart from being completely incapable of working a stadium audience, there was no way Americans would have taken to this most English of rock groups, and without a record to promote there was little point in going. Anyway, US audiences probably preferred listening to 'Free Bird' rather than 'Upminster Kid'.

10
If It's Clean ... It's Not Laundry

With a major label deal in their back pocket, Ducks Deluxe headed to Rockfield Studios to begin pre-production work on their debut album. It was their first time in a studio, and Belmont was dismayed by what he heard. "I was horrified at the sound of my voice, not that I was one of the main singers, but the bits that I did sing ... and just as horrified at the sound of my guitar playing." In October '73 they headed to Saturn Sound Studios in Worthing to record with Dave Bloxham. "I think he was from the engineering side, but along with Chris Blackwell and a couple of other people he was credited as co-producer on *Funky Kingston*," recalls Belmont. "In actual fact, when we did that first Ducks Deluxe album we had horns on a couple of tracks and the horns were The Sons of the Jungle horn section, who played on the *Funky Kingston* album."

The album featured songs written by Tyla, Belmont and Garvey, along with some well-chosen covers. Any concerns Belmont had about their sound was misplaced. Launched at the Hard Rock Cafe, the album generated solid reviews. Ducks Deluxe were called "a classic British rock band" and prophets of a "new style". Writing in *Shakin' Street*, Garry Sperrazza suggested that 'Coast To Coast' and 'Nervous Breakdown' were "so good the [New York] Dolls could have done them ... the only difference between the two bands on this cut is the make up." If anything, Ducks Deluxe had the edge on the New York Dolls because they didn't need the hair and makeup. Emerging bleary-eyed and hung over from the London pub circuit, Ducks Deluxe celebrated the release of their debut album by swapping motorways for autobahns and warm beer for ice cold lager. Europe had been enticing groups to take the cross-channel ferry for well over a decade and with good reason. "In France and Germany you pay double what you pay in England," concert promoter Michael Alfandary told the *Melody Maker*. Holland was no different and, although Amsterdam didn't have a pub rock circuit, it had Boddy's Music Inn run by local legend Ted Boddy, who was "An American, a great big guy [who] looked like Kenny Rogers with a beard and silver hair," recalls Belmont. Mr Boddy's stature was matched by his munificence which included the offer of free lodging at his hotel in return for performing at his bar. It was an offer too good to refuse and, as Belmont recalls, it made touring the pocket-sized country a breeze: "The great thing about Holland was that there was nowhere that was more than three hours [away], so you would always come back to Amsterdam after the gig. So you could go there for a week to 10 days and do a whole lot of gigs and never move out of your hotel in Amsterdam."

Brinsley Schwarz's trailblazing had whet European appetites for pub rock, Ducks Deluxe got them tipsy on it, but it was a group of bruisers from Canvey

Island who got them addicted to rhythm and booze. Dr Feelgood formed in 1971 when the late Lee Collinson (who changed his name to Brilleaux, of course) and John Sparks from the Pig Boy Charlie Band invited their friend Wilko Johnson to join them. Like their beat group predecessors, they borrowed from the R&B cabinet of curiosities to create a sound and style that was uniquely theirs. "We exist in a tradition of music and are using it to the full," explained Johnson. "It's all derived from here, there, and everywhere but it's our sound." Dr Feelgood's cocktail of blues and rock 'n' roll was the most intoxicating sound anyone had heard in years. Their gritty readings of R&B classics were, however, as unfashionable as Albert Steptoe at a Knightsbridge party. Everything about them, their attitude, image and sonic signature set them apart. Like Kilburn and the High Roads they had a menacing and disturbing outsider image that was part downtown street gang menace and part uptown American cop show chic. Originally long-haired, denim wearing ruffians, their transformation to short-haired, besuited mobsters was attributed to Joe Meek wünderkind Heinz. Dr Feelgood backed the bleached blond bombshell for a series of gigs that culminated with a slot at the '72 Wembley Rock 'n' Roll Festival. "Heinz came up one day with these two-tone shirts," Johnson explained, "and said: 'Boys, I'll sell these shirts to you for 25 bob each, alright ...'" With their two-tone shirts, skinny ties and short hair, Dr Feelgood looked like they'd just walked off the set of *Get Carter* or as Mick Farren noted "a singularly unpleasant section of the army". Chris Fenwick had returned to Canvey Island after a spell in London where he'd been trying to make it as an actor. Invited to a wedding in Holland, he chanced upon promoter Franz Moerland and impressed him with talk of the Feelgoods' savage rock 'n' roll. Fenwick persuaded Moerland to book them for a short tour of Holland that did for them what the Reeperbahn had done for The Beatles. Impressed by Fenwick's remarkable feat, the Feelgoods looked on their friend even more favourably when he put his money where his mouth was and purchased a second-hand van for the trip. The only fly in the ointment was drummer Terry Howarth. Rather than bash out the backbeat in Holland, he decided to pursue his career square bashing with the Army. Johnson got on the blower to his friend and drummer John Martin, a. k. a. The Big Figure, and asked him to sit in for their AWOL drummer. Excusing himself from his regular commitments - Martin was a professional drummer who'd worked in various pop bands - he threw in his lot with Dr Feelgood. "He was really a much better drummer and the whole thing started sounding a lot more real," recalled Johnson.

During the tour Dr Feelgood discovered that if they were to showboat by manically moving around the stage, the energy levels went up and the audiences went wild. "When we started getting in front of proper audiences, firstly in Holland, we realised we could create far more of an effect and emphasise the attack of the music by moving a lot," explained Johnson. "We'd all done this in the past ... apparently the rock 'n' roll band that Lee and Sparko had before had been into moving around and I'd also done this on occasions in bands I'd been in." Johnson and Sparko developed a mesmerising stage presence, each moving to the front of the stage and back again in perfect synchronization that created a hypnotic visual analogue to the pulsating beat of the group. Collinson was just as mesmeric. An invisible force seemed to surge through his body forcing it to twitch and his fist to pump to the beat as he growled his way through another R&B classic. Just when you thought the group had reached fever pitch, Johnson would skitter across the stage like a demonic robot plugged into the mains. "The whole intention is to create excitement," he said, "and the first person you want to excite is yourself. By moving in a violent way you create that excitement, that's why people like dancing to rock. The reason I move the way I move is an expression of what I'm feelin' - it's the same reason I play guitar, the same feelin'. A lot of the time the theatricals are for our benefit. It's a form of violence, but it's better than fighting, innit?"

The jaunt to Holland convinced Johnson that his future lay in rock 'n' roll rather than teaching. Collinson took a little more persuading but soon abandoned any idea of becoming a barrister in favour of a career as a blues shouter. Their commitment persuaded The Big Figure to join them full-time and Fenwick to swap repertory for a permanent position in rock management. But as earnest as they were it would be some time before they could afford to quit their day jobs. "We were just chugging along semi-professionally for quite a long time, a year or more, until we started to get gigs in London, on the pub circuit," Johnson remembered.

Dr Feelgood got their first gig on the pub circuit thanks to their friend, Will Birch. An aspiring musician, he'd read about the circuit in the music papers. Brilleaux recalled: "[He] saw us in a little Southend club we used to play every Sunday night and said to us 'You guys should get up to London. There's a scene up there called the pub rock circuit that you'd fit into perfectly'. Our reaction was that Will was being over-enthusiastic but we still went up to London, checked it out, and thought 'Well yeah, these other bands, like Ducks Deluxe and that, are not a million miles away from what we're doing and so there's no reason why we can't muscle in here.' - which is exactly what we did." Dr Feelgood didn't exactly muscle their way onto the pub circuit, they got lucky. Birch had been pestering Dai Davies to book the Feelgoods for some time and when the Ducks Deluxe manager discovered he'd double booked his group, he called on Dr Feelgood to fill in at the Tally Ho.

By this time the press had transformed what had been an underground scene into the next big thing. London's pubs were awash with up-and-coming groups looking for their big break with the effect that pub landlords began to exert considerable influence. Because there were more groups desperate to break into the circuit than it could handle, demand outstripped supply. The result was that some landlords expected groups to play for free simply because being seen in their pub by the right A&R manager might lead to that all important recording contract. The pub rock circuit that Dave Robinson had developed to provide new groups with somewhere to pay their dues had become big business. One time business partner with Robinson, John Eichler, told Chas de Whalley of the *NME*: "Places like the Hope [and Anchor] have taken over where the clubs were in the '60s. So instead of clubs, bands play pubs. Then they move on."

As far as some of the scene setters were concerned the original ethos had been corrupted by too much press attention. "As soon as the press started to say 'we dig pub rock, what a great idea', we were thinking, no, that's not what it's about," notes Bob Andrews. "When it gets to that level that's when it stops being a [great] idea. That's what our philosophy was. That's why it was easy to get depressed about all this stuff because you can't keep ahead of it. We weren't going to do stuff like everybody else."

Luckily, Brinsley Schwarz didn't need to rely exclusively on the pub rock circuit to make a living. They had more options than most and one of those was working with Dave Edmunds. The Welsh wizard of the fretboard had landed himself the role of musical director for the movie *Stardust*. "I went and met David [Putnam] up at Tottenham Court Road and sang 'When Will I Be Loved' by the Everly Brothers and he said 'great, that's just what I'm after.' And I had total freedom to do whatever songs I wanted," explained Edmunds.

Besides having the freedom to record what he wanted, Edmunds had carte blanche to employ whoever he liked. Putnam wanted the film to look as authentic as possible, and to achieve this he employed musicians alongside actors. "David didn't want just actors. He asked me, do you know anyone who can act and is a musician? I said 'I'll have a go'. I did an audition and had to read with Paul Nicholas and Karl Howman, and standing in the corner was Ken Russell and Michael Apted. Karl said it was hilarious: my voice got quieter and quieter and quieter. In the original script was one band member who was very quiet, didn't speak much. Because there always is one. So that was the part I got," he explained.

When the producer wanted a group to back some girl singers, Edmunds naturally suggested the Brinsleys. "We were involved with Dave Edmunds and he was involved [with *Stardust*] and first of all they needed somebody to play at the gig as a warm up band for their crowd," recalls Schwarz, "and so Dave got us in on that, and then they needed somebody to play behind three girl singers, like a Supremes-type group. I remember I got roped into playing saxophone. So we did one day of filming with that and played the gig, which we were late for. David Putnam was directing and we annoyed him quite dramatically, I think, by turning up late. He swore we'd never be in films again, which has come true."

While filming at the King's Hall, Belle Vue, Manchester, Brinsley Schwarz were interviewed for *Let It Rock* magazine. Speaking for the group, Bob Andrews aired his thoughts about the state of contemporary music. "Well, all these poofters will soon go, and all this spaceship stuff. Rock is going to become far more masculine in the future. Everything as it stands at the moment will get the elbow and we can expect a great David Niven revival - so to speak," he suggested. Perhaps David Niven wasn't the best example, but apart from that he wasn't far wrong. There was a faint whiff of change in the air and the Brinsleys had to respond or suffer the consequences.

None of the group had been happy with their attempts to produce themselves, so Edmunds was called on to beef up their sound. "People always used to come to me when they couldn't get the mix right. When they couldn't get any balls into it," Edmunds told *Sounds*. "That's how I got involved with Brinsley Schwarz." Edmunds was producing groups like they were going out of fashion (which in many cases they did). Besides producing Brinsley Schwarz, he also made records with Ducks Deluxe, the Flamin' Groovies and finished the *Stardust* soundtrack. However, by the time he began recording with Brinsley Schwarz in the early summer of '74, Edmunds was struggling to keep it together. "He was going off the rails big time. Personal problems. Drink and drugs and rock 'n' roll. He was going through all sorts of traumas. He was off his head really. One step away from madness. This is what happens to people who are really creative," recalled Ian Gomm.

Brinsley Schwarz had struggled for years to capture the essence of their sound on record. As far as Schwarz is concerned the nearest they got to it was with *Silver Pistol*. But when they began working with Edmunds any consideration of trying to replicate their live sound went out the window. Edmunds was in full Phil Spector mode and, like Mark Wirtz, before him took total control. "The production was sort of out of our hands," says Schwarz. "Only he knew what was going on." Applying ridiculous amounts of EQ and reverb to the tracks, he transformed them into the most polished pop recordings they'd ever made. But it was to no avail. "Edmunds made it sound great, the songs were good but it was a band in a wrong time," explained Andrews.

Brinsley Schwarz weren't alone in wanting a more sophisticated sound. Ducks Deluxe wanted to add a little sparkle to things too. "We just wanted to expand it, to bring out a bit more. For everybody's liking, it was far too hard-headed. It was like pushing a wall down on top of people. So we started looking for a keyboards man and we met Andy McMaster through Frankie Miller - they used to be in the same band together in Glasgow, The Sabres - and we bought him an organ," Tyla explained. But not everybody wanted the group to change. "I think we were all fairly keen on the idea of getting a keyboard player, because we felt that we were too restricted as two guitars, bass and drums," recalls Belmont. "As I remember it, the only person that was against having a keyboard player was Dai Davies, he didn't want us to change. He wanted us to stay as two guitars, bass and drums and just get a keyboard player in if we wanted one on a record. But we decided that we would have a keyboard player." Andy McMaster was the only member of the group to have written a bona fide hit. Belmont says: "[He was] definitely a pop song writer. He wrote 'We're Going On A Tuppenny Bus Ride' which was a huge hit for Anita Harris. It's a novelty pop song he wrote, but he had a pop writer's sensibility."

In May, Ducks Deluxe supported label mate and ex-member of the Velvet Underground, Lou Reed, on his 'Sally Can't Dance' European tour. Despite his time with the seminal New York art rockers, Reed had drifted into glam territory with his *Transformer* album, co-produced by the glam Übermensch David Bowie. Despite having to deal with unsympathetic audiences, Ducks Deluxe also had Mr. Reed to contend with. The grumpy old man of rock wasn't in the best of moods for the entire tour which kicked off in Stockholm with a gig at the Concerthouse. "We got treated fairly badly, as most support acts do," recalled Belmont. "But we thought it was going to be great because he was on RCA, the same label. We were lucky to get a five minute soundcheck and all the rest of that shit that goes down. But we did get to play across Europe and in various places and we got some great contacts out of the whole thing, which enabled us to go to France where we built quite a good following."

When the tour hit Paris, Ducks Deluxe met Marc Zermati, owner of the independent Skydog Records. "Marc was a one-off. He got records out to the kids through his Skydog label long before any of the major labels came and swallowed up these big names like The Clash and The Police," said Tyla. "I took him to see Joe Strummer and The 101ers in London, way before they became The Clash and he steamed right in and signed them. He just never had the cash to make these signings stick. He took me to a party once, near the Thames to meet [the late] Malcolm McLaren and watch the Sex Pistols. Malcolm wanted Marc to sign the band and me to produce them. McLaren started talking in telephone numbers and I told him the band was shit anyway and that was that. I couldn't drag Marc away - he thought they were great!" He also thought Ducks Deluxe were pretty hot too, and when they were dropped by RCA he issued their last hurrah, the *Jumpin'* EP.

If the Brinsleys and Ducks Deluxe were slipping out of time, Dr Feelgood remained five minutes ahead of theirs. In August, Nick Kent dedicated a full page in the *NME* to praising the Feelgoods. A year earlier he'd championed Kilburn and the High Roads as rock's saviours, now he claimed they'd seen better days and were "close to being cast off as last year's thing". Dr Feelgood, however, were "hot". The only thing holding them back was a lack of original material. If a group like the Feelgoods wanted to be taken seriously it had to write its own stuff. The Feelgoods would always struggle to come up with new songs, but fortunately Johnson was beginning to flourish as a songsmith. "I started to write songs then because I just always feel like I've got to make things. Previously I didn't feel the need because I thought well first of all I'm never going to be able to write a song as good as 'Route 66', and so what's the point in writing songs, because there's so many of those sort of songs around that we could do," he told *ZigZag* magazine.

With a bit of practice he'd soon be writing songs that, if you used your imagination, could be long lost R&B gems. It was only natural that he should follow in his heroes' footsteps, and if he didn't compose anything as good as

'Route 66' he nevertheless managed to come up with some convincing material that was shaped as much by the demands of the group as it was by the exemplars he admired. "The three-minute thing I think comes about because a lot of the music that we're interested in is made in that way. Also because we're very much a performing band, doing the kind of performance that we do, you can't keep that energy level up longer than that length of time in those kind of bursts, and so it falls naturally like that. We couldn't do a song for ten minutes with that kind of energy," he said.

There wasn't a rock group on the planet capable of sustaining the shock and awe Dr Feelgood created on stage for more than three minutes at a time. Many progressive groups didn't even have the energy to stand up when they performed, and their audiences were just as sedentary. Sheer intensity wasn't the only weapon in the Dr Feelgood arsenal. They were so tight you couldn't fit a Rizla between the gaps. Everything about them; their look, their attitude, their power, their street cred, drew audiences like moths to a flame. Such was their impact that without them there may never have been a following wave of musicians to stick the boot in.

Joe Strummer, who was getting The 101ers together, was a fan and played a Fender Telecaster in homage to Johnson. "Dr Feelgood were the undisputed kings of that scene," he recalled "we were the latecomers, more like the dirty cousins, because we were squat-rockers and a bit younger and a bit more incapable. We didn't know our chops, as well. Eventually we got skilled enough to be probably the second-best rhythm and blues group in West London after Feelgood, but it took a year and a half to get there."

Like Kilburn and the High Roads, Dr Feelgood were of the moment, a living, breathing counterpart to the urban decay that could be found on London's outer limits. The rows of Ford Cortinas, the small areas of open wasteland surrounded by cement works, the streets of small run-down shops and condemned housing were everywhere. Of course Strummer liked Dr Feelgood, they came from an industrialized outpost and looked like the kind of scruffy squatters he hung out with, and their music was as rough and militant as the London streets he lived on.

The best way to experience Dr Feelgood was in the back room of a pub, but those days were fast coming to an end. Playing to 200 people a night wasn't the answer. They had to break out and find a larger audience, and the only way to do that was with a hit record. The pop charts were inescapable. As Simon Frith noted in the July '74 issue of *Let It Rock*: "There's no way to avoid the current top twenty except in a nunnery. I've never had to listen to ELP or Yes or any of the other progressive prophets but I've suffered 'Eye Level' many dozens of times and, like it or not, it was part of the experience of 1973. Hit singles, whatever the sales trends and the profit figures, are still the essence of pop culture."

In 1973, 3,000 singles were issued in Britain but only a handful made it into the charts. Of course, a single didn't have to be a hit for it to be successful.

Singles were often issued to promote albums, sales of which generated more income than 45s. The problem was getting a new tune heard. First the song had to be written and recorded, then somebody at the record company had to select it for release, next it had to be promoted on radio, television or in nightclubs and finally bought. Obviously record labels were in the business of giving people what they wanted and luckily for Dr Feelgood United Artists were quite successful at doing just that. Andrew Lauder was tipped off about Dr Feelgood by Nick Lowe, but although he was fascinated by them he couldn't see them making money for the label. Not that he'd let that bother him in the past. Rather he signed them simply because United Artists could afford to nurture them and hope for the best. Lauder: "It was obviously against the run of play but at that point we had enough going on at UA to be able to say 'sod it, let's do it.'"

One of the things United Artists had going on was a planned tour by Brinsley Schwarz and Dave Edmunds. Dr Feelgood were added to the bottom of the bill with the intention of road-testing material for their debut album. Adding them to the bill might have seemed like a smart move, after all they had a lot in common with the Brinsleys and Edmunds and, despite being relatively unknown outside London, would go down a storm. But in truth it was standard record company practice. If a new group could be tacked onto a tour by an established act everyone was happy.

While Dr Feelgood were enjoying the delights of playing to enthusiastic capacity audiences, Dave Edmunds wasn't. While filming *Stardust* he'd teamed up with Keith Moon and developed an appetite for booze and drugs. "I didn't use to drink up till then," he explained. "When I was younger, I did, but during the late '60s/early '70s, I didn't drink at all, I just went off it, for the whole of my twenties. And it was when I met Keith on that movie, I was going through a divorce at the same time, leaving Wales, and getting into this movie. Meeting all new people and getting into the London scene." To make things worse he was mixing his drink with a lethal cocktail of drugs. "Everyone was doing Mandrax. I once got a prescription for a hundred Demanil and a hundred Mandrax, just by asking," he confessed. "And those are drugs that don't mix very well. If you tried to get up and do something and function on it you'd wake up under a table."

Brinsley Schwarz had the unenviable task of following Dr Feelgood each night with a set drawn from their recent *New Favourites* album. As part of their act they'd worked up a snappy medley to introduce Edmunds. "We used to have this thing worked out where we'd come on, do our set, and at the end of it we'd do this thing like a review [and play a medley of his hits]," recalls Ian Gomm. "Then Nick would say something like 'Ladies and gentlemen, I'd like to bring on one of the hardest working men in show business, Dave! 'I Hear You Knocking'! Edmunds!' And he was supposed to come on. There was this one night when our roadie was tugging at my trousers from the side of the stage to get my attention, and I'm going, 'What? What?' And he says,

'He's not here. Tell Nick he's not here. He's gone to hospital. His hands have locked up.' And then we came off and he was in the dressing room, 'Oh I'm sorry boys I don't know what happened.' I nursed him through it. I used to go back with him, [when we were] in Monmouth, at Rockfield, just to make sure he got home safe."

Edmunds did make it onto the stage when the tour hit Cardiff and two songs recorded that night appeared on his *Subtle As A Flying Mallet* album. Brinsley Schwarz and Dr Feelgood were also recorded, but not for commercial release. "Just before we were signed we were on a tour supporting Brinsley Schwarz and Dave Edmunds, and United Artists had brought the Pye mobile along to a couple of the gigs," Johnson explains. "In fact it was a result of that that the 'Bonie Moronie' track was done, and we got some 'live' tapes of that. At the time, we knew they were recording, but we didn't know if they were actually recording our set. So we just went ahead and played; we were still very much an amateur sort of thing then I suppose."

Like Brinsley Schwarz before them, Dr Feelgood wanted to keep things real. The recordings made on the 'New Favourites' tour were good, but United Artists wanted a studio album. In late August they were sent to Rockfield Studios with the late Vic Maile as producer. His production style was the very opposite of Edmunds' Spector-esque experiments, but he was no less a rock 'n' roll producer. Having captured The Who *Live At Leeds* and several other landmark live albums, he was the ideal choice to produce them. Johnson wanted to record the album live in the studio as simply as possible: "We thought when we come to record the first album, we want to do that ... play as we normally play. We thought we'd try and get the sound as it is, and to record very directly, do things in one take, with as little over-dubbing as possible," he explained. But Maile wanted to build each track by overdubbing one instrument at a time. This led to tensions, as The Big Figure explains: "Vic was someone who would stick up for what he felt should be on the record and the sound, but also someone who would talk and compromise on certain issues."

One compromise was issuing the record in mono. In the early '60s it ruled supreme, because most teenagers only had mono Dansettes on which to play their records. Stereo records were more expensive, so it made financial sense to stick with mono because you got more pop for your pound. But by the end of the decade the turntables had turned and stereo was king. As groups became more progressive and experimental, hi-fi became more sophisticated. It wasn't long before some bright spark came up with quadraphonic sound, for people with four ears. Albums like Mike Oldfield's *Tubular Bells* sold like hotcakes in its quadraphonic version. The concert experience of sitting cross-legged on the floor marvelling as the guitar panned across the stage could be recreated in the comfort of your own home. Dr Feelgood didn't make sitting-down music and Johnson was adamant that their album wasn't going to be issued in anything as bourgeois as stereo.

Part of the problem was the sound they made as a three-piece. There was little Maile could do with only three instruments and a voice so it made sense to mix the record with all the instruments in the centre because it sounded better. Although there had been a bit of a 'back to mono' revival, Johnson claimed that releasing the album in mono had nothing to do with any attempt to appear retro. "There wasn't anything behind it, we were just trying to make the band sound right," he said. "I didn't want to be like that art school vibe were you're striking poses about being retrograde. That wasn't what we were doing. We were doing something that was real…"

11
Glimpse Number Two For The Reader

In December 1973, Humphrey Ocean decided he'd had enough of Kilburn and the High Roads and quit. "My granny had died about a year before and I was left £300 and I thought, 'Well, now I can afford to stop.' I was trying to work out how many eight pounds a week that made, because that was what we earned in the Kilburns," he said. His replacement, Jerome Lucas, didn't last long before he too was replaced by Charlie Sinclair. Naturally, the new bassist was as visually striking as he was musically talented. Where Ocean had towered over Dury, Sinclair, a diminutive Scot, appeared to labour under the weight of his gigantic bass guitar. Dury's decision to recruit the pocket-sized bassist wasn't simply to maintain the group's riveting visual appearance, it was, he claimed, all part of their outsider attitude. "There is a certain outcast thing that he's got, that he knows about. Davey's got it too," he said. "It's not so much a physical thing. It's a mental thing. He knows what it's like to be outside the mainstream of society without being a hippie or a philosopher or a tramp."

The ultimate outsider, Dury had discovered that playing the fool in a five-piece band gave him certain privileges he'd been denied as a painter. "We'd do terrible yobbo things. I haven't felt the urge to do it for three years - since I've bin working with a band." For Dury, rock 'n' roll was a liberating and expressive medium that communicated ideas that were often troubling and taboo. His songs were as yet too unpalatable for most, but would soon resonate with a growing underclass readying themselves to storm the mainstream. His performances, part cathartics, part theatre and part provocation would eventually make Dury king of the hill.

In early '74, Charlie Gillett managed to secure Kilburn and the High Roads a recording contract with Warner Brothers' subsidiary Raft Records. Tony Ashton, former bassist with Family, was hired to produce the album and, despite initial reservations, found them spellbinding. "I went to see them and just fell in love with the whole thing. I had never heard a worse band - in one sense - in my life! It was so bizarre, the whole thing. But it was great and Ian Dury's lyrics were mind-blowing. So we stormed into Apple's new studios in Savile Row and began work," he said. Kilburn and the High Roads should have felt on top of the world, after all, recording an album is the pinnacle to which most groups aspire. However, the excitement of recording in the very studio once occupied by the Fab Four was short-lived. It quickly became apparent that the project was doomed to failure. Ashton found it difficult to capture their rough-and-tumble sound and criticised Newton-Rohoman's drumming. The Guyanan simply wasn't up to the task and was holding the group back. Dury decided he'd have to go and replaced him with Louis Larose. Basic tracks finished, Dury excused himself and went on holiday. It was a mistake he'd never make again. On his return he was shocked by what he heard. Ashton had added strings to complement the group's knockabout sound that made them sound like a cloth-eared cabaret band. If that wasn't bad enough, things were about to get a whole lot worse.

Joe Smith, head honcho at Warner Brothers, was in town on business and he and some of his staff caught the Kilburns, at one of their regular London haunts, Dingwalls in Camden Town. Dury told the *NME*: "One of 'em takes me aside and starts sayin' things like 'Are you going to be a superstar?' So I'm sayin' 'whooh. Well ... I dunno." Smith probably didn't understand a single word Dury said, and if he couldn't understand this chirpy Cockney chap then neither would an American audience. There was no way anyone brought up on a diet of Mountain, James Taylor and The Eagles would have bought into Kilburn and the High Roads. But Dury's fatal mistake was to undersell himself. When asked if he was going to be a superstar, Dury should have said, "Not arf"', not, "Well ... I dunno". That was hardly going to sit well with a hard-nosed businessman like Smith.

Smith's reaction was to secretly plan to drop Kilburn and the High Roads while giving the impression that Warner Brothers remained fully committed. He suggested launching the album with a big party at the Swiss Cottage Holiday Inn. According to Dury they were promised "20 hookers in the swimming pool. The week before they had 10 in the pool for some other band: We were saying, c'mon, what do we need 20 hookers in the pool for, I mean, we've all got our own things going, you know." 10 hookers, 20 hookers, it made no difference because when Gillett delivered the master tapes he was informed that Warner Brothers had closed Raft and, although the label's other acts would be transferred to Warner Brothers, Kilburn and the High Roads would not be joining them. Dury had his revenge by simply re-recording the album only months later for Dawn Records. Speaking some three years after the album's eventual release, Dury said: "The 12 cuts we recorded for Pye were almost the same ones we'd recorded for Warner Brothers. We had re-recorded them so that Warner Brothers couldn't put out an album if we were successful."

It wasn't all bad news. The band got to keep their new van, equipment and what remained of their £50,000 advance. With that kind of money they could have taken a break from gigging and worked on new material. But the allure of the road and service station food was too strong, and while Kilburn and the High Roads continued their relentless schedule of one-nighters, Gillett and Nelki tried to find them another record company. Richard Branson had recently launched his Virgin Records label with Mike Oldfield's *Tubular Bells* and was on the lookout for some more British talent to offset the company's predominantly Krautrock catalogue. The label's other British acts, Gong (well, half-British, half-French and an Australian), Henry Cow and Hatfield and The North, were no less quirky than Kilburn and the High Roads and Virgin Records offered Gillett a deal. But Dury was adamant that he wasn't going to share a label with a bunch of hippies.

In April, Larose quit the group whereupon Newton-Rohoman was reinstated. However, no sooner had they re-acquainted themselves with their funky drummer than Dury's right-hand man and musical foil decided he'd had enough. Hardy was tired of playing the same songs night after night, was stressed out from having to drive the group everywhere and wanted to play with other musicians. Hardy wasn't alone in feeling the pressure, Dury admitted to feeling the strain too: "I don't think we're built for going on the road like Penzance one night and Manchester the next. It's not as if we're 18." It had been some years since any of Kilburn and the High Roads had been teenagers, but Dury was having none of it. It was shape up or ship out. It was the very excuse the long suffering Hardy needed. He quit and was replaced by Rod Melvin who stayed for the next two years. With Hardy gone, Dury decided it was time for a radical overhaul of the way the group was managed and sacked Gillett and Nelki. He claimed it was because he wasn't happy with their day-to-day running of the group. Instead he signed with a flamboyant ex-retailer who'd owned a chain of fashionable clothes shops before moving into rock management. Tommy Roberts was a larger than life character described by Dury as a "great showman but he's not a very good grocer."

Before moving into rock management, Roberts had sold one of his stores to a recent graduate from Goldsmiths College, Malcolm McLaren. With his partner, Vivienne Westwood, McLaren had set up shop at 430 King's Road selling Teddy Boy gear to the capital's hard core rocker community. Dury's then girlfriend, Denise Roudette, recalls: "When Tommy Roberts took over there was still some money in the bank - about £1,200 - and the first thing he did was to take us all down the King's Road to Malcolm and Vivienne's shop and buy suits for everybody." The group was fitted out with demob suits and Dury with a satin boxer's gown with 'Rough Kids' emblazoned across the back. "It wasn't like a Hollywood star thing, it was just meant to be a boxer's gown," explained Dury. "But it ended up looking poofy, and Pete Erskine wrote about us in the *NME*, and said it was contrived." Compared to the ignominy Sinclair suffered, Dury got off lightly. The pint-sized bassist was told he'd have to don a grey Harrow school-boy suit and Little Lord Fauntleroy haircut. It might have worked a year or two later for Aussie rockers AC/DC, but surely Erskine was right: the Kilburns' new image was contrived. Dury informed Roberts that he wanted to record for the same record label as light-entertainment maestro Max Bygraves. The avuncular singer had recently scored a hit for Pye Records with 'Deck Of Cards'; exactly the kind of unblemished song Dury remembered from his childhood. Roberts succeeded in securing a recording contract for Kilburn and the High Roads with Pye Records, but despite Dury's initial excitement there was a sting in the tail. "It's comforting knowing they [Pye] own the London Palladium and that Lew Grade's sitting up there," Dury told *ZigZag* magazine. "And it's all show business anyway and I feel a lot safer with Des O'Connor than I would with Hatfield and the North!" But Dury was putting on a brave face. The deal was rotten and he'd have been better served had he signed with the hippie loving Virgin Records. "We all went to see a lawyer and we showed him the record contract. He said 'This clause is terrible, so is this one, dreadful, dreadful. So have you got any other record companies interested?' We said no, so he said: 'Sign it!"

By the summer of '74, Kilburn and the High Roads had become a tight professional group, but had lost some of its original impact. If once they'd looked and sounded like menacing outsiders - the kind of people you would cross the road to avoid making eye contact with - they now resembled nothing so threatening as a bunch of out of work actors from a dodgy end of the pier pantomime. They'd also added some "neo-jazz rock" to their set which didn't go down too well. Their growing professionalism had, perhaps, made them too sophisticated. Dury explained: "The next job is to get back to the basics again." Dury was also criticised by the press for overdoing the cheeky chappie stage patter. The suggestion was that rather than subverting the medium, the Kilburns had become just another flaccid attraction on what was an already over-crowded scene.

Despite the changes imposed by Roberts and Dury, the Kilburns continued to go down a storm with audiences across the country. Dury told the *NME*: "Most of the time we're inclined t'believe we went down like a load a'wet kippers." Once again Dury was being over modest. Kilburn and the High Roads were drawing respectable audiences on the pub and university circuit and going down a storm. What they hadn't done was reach escape velocity. The pub circuit was a great way to learn stagecraft, but nobody wanted to play it forever.

The only way Kilburn and the High Roads were going to break into the mainstream was with a hit record. In November '74, the Pye Records imprint Dawn Records issued Kilburn and the High Roads' debut single. 'Rough Kids' b/w 'Billy Bentley' had been recorded while the group were still managed by Gillett and Nelki and produced by Chris Thomas. Prefiguring the coming punk storm, its artless drum and bass intro and crashing dustbin lid percussion evokes a sense of the street and adolescent unrest fuelled by boredom and glue sniffing. Its B-side 'Billy Bentley (Promenades Himself In London)', heralded the kind of material that comprised *New Boots And Panties!!* If only Thomas had been allowed to produce Kilburn and the High Roads' second attempt at recording an album, it would have knocked the spots off the version that eventually saw the light of day in June '75. The single was way ahead of its time and unsurprisingly failed to bother the charts. It did, however, get them some much needed press and generated some favourable reviews.

Dury was beginning to make waves but he'd have to ride on the coattails of the forthcoming musical revolution before winning the recognition he deserved. But as unnoticed as he was at the time, Dury was influencing a small but important section of London's punk underground. Chris Thomas got to produce the Sex Pistols *Never Mind The Bollocks* album partly because he'd produced Kilburn and the High Roads. "I was approached by Malcolm McLaren about possibly doing the Sex Pistols, he set up a meeting with Steve Jones, Paul Cook and Glenn Matlock, and they wanted me to produce them because they'd liked 'Rough Kids'," he said. "I didn't think anyone had heard it."

McLaren and Westwood would drag John Lydon along to Kilburns' gigs to take notes. Sex Pistols' insider, Roberta Bayley, recalls: "He [Lydon] had a way of leaning on the microphone. For Ian it was for balance, and it was this evil thing. Just the way he would dress." Bayley wasn't alone in noticing the extent to which the future Sex Pistol modelled himself on the Kilburns' vocalist. Dury had his eyes on the spotty punk and one night bent McLaren's ear about his petty larceny. "He had a safety pin, which was the satirical elegance that I had inspired myself with, and was leaning forwards and growling and holding the microphone just like I did. And Malcolm [McLaren] had me on one side and Fred, our handler and social secretary, on the other, and I'm going, 'What's all that about then Malcolm?' 'He's copying me isn't he?' and Malcolm was there just squeaking," he recalled. Lydon wasn't the type to squeak, he was more than up for meeting his hero and asked *Sounds* journalist Jonh [sic] Ingharn to introduce him. "Ian had these earrings, he had a skin crop, they were spiritual brothers, and Ian had been into this trip for a while. John turned to me and said, 'Why don't you introduce me to this guy?' And so I did," Ingharn told Jon Savage.

Wreckless Eric Goulden didn't get to meet Dury until much later, but the first time he saw Kilburn and the High Roads he loved the tension they created: "Me and my scuzzy art school mates we loved them, because it was as though they were going to fall apart. It was on a knife edge," he said. "They had a profound and far-reaching effect on me. I suddenly realised that you didn't have to be the most accomplished musician in the world. What was more important was a kind of honesty - Kilburn and the High Roads were confirmation that you didn't have to pretend to be American to play pop music."

Graham McPherson [Suggs], later lead singer with Madness, was another who drew inspiration from the Kilburns. "It was great because it didn't seem like rock 'n' roll. It just seemed like a lot of nutty characters on stage with instruments. He seemed more of a poet than a rock 'n' roll artist. So that inspired the band [Madness] to be able to go down that route without actually having to know anything about the music business. We didn't understand the process of making records or PR or interviews. Because we'd seen Ian Dury do it, you know, someone with polio, you just saw all the possibilities for all the people who didn't look like rock stars."

Hugh Murphy was hired to record the Kilburns' album and unknown to him history was about to repeat itself. Tensions were running high and the recording sessions were fraught affairs that often turned violent as pent-up emotions surfaced. Guitarist Keith Lucas was particularly aggrieved when he discovered that a session musician replaced most of his parts. Dury's desire to make the Kilburns sound more commercial didn't help matters either. "We had played the songs a lot longer and we were probably more proficient at the arrangements, but when we got to the studios it was all changed to try and make it more acceptable," recalled Sinclair. "Everything then was the 'glam rock' and big stereo sounds and I always thought we were the first punk band and we didn't really know how to market it."

Besides having to contend with a bunch of belligerent musicians, Murphy had to fight record company politics, too. Having been told that he could take as long as he wanted, Murphy was informed that now he had to finish the album as quickly as possible. Pye Records didn't want to invest any more money in this odd little band than it had too. Murphy was given £2,000 and told to bring the sessions to an end. The result was a flat sounding album that did the Kilburns no favours. "Because the carpet had been pulled, I was only allowed one mix on the album," he said. "I think you need to get a feel of a track and mix it twice at least. But this one just took one mix and then it was shoved out," he recalled.

Little more than a flimsy vinyl epitaph that marked the beginning of their demise, *Handsome* wasn't well received by the music press or the record buying public - some sources suggest it sold fewer than 3,000 copies. To add insult to injury the Kilburns were informed by Roberts that they were broke and would have to sign on the dole. It was the final straw. Keith Lucas had never got on with Dury and with tensions between them rising he used the album's failure as an excuse to abandon a rapidly sinking ship and he was followed soon after by Newton-Rohoman and then Sinclair. Speaking of the constant turmoil, Dury said: "It was always changing, it was always somebody's a bit upset." There was little he could do but accept defeat and withdraw to reconsider his future. During the summer of '75, Dury concentrated on writing songs with Melvin, which when recorded with the Blockheads, would become sizable hits and propel Dury to international stardom.

12
Too Much Monkee Business

With the mixing desk at Rockfield Studios still sizzling from the sonic battering it received at the hands of Dr Feelgood, Ducks Deluxe arrived to begin work on their second album. The difficult second album turned out to be just that, difficult. Despite the fact that their rough hewn debut had garnered international praise, RCA wanted a more commercial record. That wasn't something Sean Tyla was willing to contemplate: "[RCA wanted] to turn us into a bloody 'pop' band because we weren't selling heavy and they wanted a more commercial sound on the next record," he said. It was a classic case of history repeating itself. Wasn't it RCA that took a dangerous and dynamic Elvis Presley and turned him into a harmless and fluffy pop star? Had they learned nothing? Ducks Deluxe was a no-frills, keep it simple, knock' em dead rock 'n' roll group. But their record company couldn't see beyond *Top Of The Pops* and the Radio 1 play lists. Its response was to knock off all the rough edges and shoehorn them into something it could understand and sell.

Dave Edmunds was brought in to produce the new album, but unfortunately his encounter with Keith Moon had taken its toll. According to Tyla, Edmunds had taken on too many commitments and wasn't in any kind of state to work his Welsh wizardry on their recordings. "Dave was burned out. He had just finished the Brinsleys' album, who Dai Davies was co-managing now, and he was struggling to finish the soundtrack for the *Stardust* movie and his own, new, solo album. On top of that he was living on a diet of cheap scotch and dangerous chemicals and was close to going financially bust. Not good!" With a lethal cocktail of drink and drugs inside him, Edmunds would leap into his Jaguar and race along the tiny roads between Rockfield Studios and his home in Monmouth, drunk out of his brain with his highly valuable Gibson 335 lying on the back seat without a case. Something had to give and, like Ian Gomm before him, Tyla found himself having to deal with the fallout. With the basic tracks cut and Edmunds incapacitated, there was nothing else to do but finish the album himself. "It was decided that I should stay and mix the album with Kingsley Ward, the studio owner and the rest of the boys went home with Nick and Andy bleating on about how I should balance 'their' tracks," Tyla explained. "I think Kingsley and I did a reasonable job in the end. We managed to screw a little bit of bass onto the thing but not a lot. That was the end of it for me, I've got to say."

Tyla and Belmont weren't happy with the pop-orientated songs that Garvey and McMasters had written to appease RCA. Although Tyla puts it down to a simple rock/pop dialectic, Belmont suggests that the root of the problem lay in the group's lack of success. "There was a lot of dissatisfaction which was probably in part due to the fact that we weren't being very successful. That's always a good reason for having an argument, blaming somebody else, it's because of you that we're not successful." One reason Ducks Deluxe didn't achieve the level of success they should have was because Tyla wouldn't compromise the Ducks' rock 'n' roll attitude. Listening to the album it's easy to hear the musical divide. Tyla and Belmont are rough and visceral, Garvey and McMaster smooth and calculated. But as far as the Tyla and Belmont axis were concerned pop was something played by men in make-up and glitter boots. "That song he [McMaster] played with The Motors, 'Airport', he wrote that while he was still in Ducks Deluxe," says Belmont. "Of course, we didn't want to do that because grand pop masterpieces wasn't our sort of thing at all. But obviously he and Nick Garvey had a strong connection in that kind of way and they left."

Besides having no idea how to market the Ducks, RCA was too busy ensuring the continued success of its established acts to bother about a group of upstarts from Camden Town. Ducks Deluxe was a small duck in a big pond and suffered because of it. "RCA were abysmal really. They signed us because they felt they had too, to stay ahead of the 'game'", says Tyla. "Dai got too tangled up in his own ambitions and let us slide. He was a Duck through and through until he smelt a better pie. You can't blame him for that. Martin kept me sane. He lived the life of the speed-driven riff-wrencher from dawn to dusk and he was totally committed to the 'cause'. We had quite different likes in music but that's what made the early Duck music so exciting."

While Ducks Deluxe had been busying themselves in a recording studio, Chilli Willi and the Red Hot Peppers had been working the live circuit like it was going out of fashion. In January they supported T. Rex on the 'Truck Off' tour. T. Rextasy was on the wane but Bolan was still packing 'em in. Not that it helped the Willis because, as Ducks Deluxe had discovered, the audience was only there to watch, and in this case scream at, the headline attraction. With lots of good press coming from the alternative music papers, *ZigZag* and *Let It Rock*, the time had come to instigate phase two of Jakeman's grand plan. This involved three steps to Rock 'n' Roll Heaven. Step one was to secure the band a record contract, Revelation having stopped trading. Step two was to capture onto tape the good time atmosphere the group created onstage. Step three, perhaps the most audacious of them all, persuade someone to put up the money for a package tour the likes of which the country hadn't experienced since the mid-'60s.

Jakeman bypassed the major labels in favour of the recently established semi-independent Mooncrest label. The company was a subsidiary of the successful Charisma Records/B&C conglomerate that was home to Genesis and Monty Python. One of the more enlightened record companies, its booking agency the Charisma Agency, had several pub rock groups on its books, so it understood how groups like Chilli Willi and the Red Hot Peppers operated.

With the ink on the contract barely dry, the group headed for Chalk Farm

Studios to begin work on their new album. They decided to take the low-key pub rock approach and produce themselves, something their record company frowned upon once it heard what they'd been up to. It wasn't necessarily that the recordings weren't up to scratch, but it was thought that a named producer would give the album a little more gravitas. Several well known people were approached but few showed any interest. That was until ex-Monkee Mike Nesmith suggested he was the man for the job and signed up to produce the record.

On paper Nesmith looked ideal. Besides being in one of the most successful pop groups ever, he was the undisputed high priest of country-rock. Nesmith's pioneering spirit as a songwriter, performer and producer gave the impression he knew precisely how to handle himself and the artists he produced. Interviewed for *ZigZag* he appeared to understand the problems groups like the Willis faced. "The record business is in a terrible decline right now," he said. "Nobody really understands it, or at least they don't seem to. It's one of the reasons Jac Holzman, founder of Elektra Records, got out, and it's one of the reasons that [my company] Countryside is in being, because it's not a record company. Our primary thrust is into exploring a new media consciousness that's on us, and I want Countryside to be the basis of that."

Nesmith's talk of "media consciousness" must have struck a chord with the Willis' media savvy manager, but it should have set alarm bells ringing. As it turned out, Nesmith wasn't the chirpy, carefree pop star who'd appeared on TV. "He turned out to be a fervent Christian Science believer, had a Bible on the mixing desk and was generally the most po-faced and humourless producer we'd ever encountered," explained Stone. The situation wasn't helped by the Willis know-it-all attitude. Having started producing the album themselves they thought they knew best. "We fiddled around with his mixes after he'd gone," said Stone. "But he was right and we were wrong. His mixes were much better than ours. I realise now that we should have listened to him." Things came to a head when Stone, Lithman and Jakeman took exception to something Nesmith said. "Professionally, perhaps, this should have made no difference to us at all, but it did - specifically to Martin, Phil and Jake," recalled Riley. "After we'd cut five tracks, Jake came out of the control room (where something had apparently 'gone down' between Martin, Phil and Mike), and announced to the rest of us that we were bailing out!"

Nesmith lasted less than a week before packing his Bible and departing with his pedal steel player for the more reverent atmosphere of southern California. Having blown out the only producer willing to work with them, there was nothing left but to finish the album as they'd begun it; without him. Like all good hippies they headed for the country to get their heads together and finish the record. "We took Ronnie Lane's mobile down to Jake's girlfriend's farm in Cornwall and recorded in the cowshed. We had Ron Nevison, who worked on *Pet Sounds*, as engineer/producer with Jake overseeing. That was a lot more fun," recalls Stone. Riley, however, remembers differently. "Nevison was a sports fan and brought a portable television with him". That would have been fine had he not insisted on watching Wimbledon and the 1974 World Cup rather than knuckle down and produce the group. It soon became apparent that tape would only roll in moments stolen from Ron's busy viewing schedule. "Having already blown-out one producer and a sizable chunk of recording budget, we had to grin and bear it," Riley recalls. "With precious little help from Nevison, who was content to take whatever was available between tennis and football fixtures, tempos raced and tempers flared. Hoping desperately that a miracle might occur during the mix-down sessions back in London, we soldiered on and finished the album."

In August the group played at London's first pub rock festival, organised by Dave Robinson at the Hope and Anchor. Since splitting with Brinsley Schwarz, Robinson had been living and working at the pub, promoting groups and building a recording studio. "I didn't know how to build a studio but I thought if I'm going to make records them I'm going to build a studio. Part of the deal was that I book the bands into the music cellar and then record them live, I thought live music was good. I was into the whole idea of it. I bought the two Beatles J 54 Studers from Abbey Road, and I had the Rolling Stones valve desks from Decca Studios, which had [recorded] everything from The Rolling Stones to 'Nights In White Satin'. They were throwing them out, I bought them very cheaply, put them all together. I'd never done that work so I spent a year welding the whole thing together and I had a great eight-track valve studio. We were ahead of our time and I recorded Elvis Costello there and Graham Parker, Bon Temps Roulez and Kokomo."

Robinson promoted the pub rock festival to create some interest in what was becoming a tired scene. Speaking to the *Melody Maker*, he claimed that the pub rock scene had become apathetic. "People were complaining that nothing was happening. But nothing will happen unless you make it." This was typical of Robinson's 'can do' attitude. It was no good sitting around complaining about things, if you wanted something to happen you had to get off your backside and make it happen.

Chilli Willi and the Red Hot Peppers' *Bongos Over Balham* album was issued not long after they'd appeared at Robinson's pub rock festival. Capitalising on the renewed interest in the scene, Mooncrest Records poured all it had into the group. Full page adverts designed by Barney Bubbles appeared in several music papers. The campaign was a microcosm of the kind of jokey, off-the-wall japery Jakeman honed to perfection when promoting early Stiff Records releases. The press adverts featured a cigar-chomping pig 'Vinyl Mogul' - recycled for Stiff Records press releases - and the album cover held in position by a hand, trotter or dildo.

No major record company would have spent so much time and money on a series of provocative adverts for an album by a group as quirky as Chilli Willi and the Red Hot Peppers. But the Willis weren't a typical group and Jakeman wasn't a typical manager. Although Mooncrest voiced concerns about the cost it went along with the wheeze. "We did it because we were on a mission," says Jakeman. "We had that collect-the-set mentality." It was a marketing ploy he'd refine once Stiff Records was in business, and it did the trick for the Willis. With support from their record company and a relentless gigging schedule the album sold a respectable 16,000 copies.

The seeds of Stiff Records had been sown. But for the moment its co-creators continued to work independently. Once they combined their talents the world would be their oyster. Robinson was exactly the kind of forward-thinking entrepreneur the music business needed. But while there were plenty of groups to record and consider making records with, it would be a while yet before it could happen. Flip City and Bon Temps Roulez weren't going to sell enough records to keep even the most prudent record company in business.

Although Robinson recorded almost every group that played the Hope and Anchor, and made demos with several new wave luminaries, little of what he'd recorded saw the light of day on vinyl. An early Stiff Records press release mentioned plans for an album culled from the recordings Robinson had made at the Hope and Anchor. But by the time Stiff Records was up and running, pub rock was dead in the water and the sharks were circling. The proposed double album was scrapped because of contractual difficulties and the tapes languished in a warehouse for years before they were lost when the storage facility was burgled.

Before Jakeman joined forces with Robinson he still had to complete the last stage of his master plan to turn Chilli Willi and the Red Hot Peppers into stars. Sales of the album had been strong; all they needed now was one final push. The final stage in Jakeman's plan was to recreate a package tour the likes of which hadn't been seen in Britain since the Motown Revue hit its shores in 1965. With Jakeman in command, Chilli Willi and the Red Hot Peppers were all set to take the charts by storm.

13
A Present ... For The Future

If London was struggling to maintain a vibrant music scene, outside of the capital things were a whole lot worse. A few years previously Liverpool had been at the heart of the British beat boom. Now it languished in the rock 'n' roll doldrums. As in the good old bad old days, if you wanted to make it in music you had to move to London. Declan MacManus, who would emerge as Elvis Costello, had recently returned to London from Liverpool and to his delight found its pubs full of groups playing the kind of music he loved. A fan of The Band, he found inspiration in Britain's answer to Dylan's backing group, Brinsley Schwarz.

MacManus saw the Brinsleys at the Cavern Club, Liverpool, and met Nick Lowe at the bar for a beer and a chat. It was a minor revelation. It was, he told *Rolling Stone* magazine, the first time he'd ever spoken to anybody in a group and, more importantly, it was Lowe's attitude that came as a minor epiphany. MacManus struck up a relationship with the group and whenever he was in London he'd roadie for them. Like Martin Belmont before him, he used the experience to his advantage and decided to move to the capital and form his own outfit. He met bassist Michael 'Mitch' Kent at a Brinsley Schwarz gig and with Malcolm Dennis on drums formed Mothertruckers. The trio played a handful of gigs before changing their name to the Bizaro Brothers and finally Flip City. Modelling themselves on Brinsley Schwarz they added Steve Hazlehurst (lead guitar) and Dickie Faulkner (percussion) and moved into a house together.

Ever since Lennon and McCartney breathed life into the nation's moribund pop scene, it had become imperative for groups to write their own material. Flip City was fortunate that it had a budding songwriter, even if he was still finding his feet. MacManus was a sucker for a well-constructed song and looked to the singer-songwriters that were all the rage for inspiration, but something told him it wasn't the right road to travel. "For a time I resented liking things like the singer-songwriters of the early Seventies," he said. "But that was what was happening then." His early compositions reveal his influences, but he soon learnt to disguise his borrowings as his style developed.

Flip City performed several MacManus originals that, with a little remodelling, would become New Wave classics. As good as some of his early songs were, Flip City simply couldn't do them justice. Early versions of 'Radio Radio' and 'Pay It Back' bear more than a passing resemblance to the R&B swing of his heroes, but a few grams of speed and a big dose of attitude would change that. With the Attractions behind him, these songs would be transformed into sonic sputum that galvanised a generation.

Flip City worked up an unadventurous set of covers and originals with an eye to launching themselves on the Pub Rock circuit. "In the evenings we'd try and play rock 'n' roll, R&B numbers, some country songs - a real Pub Rock mixture," Costello said. Trying too hard to be like Brinsley Schwarz and lacking focus, Flip City debuted at the North Pole, a pub in north Kensington. By the summer the group had secured a short-term residency at the more famous Kensington, but although they had regular gigs, they couldn't afford to give up their day jobs just yet. "We played for peanuts. The most we ever made was £25, on a Saturday night," Costello recalled.

Across town, John 'Woody' Mellor, who'd reinvent himself as Joe Strummer, was planning his own attack on the capital's music scene with his group The 101ers (they got their name from the address of their squat at 101 Walterton Road, off the Harrow Road). If Flip City was born from a backseat quickie between Brinsley Schwarz and Little Feat, The 101ers was the bastard offspring of Ducks Deluxe and Dr Feelgood. London's squatter community had already produced one group of note - Ducks Deluxe - and was about to produce another. Large parts of the city were scheduled for redevelopment, but left vacant because the Greater London Council couldn't afford the improvements. Scores of empty properties were occupied by a mixture of homeless families, musicians and politically motivated twenty-somethings. A network of squatters developed with Elgin Avenue, a stone's throw from Strummer's squat at 101 Walterton Road, a hot bed of squatter activity. The community was well organised; providing restaurants, tea rooms and even support in the form of the All London Squatters Federation (ALSF) for its members.

Strummer was an active participant in the local squatter community, to the extent that he earned money to buy food for his fellow squatters and decided to form a house group to entertain them. "This was '74," he told Jon Savage. "I went back to 101 and tried to put a group together. Big John was trying to learn saxophone, and I got Patrick to play bass, but we had no money or equipment. I borrowed a bass guitar and amp and speaker, and suddenly we were happening." Strummer gave conflicting reasons for forming the group. Either it was because he wanted to be a rock 'n' roll star, or because the Transport Police were cracking down on busking and playing pubs was both safer and more profitable. Like many of his generation he was inspired by the rock 'n' roll and R&B he encountered in his youth. Recalling his school days and the impact beat music had on him, he told Gavin Martin: "I heard the start of The Rolling Stones 'Not Fade Away'. It was turned up really loud, those things (valve wireless sets) had massive bass. I just thought, 'This is it.'"

Strummer had already earned money from busking, so why not take the next step and do it with a group? "We saw it as maybe we can keep body and soul together if we can get a few gigs in these Irish pubs," he told Chris Salewicz. Strummer borrowed some money from the late Arabella Churchill [Granddaughter of Sir Winston] to buy a very small part of Pink Floyd's PA and installed it in the basement of 101 Walterton Road as a rudimentary rehearsal space. Here he formed El Huaso and The 101 All Stars. The group comprised Antonio Narvaez (drums), Pat Nother (bass), Simon 'Big John' Cassell (saxophone) and Alvaro Pena Rojes (saxophone). The group hardly had a chance to rehearse before it was booked to play a benefit for the Chilean Resistance. "We had five days to knock something together, we could only play six numbers. Then our fucking drummer went on holiday. That's when the Snakes joined for the first time," Strummer told Allan Jones. A student at Chelsea University, Richard (Snake Hips) Dudanski had never played the drums in his life. "After a couple of days of frantic practice I thought I could handle it," he said. "It wasn't too difficult. I just bashed everything in sight. I still do."

Rehearsed or not they headed to The Telegraph Inn, Brixton, to support local reggae group Matumbi. With little in the way of their own equipment they hoped to persuade the headliners to lend them theirs. It was an early coming together of rock and reggae that made a lasting impression on Strummer. "They lent us their drum kit," he told the *Melody Maker*'s Paolo Hewitt. "Can you believe that?" Matumbi saved the day, but as Clive Timperley recalls: "They [the 101ers] did their six songs and ran out of material, and that was it. They weren't very good, but they tried hard, and it was nice to see your mate on stage." It didn't matter that their riffs were rough or that they sounded amateur, the 101ers created a clenching, shocking blitzkrieg of sound that poured from the tiny stage and electrified their audience.

The 101ers were everything the mainstream wasn't; they were everything Pub Rock wasn't. Brinsley Schwarz gave the impression they weren't interested in musical virtuosity, but in their own way they were. The Brinsleys' determination to eschew the mainstream was as prescriptive as the ghastly corporate rock and pop they wanted gone. Their virtuosity wasn't in question, they always played with exquisite taste and style; their arrangements, solos and sound were polished to perfection. The 101ers weren't. Roger Armstrong, who formed Chiswick Records with Ted Carroll, suggests: "The 101ers were coming slightly out of that, with more of a ramshackle approach. They weren't pro musicians the way a lot of the Pub Rock musicians were."

The 101ers took their inspiration from the kind of rough and tumble R&B Dr Feelgood were perfecting, but were cruder and looser. Anarchic in a way that no other Pub Rock group dared to be, they were de facto punks, but not in the 1976 'safety pin through the nose' kind of way. The word punk was in common usage at the time, but like the term Pub Rock it could be applied to a variety of stylistically diverse groups. Before punk rock was appropriated by the Bromley Contingent, Malcolm McLaren and Bernie Rhodes, it referred to the American beat groups that emerged in reply to the British Invasion of 1964. According to Mick Houghton, punk could be used to describe "any rock performer who camps it up to any degree, on or off stage, or who displays an arrogance and contempt for his audience."

The term had re-entered rock's vocabulary thanks to Lenny Kaye's compilation of American garage bands, *Nuggets/Original Artyfacts Of The First Psychedelic Era 1965-1968*. As Houghton went on to explain, "In its heyday the punk tag was more a qualitative one. Punk, punk, adj. - rotten worthless. Like bubblegum [the music, not the sweet] it was seen as the dross of its day. It seemed totally ephemeral and not to be taken seriously." Britain was experiencing its own proto-punk revolution. The charts were full of tawdry pop groups. Some were more knowing with their influences than others, and to tar them all with the same brush would be unfair. But as Michael Watts noted: "To a large extent the new British pop is closely tied up with the punk rock scene, itself based on the ethic of trash, which represents a backlash against the more high-minded aspects of rock that developed in the Seventies."

Call it what you will, mainstream glam/bubblegum/punk/pop of the mid-'70s was often a bland confection commercialised by major record companies for maximum airplay on wonderful Radio One and *Top Of The Pops*. It was product, pure and simple. It wasn't made by the kids, it was made for them by businessmen who saw a gap in the market and waded in to profit from a generation too bored and apathetic to do it themselves. When it came to pop music there was nothing driving change. Subcultures had, it seemed, stopped mutating and were producing new subsets of bored teenagers. Rockers and Teddy Boys were only fit to be parodied by groups like Mud and Showaddywaddy. The Mods had mutated into skinheads and the hippies were little more than targets for ridicule. Pop had eaten itself and was suffering from a severe bout of constipation.

Step outside the mainstream and the picture was a little different. Not everyone was satisfied with a diet of Cockney Rebel, Sparks and Gary Glitter. Disaffected by a gradual breaking down of social and cultural networks, there were some who took the first generation of punk rockers trash ethic and instead of wrapping it in glittery lurex rubbed its face in the dirt and kicked it in the bollocks. Houghton's definition of the original punk groups describes The 101ers perfectly. Like the earliest British beat groups and their American garage/punk counterparts, The 101ers performed rudimentary rock 'n' roll on cheap equipment. Their early repertoire appropriated influences from Britain and America and their amateurism and casual indifference made them sound unique. "There was a real individuality about them, they weren't so self-consciously retro R&B. They were more shambolic, especially early on," recalls Armstrong.

Ignored by the mainstream this type of rock music was beginning to develop a considerable cult following. Entrepreneurs like Ted Carroll were importing old American rock 'n' roll records by the lorry load and the more obscure, energetic and primitive it was the better. The 101ers had tapped into a revivalist scene that was both underground and overground. On the street, rockabilly kids were replacing traditional Teddy Boys, while mainstream pop acts like Mud and Showaddywaddy camped it up on *Top Of The Pops*. Even the major labels had cottoned on to what was happening and issued budget rock 'n' roll compilations for those who missed the rock 'n' roll revolution first time round. Recalling the heydays of his rock 'n' roll emporium, Carroll said: "I remember Jimmy Page coming in with BP Fallon and buying a load of Sun 45s at the Goldhawk Road stall. Lemmy also used to visit regularly. John Peel would come in and lurk in the background ... and then disappear, though he subsequently became a regular customer in Soho. Joe Strummer was in all the time."

When he wasn't hanging out at Carroll's stall, Strummer worked on perfecting his group. Like Ian Dury, Strummer's search for the right musicians meant that the line-up was constantly changing. "We got through two or three guitarists a week, who Woody [Strummer] was into attacking. It was just fucking around on crap instruments with a bunch of crap musicians, you know," says Pat Nother. The group's line-up changed from performance to performance because any friend who had an instrument and could play was welcome to sit in and jam.

The 101ers were as much a product of their environment as they were of Strummer's love of rock 'n' roll. Politics had never been the driving force behind Pub Rock, but that's not to say that they weren't political. Dave Robinson's involvement with the Greasy Truckers, the Brinsleys' tireless support of benefit gigs and free festivals and Jake Riviera's attempts to democratise the music industry were all politically motivated. As part of the squatter community The 101ers couldn't avoid politics. "Actually, there was as much, if not more, politics about the 101ers as there was with The Clash," says Armstrong.

In the weeks and months following their gig at the Telegraph, The 101ers made a handful of appearances at local squats. "To call them gigs is stretching it," says Pat Nother. "My memories are more of things like standing in a cinema in puddles of water, very worried about the effect on the electricity supply." At this stage The 101ers were still testing the water, but that was about to change thanks to some preparatory work carried out by another squatter group, The Derelicts.

Contemporaries of The 101ers, The Derelicts had progressed to playing both the Chippenham and Elgin pubs, but were about to be usurped by Strummer and Co.. Neither pub was on the Pub Rock circuit, and like most Irish pubs the Chippenham's live music was provided by acoustic folk duos. That changed when The Derelicts moved in and introduced the landlord to rock 'n' roll. Richard Williams, drummer with The Derelicts, recalls: "We set up and played at a squatters benefit at the Chippenham and subsequently The 101ers moved in with their weekly Pigdog club. Similarly we had a residency at the Elgin but when we took a two week summer break, The 101ers moved in and we never got our residency back!"

The 101ers fortunes changed dramatically once they got a residency at the Chippenham. The group would have been happy to keep playing in basements and old cinemas, but were galvanized into action by Liz Lewis who booked the pub's upstairs room for them on 4 December. The idea was to run a club for the local community that would comprise a rudimentary disco, provided by Strummer's Dansette, and live music, provided by The 101ers. The room cost £1 to hire and entrance was set at a very reasonable 10p, considerably less than it would cost to see one of the established Pub Rock groups. The group wasn't interested in making a fortune from performing, once they'd made enough money to buy a couple rounds of drinks that was enough. What they were more concerned about was getting their act together and, like every other group on the Pub Rock circuit, they could only do that by playing regular gigs. "We never really got off the ground until this girl pushed us into renting the room above the Chip. Because we couldn't play, how could we get any gigs?," Strummer recalled. The residency at the Chippenham would transform The 101ers from an informal amateur group of mates into one of the tightest, hard-rocking groups on the pub rock scene.

14
It's Hello From Us ... And Goodbye From Them

The lights along Southend-on-Sea's seafront glittered and twinkled in the breeze, illuminating the fish and chip shops and amusement arcades along its golden mile, which ended at the famous Kursaal Ballroom, a stopping-off point on the tour schedule for most bands of note in the 1970s [It is now a bowling alley]. The Blue Boar pub is a mile or so from the Kursaal and a mere stone's throw from Roots Hall where Southend United ply their trade in the lower reaches of the football league. It wasn't quite as well known as the Kursaal Ballroom, but twice a week this pub was home to the Kursaal Flyers. Only weeks earlier they'd risen phoenix-like from the ashes of the Surly Birds and having secured a residency at the pub won over the hearts and minds of its tipsy regulars with ease. The Flyers went down a storm with the locals, but drummer Will Birch was hungry for success and briefly flew the nest to try his hand with Charlie and the Wideboys. It didn't take him long to realise the error of his ways, whereupon he re-joined Graeme Douglas, Paul Shuttleworth, Vic Collins, Richie Bull and Dave Hatfield in their quest for stardom. With Birch back bashing the skins, the Flyers set their sights on the dazzling lights of London and bigger and better gigs.

It was only forty miles to the heart of London, but for this group of local wannabes it might as well have been a million. They desperately needed a way into the Pub Rock circuit that Birch knew would be their making. Luckily for them good fortune was on their side. Birch had helped Dr Feelgood secure their debut London gig, now it was time to call in the favour. The Canvey Island four persuaded Matt Farley, landlord of the Kensington, to book the Kursaal Flyers for a couple of Sunday gigs. It was an important move and the Kursaals knew it. "There's a lot of bands trying to use the pub rock scene to get up quickly," Douglas told *Let It Rock*. "I think we're the last band to come up through it, it's come full circle." Douglas was a bit off with his prediction. The pub scene was changing but hadn't yet gone full circle. The Kursaals weren't the first and they wouldn't be the last to benefit from playing London's pubs. They wouldn't even be the last group from Southend to sup deep from its intoxicating pool.

The Kursaal Flyers London debut turned out to be the lucky break they'd dreamt of. They were spotted by Pete Thomas, who returned the following week with his manager, Andrew Jakeman. The Flyers impressed the irascible custodian of cool who recommended them to Paul Conroy at the Charisma agency. Conroy loved the Flyers and signed up to become their manager and agent. The Kursaal Flyers had come up through the ranks fast. They'd only turned professional in January '74 and by February they were in negotiations with Jonathan King's UK Records, with whom they signed a two album deal. Lucky breaks were coming thick and fast and while the Kursaal Flyers were beginning to enjoy the first fruits of success, another up and coming group emerged that would soon eclipse everyone except Dr Feelgood.

Rising from the ashes of The Action, Mighty Baby and Warm Dust, Ace - guitarists Alan 'Bam' King and Phil Harris, bassist Terry 'Tex' Corner, keyboard player Paul Carrack and drummer Steve Witherington - would, for a brief period, become Pub Rock top dogs. Mighty Baby having gone for a Burton, Alan 'Bam' King teamed up with guitarist Phil Harris at the tail end of '72 to form the oddly named duo Clat Thyger. It wasn't long before they decided to expand the line-up to include Terry Corner and Steve Witherington. Emerging as Ace Flash and The Dynamos in the early months of '73, the group struggled to define its sound until King and Harris decided they needed a keyboard player. Terry Corner had been in the much hyped progressive rock group Warm Dust with Paul Carrack and recommended him for the job. A drummer by trade, Carrack taught himself to play keyboards but only in the key of C. When he joined progressive rockers Warm Dust he quickly found himself out of his depth. He told the *Melody Maker*: "Progressive music was the thing and being technically able to play your instrument was important. I got a bit paranoid about it and I did all the exercises." The exercises paid off, but Warm Dust were quickly swept under the carpet and Carrack reduced to washing cars for a living. Joining Ace saved him from a life of chapped fingers.

Ace avoided the usual Pub Rock practice of augmenting their set with cover versions and concentrated instead on playing original songs that showed off the group's blend of country-rock and blue-eyed soul. Following in the footsteps of previous Pub Rock hopefuls, Ace built a strong London following that quickly spread to the provinces. Spotted by the newly formed Anchor Records they wasted no time in signing with the American based company and began recording their debut album. Sessions began in London but didn't go well. Steve Witherington quit the group and was replaced by former Bees Make Honey drummer, Fran Byrne. Relocating to the more relaxed atmosphere of Rockfield Studios, they finished the album without further to-do. The resulting record, *Five-A-Side*, was issued without fanfare and might have sank without trace had it not featured the Paul Carrack composition 'How Long'.

A semi-autobiographical account of inter-group politics, Carrack was inspired to write 'How Long' when Corner was offered a job with rivals The Sutherland Brothers and Quiver because future bassist with Elvis Costello and The Attractions, Bruce Thomas, had quit and they needed a replacement. Carrack thought Corner had gone behind his back and decided to vent his spleen in song. "I felt a little bit bitter at the time but really I shouldn't have. They just offered him a job, it's as simple as that," Carrack explained. Carrack couched his bitterness in such a sweet way that many thought he was singing about a failed love affair. 'How Long' was the kind of song that comes along once in a lifetime, if you're lucky, and turned Ace into pop sensations. "Everyone in the business seemed to like 'How Long' which was good 'coz we're a bit thin skinned and heavy criticism would've definitely hurt us," said Carrack. Issued as a single, it was helped on its way by Anchor Records hunger for a hit. "I mean we could have gone with EMI or somebody and they wouldn't've put in half the effort into it," Carrack told the *Melody Maker*.

Ace's remarkable success with 'How Long' was proof that, with a little luck, Pub Rock groups could break out of the boozy circuit and sell records. Writing in the *Melody Maker*, Geoff Brown claimed that "They've proven that, with the right song, a band with absolutely no image other than their music can sell singles." The Pub Rock circuit was beginning to deliver the kind of results Robinson long believed it would. But it was something that had to be endured and every group that played it wanted out. Speaking to the *NME*, Corner said: "We were lucky, I suppose, to get out when we did, because when 'How Long' took off we were just about at the end of our financial tether like." Ace had ambitions, and who could blame them? Alan 'Bam' King had been scratching a living from music for the best part of a decade. When success and money came a knocking they weren't going to turn it down. Although there was no discussion within the group about what they'd do if and when fame hit, there was a tacit understanding that when the chance came they'd leave the pubs with guns blazing. "We'd just concentrate on the music and took it from there, but we wanted to get out and about and reach as many people as possible," explained Corner.

Having broken free of the Pub Rock circuit, Ace now faced the even bigger quandary of how to muscle in on the action on a bigger stage. Corner said: "We're seen as a threat to the establishment because we're reaching out and also becoming established and a lot of people don't want to see that happen." Ace also discovered that a hit single had as many disadvantages as advantages. When they'd been playing to 150 seasoned drinkers at the Hope and Anchor, they hadn't given any thought to their appearance or their stage presence. With a hit single under their belts all that changed. Ace began attracting a more diverse audience that Paul Carrack told *Rolling Stone* magazine now comprised everyone from mums and dads to soul freaks. That made the group concentrate on developing a stage-show, possibly with a detrimental effect on the music.

With no image or show to speak of for a lot of the time there was nothing happening on stage other than five blokes playing their instruments. What might have gone down well after a few pints, in the harsh light of a theatre looked dull indeed. "I think we're a very subtle band. People have to listen to us as opposed to getting a visual vibe. We're just a band of musicians enjoying music," said Phil Harris. Ace weren't a goodtime boogie band, they didn't rock and they didn't wind up audiences with high-energy R&B like the Feelgoods. The way they presented themselves on-stage was just as dull as the progressive groups they'd turned their backs on. In short, they were perfectly suited to support the kind of turgid stadium rock acts the Americans loved. Finding it difficult to make ends meet in Britain, they jumped on the first aeroplane to America to support Yes and found it to be a revelation for them. "Anyway we came over ... and working over here is like incredible. Like the whole thing is much more professional and much more active," Corner told *Melody Maker*.

A revelation was exactly what Brinsley Schwarz needed. Disillusioned with the music business, financially drained and divided over management issues they were nearing the end. Exhausted by the endless one-nighters that took them the length and breadth of the country, they considered following Ace to the United States. "We'd had lots of interest from America and we thought we'll try and make an album for America," recalls Gomm. "So they [United Artists] got Steve Verroca in and the idea was to try and make [an album] for the American market, to try and break [us] in America."

Brinsley Schwarz began recording what would become their last album at Rockfield Studios with Verroca in the autumn of '74. If they'd learnt anything from working with Dave Edmunds it was the difference a good producer could make to a record. For too long they'd struggled to produce themselves without much in the way of creative or commercial success. They'd always wanted to be a top end pop group, but had resisted working with a producer because that would have meant compromising themselves. It had taken Edmunds to turn good songs into a great record, now everything rested on Verroca's ability to do the same. The album featured several gems, including the Gomm-Lowe hit-in-waiting 'Cruel To Be Kind', and the Brinsleys even attempted to make a video to promote one of the songs, but as their manager Dai Davies recalls, Lowe wasn't prepared to take it seriously. "One time we were trying to make a sensible video of the band, and Nick ended up playing 'God Bless Whoever Made You' with his trousers down."

Was this farcical act an attempt to destroy any chance the group had of success? Looking back, Lowe claims he could sense that things were changing and it was time to move on or be left behind. "When the Pub Rock scene started going downhill, largely due to Dr Feelgood, who were so great they spawned many duff copyists, it was time to move on," he told *Mojo*. "It was almost like a voice saying, 'You've been bitching and moaning about the state of things, well, now it's your turn, pal. What are you going to do about it?' So we took a look round and thought it was all so terrible the only thing to do was pull it all down and start again. I had to banish earnestness, take the piss."

The music scene was indeed changing and after four years hard toil Brinsley Schwarz were still struggling to make ends meet. Speaking to *ZigZag*, Dai Davies revealed that for a group like Brinsley Schwarz gigging was no longer financially viable. "At £410 a night it's a waste of energy. As soon as you move from having one vehicle and earning £100 a night you start losing money and you carry on losing it until you start making a grand a night. it's nobody's fault, it's just the way things are." The system had finally beaten them.

According to Davies there was only one way they were going to earn anywhere near £1000 a night and that was if "there's three hit singles and a hit album". Lowe's antics had seen to it that that wasn't going to happen and without a hit all Brinsley Schwarz could do was survive. "That's all we did," says Schwarz. "We improved our equipment, but that's an ongoing thing, the van is an ongoing thing, you've got to pay roadies, we had no wages ourselves for quite a long time. It was only at the end that we paid ourselves a few quid so that we could go out."

The Brinsleys simply didn't have the will to undertake another round of disheartening and financially crippling gigs to promote an album that none of them really believed in. The previous year they'd re-signed with United Artists, but weren't happy with the deal. Not long after they got a better offer from Island Records but were stuck with UA. "We'd had an approach from Island Records, who offered us a deal, which was everything we wanted, which was to take us to America," recalls Gomm. "We thought, 'this is the only way out', because we felt strangled by the UK. We couldn't break out of it. The only thing was United Artists wouldn't release us, and that's when we split up. We said, 'it's either [America] or nothing.'"

United Artists would rather see the group wither under them than flourish with Island Records. At least United Artists continued to issue their records, but without success. In January '75, the company issued the Brinsleys' pounding cover of Tommy Roe's 'Everybody', but it was too little too late. The final straw came when Andrew Jakeman suggested he replace Davies as their manager. It was a suggestion that divided the group. "Three of us wanted to go with Jake, two of us didn't. Because they didn't want to go with Jake, he said, 'Oh sod it, I'll just take Nick,'" explains Rankin. "I wanted to go with Jake because I thought he was the guy we needed to give us a good kick up the arse and break down a few doors. As a manager I thought he was outstanding."

Outstanding or not, Jakeman wasn't about to get his hands on Brinsley Schwarz. They made one final tour of the country supporting Al Stewart before playing their final gig at the Marquee Club on Tuesday 18 March '75. It was by all accounts the highlight of their career. Myles Palmer reviewed the gig for *ZigZag*: "The atmosphere in the packed Marquee was boisterous and festive as they kicked off their first set with 'Small Town', a number I've always found stiff and peculiarly banal, moved swiftly into a brilliant version of 'We're Having A Party', then into 'Play That Fast Thing One More Time', featuring two tight, waspish guitar solos from Brinsley." Everyone who was there agrees it was the best gig they'd played in years. "One of the best gigs we ever played was the last one at the Marquee," says Schwarz. "It was the best gig we'd done for years," Rankin concurs.

Less than two months after Brinsley Schwarz played their farewell gig, The Kursaal Flyers were preparing to issue their debut album for UK Records. Label boss, Jonathan King, had produced a string of pop and bubblegum hits and achieved great things with 10cc, before they jumped ship for Mercury Records and bigger and better things. The Kursaal Flyers were in the enviable position of being the only act signed to UK Records. "That's a much better thing for us because others have got 20 or 30 bands on their books and all their energies are diverted between them," Shuttleworth told the *Melody Maker*.

One reason few Pub Rock groups achieved commercial success was because they weren't promoted properly. Had United Artists backed Brinsley Schwarz the way Anchor Records backed Ace they might have fared better. But they were only one group among many signed to United Artists, and it was the groups with hit making track records that got the promotional push. UK Records had recently signed a new deal with Polydor and that gave it real clout. "The deal with Polydor is that we nominate an act to get not less than the promotional and marketing drive comparable to the most popular acts on Polydor," UK Records general manager Clive Selwood told the *Melody Maker*.

As the Kursaal Flyers were the only group signed to UK Records they should have been well set for success. However, King simply didn't know what to do with them. Their album, *Chocs Away*, was recorded in a hurry to capitalise on their popularity as a live act and suffered for it. Recording sessions were grabbed whenever the Flyers had time off between gigs, with the results that there were annoying defects the group would have liked to change. "We were happy with what we got down," said Shuttleworth, "but ... little things. Not enough rhythm guitar, something wrongly positioned on the stereo [niggled]." The album was remixed but the result was, according to Selwood "an excellent, competent rather polite album. But that's not the Kursaal Flyers. They're raunchy and fun!" Despite the promotional push it supposedly received from Polydor Records, the album failed to sell in the kind of numbers they'd hoped for. Perhaps part of the problem was UK Records' deal with Polydor. The album was delayed and Selwood suggested that Polydor had failed to get it into the shops. "If the Kursaal Flyers' album isn't there they'll pick another without blinking," he claimed.

Issued with a jokey Barney Bubbles sleeve, the Kursaal Flyers' debut had more than its fair share of quality pop songs. Had one of them been a hit it might have encouraged record retailers to stock the album and it would have been double brandies all round. When UK Records issued 'Speedway' as a single it flopped. Despite being hailed as representing the next new wave in rock, the Kursaal Flyers weren't going to make it onto *Top Of The Pops* while signed to UK Records. Although they'd developed their own distinct style that owed much to the back to basics approach pioneered by the originators of Pub Rock, for the moment they were still out of step with the record buying public. Ever perceptive, Birch could sense that change was in the air. "I can feel that other people are gonna get hip to it and maybe in six months' time you'll get other bands playing what we're doing now." Prophetic words Will.

15

Naughty Rhythms

As the summer of 1974 drew to a close, Andrew Jakeman's fertile imagination began working overtime as he planned the rise of Chilli Willi and the Red Hot Peppers. With their first proper album about to hit the shops, it was time for Jakeman to initiate the final phase of his master plan. In the previous year the group had played 260 gigs and worked itself into the ground. Sick to the back teeth of the endless one-nighters, they were becoming frustrated by the lack of progress. Speaking to the *NME*, Jakeman made it clear that the group had grown tired of paying its dues. "It's simply too obvious a fact that there is not one iota of kudos or prestige in the whole graft process of 'trying to make it.'"

Something had to be done to transform the Willis from rickets ridden Pub Rock stalwarts into chart heroes. But to do that Jakeman would need a little help from two other up and coming Pub Rock acts, Dr Feelgood and Kokomo. Chris Fenwick was in the same position as Jakeman, somehow he had to create an opportunity for Dr Feelgood to make the leap from the 400 capacity pub/club rut to the larger and more profitable university and theatre circuit. Most of the Pub Rock groups had tried touring as support acts to more successful bands but with little reward. Jakeman and Fenwick's plan was to offer three of the hottest up and coming groups in the country at a very affordable price (75p) and hopefully reason a small profit. To achieve this all the usual excesses associated with touring were foregone in favour of the Pub Rock 'less is more' ethic.

Jake's next plan was 'The Naughty Rhythms Tour', a reconstruction of the pop/R&B package tours of the '50s and '60s: Kokomo, Dr Feelgood and us taking turns at headlining," explained Stone. Package tours had been a staple of the 1960s gig circuit. Arthur Howe, the undisputed king of them, had the power to make or break new groups, and he did. His idea was simple, book half a dozen acts, give them each 15 minutes to perform their hits and watch the cash roll in. Package tours made stars of The Rolling Stones, The Who and The Beatles. When Brian Epstein cottoned onto the idea most of his stable of Merseybeat groups became stars too. Berry Gordy did the same with the Motown Revue as did Dave Robinson with the Downhome Rhythm Kings package tour in 1971. Now it was Jakeman's turn to take a handful of six-time losers, with one eye on success and the other on the bar, around the country.

Jakeman and Fenwick planned to pool resources, share equal billing and keep ticket prices low. If the 'Naughty Rhythms' tour worked as planned it would transform the way live music was promoted and the prospects of the three groups it featured. Neither the Willis nor the Feelgoods had huge debts to worry about, but neither did they have large amounts of ready cash with which to finance a national tour. The only option open to them was to turn to their record companies to finance the enterprise. This they duly did, but they got much less cash than the £12,000 they felt they needed. "We ultimately settled for £2,000 apiece which UA provided for the Feelgoods, Mooncrest provided for us and O'Rourke's 'E.M.C.A [Kokomo's management company].' also splashed out." Jakeman told the *NME*.

Jakeman commissioned Barney Bubbles to design a graphic that would convey the spirit of the tour. Having already created a series of irreverent adverts to promote Chilli Willi and the Red Hot Peppers' *Bongos Over Balham* album, he designed a striking black and white 'Naughty Rhythms' logo that was used to brand the tour. Paul Conroy, who was then working as a booking agent for the Charisma Agency, says: "Barney did these huge posters and also flyers and badges, so it was a total package, which suited the spirit of the tour." The puns and tongue-in-cheek visuals were an important part of the package and prefigured much of what Jakeman brought to the table when he joined forces with Dave Robinson.

The tour was intended to establish a feeling of concord but, as it progressed, this soon fell by the wayside and the old rivalries and jealousies surfaced. But it was, perhaps, the first time a rock 'n' roll tour had been promoted as a complete package - visuals and music being given equal credence. It was certainly the first time Pub Rock groups had been promoted in such a knowing way. The 'Naughty Rhythms' package tour effectively extended the anti-rock idea first propagated by the Brinsleys, but gave it a striking image, something that Pub Rock groups deliberately ignored. Jakeman was doing more than simply promoting a handful of Pub Rockers, he was championing a style that poked fun at the mainstream and tapped into an audience whose tastes were mostly ignored by the major record companies. One had to be part of the scene to get the in-jokes and knowing visuals. Who could resist belonging to such a cool gang of rebellious good time Charlies? It was either that or join the Osmonds' fan club!

Jakeman and Bubbles were way ahead of their time. The best United Artists' marketing department could come up with to promote Dr Feelgood was the tried, tested and somewhat obvious step of issuing the group's debut album to coincide with the tour. Bereft of original ideas, all United Artists' marketeers could dream up was the uninspired strap-line 'destined to become one of the most played albums of 1975'. United Artists' grand plan was to promote the group as anti-social outsiders along the lines of the media campaign Andrew Oldham created for The Rolling Stones the best part of a decade earlier. "Like next week, there's a Shirley Bassey concert and I want to get 'em front row seats. They'll have to walk in five minutes late, of course," a United Artists marketing manager told the *NME*. How original. Did he really think the Feelgoods would take part in such a hare-brained scheme? One can imagine the response he got when he made his cunning plan known. Luckily, United Artists had issued the Feelgoods debut single, 'Roxette', which was getting heavy rotation on the nation's airwaves and doing them more good than a half-arsed publicity stunt.

Although the tour was a bit of a gamble, all the big name promoters bought into the idea and were more than happy with its concept. "Promoters have been very good to us, even people like John and Tony Smith and Harvey Goldsmith who are promoting about four of our concerts," Jakeman told the *NME*.

The tour may have been sold as a light-hearted romp across the country by a bunch of wild-eyed musicians, but it had the backing of major record companies and promoters. Despite everything Robinson and the Brinsleys had fought for, there was no escaping the hand of Big Brother. Money doesn't talk, it screams and the only way any of the 'Naughty Rhythms' groups were going to get anywhere was to work with the money men, not against them. Jakeman's idea might have looked revolutionary, but had it looked like losing money none of the major labels or promoters would have touched it with a bargepole.

The tour opened with two warm up dates in Bristol and Guildford and it soon became obvious that one group in particular would come out of the tour ahead of the others. "It quickly became apparent that the Feelgoods ought to top every night; the Willies were too diverse, Kokomo were too disco and the Feelgoods were too good," recalled Stone. By the time the tour closed at the Rainbow Theatre, London, Dr Feelgood were unstoppable. For them the tour had been a resounding success. It moved them further up the rock'n'roll ladder and a little closer to achieving the holy grail of rock, a hit single. Speaking to *ZigZag* magazine in January '75, Johnson explained why Dr Feelgood had to keep moving onwards and upwards. "So we had to get into a position where we could just become a touring band rather than a gigging band, because then it means you can organise yourself with a tour of a certain number of dates, and then each gig becomes significant again. In the early days when we started doing the pub thing, every gig was significant then because it was a whole new audience, and we were building up a reputation, and it all meant something. Every gig you feel is important, and it's the same with the tour ... every gig becomes part of the tour, and there's an end in sight."

If the tour had been the making of Dr Feelgood, it had all been too much for the Willies, who decided to call it a day. According to Jakeman, Dr Feelgood's good fortune was too much for Lithman. The virtuoso multi-instrumentalist became very disillusioned at his group's lack of success. "When he saw audiences lapping up Lee Brilleaux, who was nothing more than a bank clerk who could hardly get two chords together, the old bitter and twisted came out," explains Jakeman. However, Lithman later suggested it was more to do with feeling stagnant than bitter. "When you get a view close to the top you kind of think what it is all leading to, and what do we do when we get there. I mean the interest just goes," he said. "You've built something up and there's nothing more for you to do than maintain it. It was just boredom on behalf of everyone. We didn't want to spend years of our lives maintaining some illusionary position that we have close to the top, and the idea for me is to keep going onwards and upwards." The rift between Stone and Lithman was driving a wedge through the group. The situation had got so bad that Paul Bailey thinks Jakeman may have had a hand in the group's demise. "My guess is that Jake had got fed up with Phil and I think he'd chosen to light a bit of a fire underneath it and use it as an excuse to go off and do something he'd rather be doing," explained Bailey. That something else was working for Dr Feelgood as their tour manager.

Although the tour had been a financial and critical success, it hadn't turned out as Jakeman and Fenwick had hoped. There wasn't the affinity between the groups that they'd hoped for. It turned out that Kokomo's management had put in twice as much money as either United Artists or Mooncrest, and as far as it was concerned that gave them certain privileges. In return for supplying the PA and Pink Floyd's lighting rig for the London show, Kokomo's management company, E.M.C.A., insisted their act headlined the prestigious gig. There was also some resentment among certain members of the Willis and the Feelgoods because Kokomo could afford to stay in better hotels and were paid more. So much for the spirit of mutuality. In the end it was the management company with the biggest bank balance that called the shots. 'Twas ever thus.

By the time the tour ended, Chilli Willi and the Red Hot Peppers had imploded and Kokomo were headed for America. Only Dr Feelgood came out of it stronger, wiser and better positioned to capitalise on the hard graft they'd put in the previous year. But could they put this new-found knowledge to good use?

16
Taxi To The Terminal Zone

If ever an album had a fitting title it was Ducks Deluxe second outing, *Taxi To The Terminal Zone*. Having recently moved into a communal house in Hendon, Garvey and McMaster decided they'd had enough and quit, leaving the others to freewheel onto the group's final resting place. "I can't remember the exact reason, whether it was a gradual thing or a big argument," recalls Belmont. "They left so me and Tim and Sean were carrying on and we auditioned for a bass player. We hired a rehearsal room and all these appalling people turned up, one after another, just terrible, until this guy Micky Groome turned up and he was a good bass player and he was a great harmony singer, he had all the same musical references as we did and he was great. He was obviously the person so he got the gig."

Back to performing as a four-piece, Ducks Deluxe recorded a revved up version of Sonny Curtis' 'I Fought The Law' in a last ditch attempt to storm the charts and save their deal with RCA Records. Like their previous 45s it failed to catch the public imagination and flopped. "RCA released 'I Fought The Law' as a single but they might as well have set fire to it publicly for all the promotion they did!" complained Tyla. It fared no better when issued in Europe by Skydog Records as part of the four-track *Jumpin'* EP, but The Clash had more success with the song, of course. RCA Records had lost interest in the group to such an extent that *Taxi To The Terminal Zone* wasn't even issued in America, and with the failure of 'I Fought The Law' Ducks Deluxe were dropped. "We were signed to a huge American-owned record company for two years but they never really got behind us," laments Tyla. "Dai did a great job in the early days but he should have kicked a bit more arse at RCA."

The Ducks were down but they weren't out for a duck. Not long after recording the *Jumpin'* EP, Tim Roper jumped ship and was replaced by Billy Rankin. "He [Roper] played on the *Jumpin'* recordings but we fell out with him over his girlfriend, who was somebody who nobody else in the band got on with. He had to choose between the band and his girlfriend and he chose his girlfriend," explains Belmont. Ducks Deluxe couldn't get arrested on home turf but they were stars in Europe. If RCA Records wasn't interested, Marc Zermati was and booked them into a lengthy European tour that would be their last. "Billy and Micky fitted in like gloves and we played our socks off," recalled Tyla. "Marc had virtually turned us into living legends in Europe and especially France. The tour was sold out wall-to-wall. The whole thing was ironic but we had a ball - ah, until we got to Amsterdam."

When the group arrived in Amsterdam they were surprised to see posters advertising 'Ducks Deluxe featuring Brinsley Schwarz'. Unknown to any of the Ducks, Dai Davies had decided that while he still represented Mr Schwarz he'd get him some work and added his name to the posters. "I couldn't believe it. Nick Lowe was hanging out with us at the time and he hadn't got a clue as to what was going on," explained Tyla. "Dai had arranged the Dutch end of the tour and had planned to add Brinsley to the leg without any rehearsal or a by your leave from us. We were a hot unit coming out of France and I thought that trying to fit another musician in like that was going to bugger the job up all together. I was livid. It wasn't Brinsley's fault, he's a great guitar player but Dai had his head up his arse when he concocted that idea. Apparently, the promoters didn't think the Ducks would sell seats on their own and the Brinsleys were as popular in Holland as we were in France but he could have told us. As it happened, we had a good time and kept gigging in that formation right until the end."

That end happened on 1 July 1975 when Ducks Deluxe bowed out at the 100 Club. With the group haemorrhaging members, record company apathy and declining record sales, Ducks Deluxe found it difficult to survive on their reputation alone. The time had come to split up the group. If Brinsley Schwarz had ended their career on a high, Ducks Deluxe were about to bow out with one of the worst gigs of their career. The club was a little over half full, the sound was atrocious and the group just wanted to get it over and done with. "I don't know why we did it," says Tyla. "It was badly advertised and our heart wasn't in it. In retrospect, we certainly 'made it' as a live band but we just couldn't rack up the record sales."

As Ducks Deluxe slid down the snake of misfortune, Dr Feelgood climbed up the ladder of success. The group was experiencing the kind of adulation usually reserved for rock gods. Since moving out of the Pub Rock circuit they'd developed a powerful visual image, electrifying stage act and hard driving sound that was commercial yet authentic enough to appeal to R&B cognoscenti. Lee Brilleaux had begun wearing a white stage suit that contrasted with Wilko's bible black outfit. It was as if the stark black and white image that adorned the group's debut album had come to life before your very eyes. As Brilleaux's white suit got more soiled and creased it took on the mantle of the ultimate anti-rock statement. It was a look anybody could achieve and said more about the group than words ever could. "We were just bashing away at guitars and drums, wearing clothes you could walk down the street in, with a look you could get together for a fiver," explained Johnson.

When the group progressed to larger theatres they faced the same problem that had beset Ace when they moved onto that circuit. But unlike Ace, Dr Feelgood knew how to adjust and evolve. With larger stages to fill, they'd developed an inflated stage presence and theatrical routine. Speaking to Andy Childs, Johnson explained how he adapted to playing larger venues: "I prefer playing to a big audience in a way actually, because for one thing it's nice to have a great big stage ... You've got that much more scope with what you're doing onstage, you're not in danger of poking peoples' eyes out with your guitar and things like that; and also it gives you a bigger rush if there's a great big audience - there's blinding lights and things, it's a different feeling, but it's potentially a much bigger feeling, so I like it for that."

The Feelgoods conveyed that bigger feeling effortlessly. Johnson became even more animated, while Brilleaux stalked the stage or simulated sex to the heart stopping beat laid down by the Big Figure and Sparko. A highlight of the set came when Johnson and Sparko joined Brilleaux centre stage to introduce 'Riot In Cell Block No. 9'. Holding their guitars like Tommy guns, they glared into the audience like prison guards daring them to make the first move. It was a touch of showbiz magic, simple but effective, and it made the world of difference. They were also reacting to changes in their audience. Speaking to the *NME* in June '75, Brilleaux described how the typical Dr Feelgood audience had changed: "Now it's the kids who support Man United who come to see us the same kind of kids who were in Paris last week in the (Leeds) match." The football fans Brilleaux referred to had rioted after the 1975 European Cup Final when their team lost to Bayern Munich due to some dodgy decisions by the French referee. They were also turning up at Feelgood gigs.

The Feelgoods' audience was more rambunctious than the typical Pub Rock crew. It was, as Bob Andrews had predicted, more macho. Reviewing a Feelgoods' gig at the Liverpool Stadium in late '75, Mick Farren wrote: "There seems to be a peculiar streak of male masochism that is brought out into the open at a Feelgood concert. Only a small minority of the audience are women." These kids were too young to visit the boozer to get their musical fix; their intoxicant was the feeling of community they experienced as the Feelgoods powered through their set. This was rock 'n' roll communion for a generation growing up with recession, unemployment and alienation. Sound familiar? Rock and pop had become distanced from the mundane realities of everyday life that most teenagers experienced. Dr Feelgood were the scruffy working class answer to the preening extravagance that popular music had become. Visually and musically, they were a potent antidote to the excessive styles that had dominated British music for too long.

What they offered was a third way; a new style that could be adopted by their audience and used to resist the mainstream culture they found so meaningless. When asked if he thought Dr Feelgood filled a gap in the contemporary music scene, Johnson said: "I think a lot of the reason that we got on was because we were doing a certain thing at a time when there was a need for it. Probably nobody even felt the need until some people had started doing it, but I think generally there's a feeling now of people wanting to get back to basic music. I think the 'Naughty Rhythms Tour' has proved this really, because you've got three bands that are all playing basic music. There's no kind of hype or fantasy or anything - well there's always fantasy with any performance I suppose, particularly ours - but these three bands are quite different and they've all been going down very very well. And I think that's because people want it, they want something more direct."

For those unable to see and hear Dr Feelgood in concert there was always the records. The release of the second Dr Feelgood album, *Malpractice*, did much to reinforce their anti-rock image. Like their debut, its cover was a stark black and white photograph of the band hanging out in front of a typical blue collar barbers shop on Canvey Island. This was their natural habitat, as realistic and unpretentious as they were. They'd also refined their sound, although Neil Spencer of the *NME* suggested the album didn't make sense unless it was played loud - confirmation that Dr Feelgood was best experienced live. "I think we've got just about the sound we wanted," Johnson claimed. "People ask us why we don't use more effects and overdubs. The simple answer is that we don't want them." The album slipped easily into the Top 20, a sign that the Feelgoods had established themselves as a viable alternative to the grinding attrition that glam, in both its uptown and down-town forms, had to offer. Hallelujah!

17

Teenage Depression

Southend, out of season, can be a depressing place. Pleasure gardens offer little in the way of enjoyment, boarded up amusement arcades and peeling advertisements for jellied eels and whelks do little to lift the spirits on days when the sea and sky both appear as uninviting and grey as a battleship. Viewed under a leaden sky, everything looks as flat and monochrome as a black and white postcard. Unemployment stalked its streets and, if you were lucky enough to have a job, inflation stood at a wage sapping 27%. As if that wasn't bad enough, Telly Savalas topped the singles chart with 'If'. But it wasn't all doom and gloom. Dr Feelgood were rapidly becoming bona fide rock stars, the Kursaal Flyers were hot on their heels and Eddie and the Hot Rods were about to complete Southend's rock triumvirate.

The Fix and The Southside Blues Band had already given the world Dr Feelgood and would soon be responsible for another offspring, Eddie and the Hot Rods. Dave Higgs had been in The Fix with Johnson and Brilleaux before abandoning the local music scene to pursue other interests. Returning to Canvey Island he began working for Dr Feelgood as a roadie. "They [Dr Feelgood] suggested I should get my own band together," he said. Higgs placed an advert in a Southend music shop and got a phone call from Pete Ward, the guitarist with local beat combo Buckshee. Ward rehearsed with his mates Steve Nicol, Rob Steel and Barrie Masters in his parents' garage and arranged for Higgs to attend their next jam session. "When I got there he [Ward] knew about one chord and the bass player didn't know you had to be in tune with everybody else," Higgs recalled. Not to put too fine a point on it, Buckshee were crap. A mediocre garage band born of the same teenage frustrations and desires that spawned The Sonics, The Standells and The Seeds, they were so primitive their bassist's idea of tuning his guitar was to make the strings as tight as possible without breaking them. Higgs saw it as a challenge and set about transforming them from a ramshackle group of amateurs into a powerhouse beat combo. "He was the one who really got the band sorted out," recalled Nichol. "He'd been in quite a few bands before, but none of us had."

Buckshee took its repertoire from American R&B and played it fast and hard. "We used to do mainly R&B - Chicago things, old Jimmy Reed numbers. We used to do a few soul numbers as well, Otis Redding things," Higgs recalled. Playing such arcane beat music with obvious over enthusiasm was a defiant 'V' sign from the street aimed at what passed for pop music. Buckshee's music making was as much a negative reaction to mainstream pop as it was a positive reaction to the original beat music that inspired their brothers and sisters ten years earlier.

No matter how bad Buckshee was, the important thing was that they were actually doing something. In March '75, Mick Farren wrote a lengthy piece in the *Melody Maker* bemoaning the state of teenage rebellion and music in general. His heartfelt plea was that "The very last ray of hope in this whole depressing examination is that there is The MC5 of '76 working out in a church hall somewhere." If Farren wanted to find the next MC5 he'd need to take more than a cursory look round his local church hall. There were plenty of kids starting up groups who weren't interested in imitating the big retro-stars of the day such as Showaddywaddy, Mud or The Rubettes. As the name Buckshee suggested, they'd tapped into the punk/garage aesthetic that reflected the way society valued them and their music (worthless). It was a great name but one soon ditched in favour of a more pedestrian sobriquet Eddie and the Hot Rods. "We went through hundreds of silly names," recalls Higgs, "I was just lying in bed one night and thought of 'Eddie and the Hot Rods.'"

Inspired as much by the frantic shock and awe-filled performances of the MC5 as old school R&B and rock 'n' roll, Eddie and the Hot Rods began forging a reputation as the loudest and fastest group in Southend. "We got a good little set going and we started playing working men's clubs and things like that," recalls Masters. Mental hospitals, British Legion halls and pubs all experienced the full Eddie and the Hot Rods treatment. But no sooner had they got a few gigs under their belt than Ward left to concentrate on his apprenticeship and starting a family. A gig at the Anchor pub in the tiny village of South Fambridge brought them to the attention of Ed Hollis. Something of a local legend, Hollis had a large and impressive record collection which he used to entertain customers at the Top Alex pub in Southend, where he was the resident DJ. His knowledge of music, gift of the gab and fiery enthusiasm made him the ideal person to manage the rowdy Hot Rods, who lost no time in obtaining his services.

Rather than look for a replacement guitarist, Higgs recruited another ex-member of The Fix, harmonica player Lew Lewis. The wizard of wail was desperate to join a group and the Hot Rods were keen to recruit him. "I said to Dave, 'Look, Dave, I've got to get playing,' so he invited me along," he recalled. Lewis' ability to blow a mean blues harp gave the group a shot of bluesy authenticity and beefed up what was already an impressive sound. While Lewis couldn't get enough of playing with the Hot Rods, bassist Rob Steel was having second thoughts and decided to quit. The search for a replacement led them to Paul Gray. All he'd wanted to do since childhood was play rock 'n' roll. Inspired by Hawkwind's bassist, Ian 'Lemmy' Kilmister, he developed a simple yet powerful style of playing. "When people asked me who my favourite bass player was I'd say I admired Lemmy. And they'd say 'Lemmy? What an idiot - he's nothing!' But I thought he was great because he had the power and energy and kept it all going. He's a very physical player." Lemmy would have been the ideal bassist for the Hot Rods, but he was too busy taking huge doses of speed and being sacked from Hawkwind. Higgs invited Gray to audition for the group and offered him the job because he could keep up with the Rods' relentless adrenaline rush.

Eddie and the Hot Rods looked like any other bunch of scruffy streetwise kids, but sounded like the bastard offspring of The Yardbirds and The Downliners Sect fuelled by copious amounts of cheap booze and amphetamines. When they played they gave 100% and expected the same from their audience. But few were ready for the Hot Rods' brand of frenzied garage/punk/rock 'n' roll. Interviewed for *ZigZag* in May '76, Higgs claimed that on home turf they were greeted with apathy. "A band's got no chance in Essex," he said. "Like we were playing up at this place called The Double Six only the other night, and the main attraction there is the pool tables ... they got more applause than us." The Hot Rods were so out of step that Masters suggested they were viewed as freaks with no fan base. "A few people used to pop along - maybe. They were curious. Mouths open job. They'd come and see us again, but you'd never get any claps or anything," he complained.

Like elsewhere in the country, the club scene was dying on its arse and being replaced by discos. According to local hero Mickey Jupp, discos had all but replaced the live music scene in Southend. "There's nowhere to play here anymore, place is dead as a doornail." he told the *NME*. "It's all discos now." There can be no doubt that discos were booming. In late '74 there were between 7,000 and 8,000 in Britain that catered for an audience hooked on the latest hits; hits that were designed with discos in mind. Many had probably never experienced a live band and they would have been horrified at the sound Eddie and the Hot Rods made. Southend had more than its fair share of discos with Tots (The Talk of the South), Zero 6 and the Goldmine on nearby Canvey Island all catering for those who didn't need their music to be live.

In October '75, Pete Fowler interviewed some Roxy Music and Bowie fans for *Let It Rock* magazine. He described them as "sophisticates, smooth smart and dapper." Art students specialising in commercial or interior design, he claimed "They are not popular and are intensely disliked by the Man United Boys." They may not have been typical disco goers but what they said was revealing. When asked what kind of music they liked they said: "Very weird music - Roxy, 2000ish - something that's futuristic, something very weird, kinky, anything like that. Roxy are the nearest to it - they fit into the disco atmosphere. It's popular music that a lot of people like, so I can get along with a certain group of people and fit into a society then." Like many they felt disillusioned and dreamt of a hi-tech, shiny future full of "bright buildings, cars, really expensive gadgets, everything, the women really fantastic, perfection itself." What they experienced was anything but that. Nevertheless, for them Bowie and Roxy Music looked to the stars while groups like Eddie and the Hot Rods had their feet in the gutter.

If Eddie and the Hot Rods were playing to sophisticates, smoothies and dapper Bowie fans in Southend's discos and clubs it's little wonder they were viewed as freaks. Most teenagers didn't want to be reminded of how grim things were, they sought escape in a fantasy world and wanted to dance the night away. Discos grew in popularity precisely because of the dire state of the economy, plus they were cheaper to put on and more profitable than live music. Barry Dickens of the MAM organisation explained the situation to the *Melody Maker*. "It cost virtually nothing for club owners to put a disco in, and I believe most of the records are sent [free] from record companies." Free records, no need to book a group or worry about punters liking the music, no wonder club owners turned their backs on live music in favour of DJs.

Yet Southend had produced some solid groups, not nearly as many as Liverpool in the early '60s but, according to Will Birch, rock 'n' roll went through Southend like Southend went through the sticky pink rock sold on its seafront. "Southend's a rock 'n' roll town," he told the *Melody Maker*. "Y'know back in the Fifties and Sixties it was all amusement arcades along the front. Everyone had a jukebox." Rock 'n' roll had been the soundtrack of choice for fun fairs and seaside towns, but that had changed. Eddie and the Hot Rods couldn't get arrested in Southend and had to look elsewhere for gigs. When they did the reaction they received was often the very opposite of what they experienced at home. "Every time we played [...], there was a fight - that's just the sort of scene it is," Masters said.

Like Dr Feelgood, Eddie and the Hot Rods were playing to a young, boisterous audience that liked to drink and play hard. They were the same kind of fans that rioted at football matches and liked to stick the boot in. Eddie and the Hot Rods simply provided them with a soundtrack that elicited a violent reaction. "They've had enough of the perfect sound bit, sitting down and doing that ... They want to get up and boogie now," Masters told the *Melody Maker*. Naturally, the response was going to be more frenzied because the Hot Rods actively encouraged dancing, as had groups like Brinsley Schwarz. But Eddie and the Hot Rods rocked harder and worked harder to break down the barrier between band and punter. Crushed together in front of the stage, the audience resembled the crowded terraces at a packed football game and experienced the same sense of camaraderie. "Our kids are more like a football crowd," Masters said. "They just want to be part of it. Instead of band-audience, it's all one, a basic group." Bopping to Eddie and the Hot Rods, the average Rods fan was saturated with music and overwhelmed by the experience. They became victims of a passion that deprived them of individuality. That's why they threw themselves at the stage time and time again. They wanted to be one with the group, to experience the same things and share in the communion of rock 'n' roll. It may have looked violent but was, in fact, the same kind of controlled, symbolic violence that Wilko Johnson created on stage. Dancing to the Rods was an expression of unity that, as Johnson recognised, was a lot more enjoyable than actual violence.

The one gig Eddie and the Hot Rods desperately wanted still remained out of reach. "The London circuit had a moat around it," recalled Higgs. "We'd get to Poplar, Leytonstone, Crawley, Camberley, but we could never get into

London. But somebody puts in a good word for you and you're in straight away." Once again Dr Feelgood came to the rescue and secured Eddie and the Hot Rods a gig at the Kensington. Their London debut led to a six week residency and more gigs on the pub circuit at the Red Cow and the Nashville Rooms. But having got themselves onto the London circuit they discovered that they weren't alone in plundering their record collections. "When we got to London we found that three other bands were doing all the same stuff. We had to get a new set together really snappy, didn't we," recalled Higgs. Competing with other groups and a weekly residency at the Kensington forced them to re-think their repertoire. But even with a new batch of songs they struggled to win over what could be a fickle audience who didn't understand the band. "And we got to the stage of thinking: 'well, if they don't want to know, we'll just play for ourselves'. We started going down well and getting a following. Small but strong," Masters explained. It wasn't long before the national music press picked up on the group and began the process of building them up into the next big thing. Still looking for a group to shake up what was a tired and dull music scene, the music press thought Eddie and the Hot Rods held the answer. And for a while they most certainly did.

18
A Howlin' Wind

With little else to do other than hang out, ex-members of Brinsley Schwarz, Chilli Willi and Ducks Deluxe gravitated to the Hope and Anchor pub in Islington. Since splitting with the Brinsleys, Dave Robinson had been living and working at the venue, slowly transforming it into one of the most vibrant music places in the capital. Its tiny 150 capacity basement, which had previously played host to Irish Showbands, became the centre of the capital's pub rock scene. "I was booking the pub bands and I knew quite a lot of bands, so the classy pub bands who had really got their stuff together, we would book into the Hope and Anchor," Robinson explained. "The problem was it was a very small space so you had to get the best to try and make a bit of money on the door and be able to pay them."

The ground floor bar was co-managed by Martin Belmont. "I was living at the Hope and Anchor, and was running the music bar," he recalled. "Dave Robinson had an eight-track studio up on the first floor, which people used to come in and make recordings. You could record people playing live downstairs, but that wasn't the main purpose of it, it was more for people to come in and make demos." Robinson's plan was to turn the Hope and Anchor into the North London equivalent of Berry Gordy's Detroit-based "Hitsville USA". As previously mentioned he booked groups to perform in the basement and, if they were any good, recorded them in the studio with the intention of releasing them on the record label he was hoping to start.

A combination of good luck and happenstance delivered to Robinson's door some of the hottest out-of-work musicians in London. Brinsley Schwarz was searching for somewhere for him and his family to live but had kept in touch with his old band mate Bob Andrews, who was trying unsuccessfully to get a visa to work in America. Pete Thomas had better luck than Andrews and had already moved to California to work with John Stewart. Fellow Willi, Paul Bailey also found himself drawn to the Hope and Anchor where he teamed up with Steve Goulding and Andrew Bodnar. Bailey, Bodnar and Goulding joined forces with Steve Bennett and Tony Downes to form Bon Temps Roulez. Based at the Hope and Anchor they rehearsed a set of blue-eyed funk that got Robinson's pulse racing. At about the same time an aspiring singer songwriter from Camberley, Surrey, entered Robinson's life. Graham Parker had recently returned to England from Morocco and was working with a publisher, Stuart Johnson, who owned a studio at which he recorded a few demos prior to meeting Robinson. Johnson hawked Parker's songs around all the usual record companies, but without any interest. "The singer/songwriter boom was over, and they weren't signing people up just because they could write songs

Mighty Baby: Martin Stone, Ian Whiteman, Michael Evans, Alan King and Roger Powell. Head Records publicity photo.

Nick Lowe, Bob Andrews, Ian Gomm, Billy Rankin and Brinsley Schwarz in the garden at Carew Road, Northwood.

Ducks Deluxe: Back row: Nick Garvey, Sean Tyla. Front row: Martin Belmont, Andy McMasters and Tim Roper.

Dr Feelgood at Friars, Aylesbury. Wilko Johnson, John Martin aka The Big Figure and Lee Brilleaux.

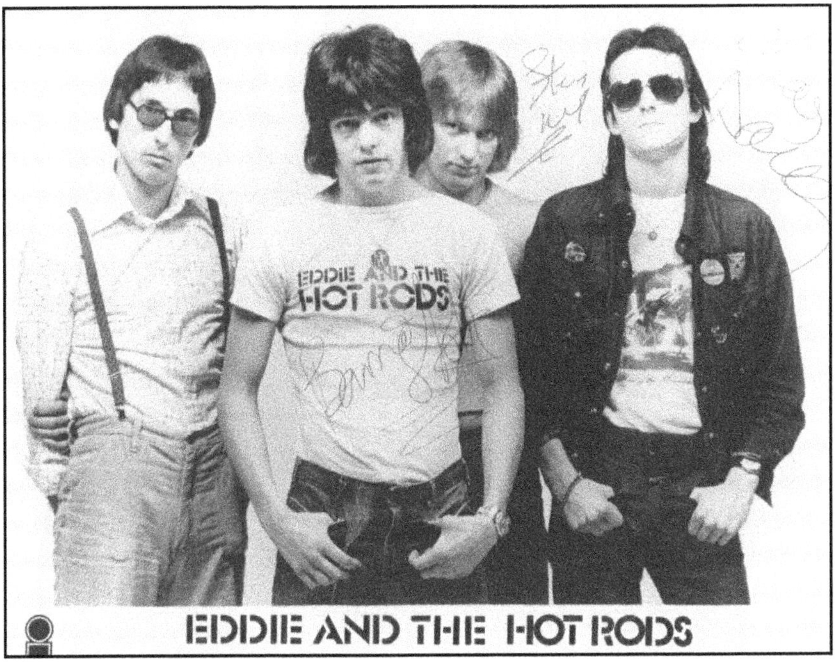

Dave Higgs, Barry Masters, Steve Nicol and Paul Gray. Island Record publicity photo.

The Kursaal Flyers: Graeme Douglas, Dave Hatfield, Paul Shuttleworth, Richie Bull and Will Birch.

Dave Edmunds and Billy Bremner at Reading University.

Ian Dury.

Chilli Willi and the Red Hot Peppers: Paul Bailey, Martin Stone, Philip Charles Lithman, Pete Thomas and Paul "Dice Man" Bailey.

Lene Lovich.

Elvis Costello at the New Theatre, Oxford 1981.

Graham Parker and the Rumour performing on stage at the Auckland Town Hall.

Nick Lowe returns to the Pub Rock circuit. Playing the Sir George Robey 1985.

Wreckess Eric, Jona Lewie, Rachel Sweet, Lene Lovich and Mickey Jupp. Stars of the 'Be Stiff' tour.

anymore," Parker explained. "But I did a publishing deal with Stuart... That's Tower Bridge Music - he's got 'Back To Schooldays'. He's also got a load of my very old stuff which is no good really."

Parker's group had a regular gig at a cafe, the Southern Comfort, in Finsbury Park, but were going nowhere. Noel Brown, who played slide guitar in the group, introduced Parker to Paul Riley who gave a copy of Parker's demo tape to Robinson. Impressed by what he heard, Robinson suggested Parker record some more songs at the Hope and Anchor. "Graham Parker came in and made three demos, which is where we all heard him the first time, including Dave," explains Belmont. "I remember when he played me the demos of 'Between You and Me' and 'Hey Lord Don't Ask Me Questions'. I was just fucking gobsmacked. God this is fucking great! It was all the stuff I like, it's like soul music, it's reggae, it's Bob Dylan, it's Van Morrison, it's just kind of everything that I like all mixed up in the sort of guy's songs.

By now, Bon Temps Roulez had called it quits and their rhythm section, Goulding and Bodnar, had teamed up with Brinsley Schwarz, Bob Andrews and Martin Belmont. "We kind of did some rehearsing and worked out some numbers that we liked playing. We didn't really have a plan but we kind of knew what we didn't want to do," explained Belmont. Apart from rehearsing, they drifted aimlessly until Robinson had a Eureka moment. "Graham [Parker] obviously had something, and he wanted me to do something [to help] and meanwhile the Brinsleys weren't doing anything, so these very good, highly trained musicians were hanging around looking for something to happen, so it was just an opportunity. There's always a little destiny involved, it just fitted together at the right time," Robinson says. Robinson suggested that Parker front the as yet unnamed Pub Rock super group. Unconvinced, Parker went on holiday to think things over. "At first I didn't know. I was going on Dave's decision. All I knew was that they could play and that they had gone through the same things as me. They weren't into playing bland Les Paul guitar solos. They were playing off the wood. Eventually I just realised it was right," Parker told *ZigZag*. Parker had the songs, a publishing contract, a new manager in Robinson and, to top it all, one of the hottest groups on the Pub Rock circuit to back him. Rehearsals commenced at the Newland Tavern, Peckham. "There was a very nice couple who used to run the place [and they] let us rehearse there in the afternoons. That was where we built up a repertoire and did a lot of Graham's songs and when we first kind of started out, the first couple of gigs [were] at the Newland Tavern," recalled Belmont. The model for this was obviously Bob Dylan and the Band. That's how we saw ourselves." Crammed into a small back room, the first rehearsal didn't go well. Both parties were nervous, but despite the group's initial lifeless performance, Parker knew something special was brewing. The group were still without a name so everybody chipped in with ideas, but it was Schwarz who came up with the keeper. "It was [at the] Newlands Tavern that we took the democratic task of coming up with names for the band and then voting for the winner," recalled

Parker. "I came up with Graham Parker and the Questions, but Brinsley's the Rumour obviously won."

While Parker and the Rumour were working up a set, Parker's recent Hope and Anchor demo tape found its way to Charlie Gillett, who played it on his Radio London show, *Honky Tonk*. "Nigel Grange got in touch. He'd heard a track on Charlie Gillett's show one Sunday and the following day, Charlie gave him my number and he was keen, we were obviously keen, and the Hope and Anchor days were coming to an end so everything fitted together. It's always great timing or blind luck whichever way you see it," Robinson explained. With a recording contract in his back pocket, Parker began planning his first album with the Rumour. "I had about 15 songs together for *Howlin' Wind*; it was about autumn 1975 that I signed the deal, and everything since then has happened extremely quickly," Parker told *ZigZag*. The original idea was for Tim Moore - an American singer and songwriter - to produce the album, but he cancelled because of exhaustion. Nick Lowe was anything but exhausted, having spent the last few months resting, and was offered the job by his old manager. "I didn't know Nick Lowe, what he could do or what he couldn't do ... I hadn't even heard him sing or anything," recalled Parker. "I hadn't heard the Brinsleys. So I said, 'Yeah, okay, I've trusted you so far, I'll go along with it'. And Nick Lowe was just right."

Graham Parker and the Rumour probably played their first gig at the Newlands Tavern, although Martin Belmont has a vague idea that it might have been at the Nags Head in High Wycombe. Wherever they debuted it was a low key affair because they were still working on how to present themselves. "What we did was Graham would do three or four songs, and then we'd do three or four songs without Graham. It was a very bad move because it very quickly became apparent that Graham's songs were so much stronger and his presence, he was such a focus for the audience that it was silly doing it without him," says Belmont modestly. Although they'd played a few low key gigs on the pub circuit, there was no way Parker wanted to be associated with pub rock. "To me, playing in a London pub was the biggest thing possible, it was like stardom. But I soon realised that pubs are where people play because they haven't got anywhere else to play, right? And the band were really fed-up with being tagged 'Pub Rock', so they helped me to realise what direction to go in," Parker explained.

Having sorted out how to present themselves, their thoughts turned to recording their debut album, which was significant for several reasons. "We [played] a few of these little gigs towards the end of '75, and I guess it was around November/December [that] we went in and started recording the first album, which Nick Lowe produced. His first production, our first record. Graham's first record ever, so it was a first in a lot of ways for a lot of people," suggests Belmont. Everybody in Brinsley Schwarz had been impressed by the way Dave Edmunds transformed their pedestrian recordings into sparking, exciting delights when recording their *New Favourites* album at Rockfield

Studios. Lowe was as impressed as the rest of the group and learnt a lot from the Welshman's ways with a mixing desk, though as he developed his own style he became less enamoured with Edmunds' methods. "I studied him and used him and stole any idea I could off him and now, well, there's certain incompatibilities." explained Lowe. Edmunds was the catalyst for another important but all together unforeseen lesson in record production. Lowe had taken to hanging out with Edmunds at the recording studio and tagged along one day when the guitarist dropped off some tapes at a cutting studio. The cutting engineer was none too impressed with Edmunds' offering and told him so. "This guy had a reputation for being quite blunt with his clients," recalled Lowe. "Edmunds hit the roof, grabbed his tapes, and off he went." With nothing better to do, Lowe stayed for a chat with the engineer and learnt a valuable lesson in record production, that it wasn't all about making things as loud as possible for radio airplay. "It all comes down to the arranging, and using as little as possible," explained Lowe. "I got a fabulous lesson from this rather grumpy little man."

Lowe developed a "less is more" production style which, thanks to the speed at which he worked, earned him the moniker Basher. Lowe threw the rulebook out the window and did whatever he had to do to make great sounding records. "There are no rules," he explained. "If the drums sound bad, just leave it and see if the record works, and then deal with it afterwards." Lowe's approach caught the spirit of the times perfectly. He made records that captured the excitement of the new musical movement and sounded fantastic on the radio.

Although Parker was produced by a stalwart of the Pub Rock scene, and was backed by a Pub Rock super group, he managed to escape being branded a Pub Rocker himself. Graham Parker and the Rumour were another span in the bridge between old and new that avoided categorisation. Parker was part of a wider cultural movement that articulated its frustration through music in ways that hadn't been heard for years. Parker's Mod background informed his sensibility. Like the original Mods who saw Afro-Caribbean culture as symbolic of an alternative lifestyle, he felt an affinity with the country's alienated inner-city communities. "I feel more like a black man than a white man a lot of the time," he told the *NME*. "There's a thing about it, that feeling. You can't put it into words."

Taking inspiration from soul, R&B and reggae, Graham Parker and the Rumour delivered a heady musical cocktail that enlivened the arid mainstream music scene. They played black music, twisting and inverting its meanings. It was R&B based pop but played with the kind of attack associated with the coming Punk scene. Parker's voice was described as "a nasal punk drawl", the Rumour as "rough and raw" and Lowe's production as "earthy". Writing the sleeve notes to the official bootleg Graham Parker and the Rumour at the Newlands Tavern, Parker says: "What strikes me most about this tape is the full-grown ferocity of the performance. Not only do I sound as if I was already competing with the punk bands that were not to fully emerge until over a year later, but the Rumour sound as if they've been playing my stuff for years, and are rocking in suitably ferocious form themselves."

With acres of good press in the nation's music weeklies, a lot of hard work, solid management and record company support, Parker and the Rumour couldn't fail. But while record company support was forthcoming in Britain, it was a different story in America. Having watched the slow demise of Brinsley Schwarz, Robinson knew everything depended on breaking Graham Parker and the Rumour in the US and arranged for PolyGram's sister company, Mercury Records, to see them perform at London's Marble Arch Studios. "The premise of this gig was that they were going to get all the executives from Mercury Records, which was the American arm of Phonogram, to actually see us perform a special concert for them in this sort of big basement studio they had, and it was recorded," explained Belmont. "Nick Lowe oversaw the recording and interestingly the engineer in the studio was a guy called Steve Lillywhite who went on to become a very successful producer. So we did that and the Americans were duly impressed and we got a record deal with Mercury and we went and did our first American tour that summer, which was not a long tour, we only did the East Coast." There would be no big hype job as there had been for Brinsley Schwarz, but a slow burn that would see the group's fan base grow organically. A whistle-stop tour of the East Coast was followed later in the year by a longer jaunt that took them from coast to coast. But limited support from their American record company ensured that the tour would be both hard work and frustrating. "We were travelling in station wagons and driving ourselves and we were just getting gigs wherever we could, and we would open for the most inappropriate bands," revealed Belmont. "You won't believe some of the people we opened for. Blue Oyster Cult to Richie Havens, it was very bizarre."

More bizarre was Mercury Records' lack of support for its new signing. The sole reason for Parker and the Rumour touring America was to promote their new album *Heat Treatment*. But in true Spinal Tap style few cities they visited actually had copies of the album for sale. Parker put the blame fairly and squarely on Mercury Records. Allen Frey, Parker's American representative, told *Rolling Stone* magazine that Mercury initially pressed only 8000 copies of the album and that that wasn't enough to even ensure one copy in each record store in every city the group played. Although Mercury refuted the allegation by claiming that "substantially more records" were in the shops by the time the tour opened, its lack of support set the tone for every Graham Parker and the Rumour album that followed. Despite claims that Mercury Records hadn't done enough to support *Heat Treatment*, the album gave Graham Parker and the Rumour their first taste of success in America. Its modest chart peak of 169 was scant reward for a gruelling two month tour of the country, but proof that with a lot more hard work America was theirs for the taking.

19
There's A Riot Going On

In the months following their debut at the Telegraph in Brixton, The 101ers had made a name for themselves as serious garage/punk rockers at the Charlie Pigdog club. Long before the Sex Pistols carved out a reputation for violence, The 101ers attracted the kind of audience that did more than threaten to riot, it did. Things came to a head in April 1975 when the landlord of the Chippenham closed the Charlie Pigdog club because it had got out of hand. Alan Jones witnessed a typical night at the club and wrote about it for the *Melody Maker*: "It was the kind of place which held extraordinary promises of violence. You walked in, took one look around, and wished you were the hell out of there."

Barred from the Chippenham, The 101ers headed to the Elgin where they secured a Tuesday night residency from 12 May. The group was generating quite a name for itself thanks to its riotous gigs and a select handful of journalists writing about them in the music weeklies. It was an Elgin gig that got them noticed by Roger Armstrong, the assistant manager at the Rock On stall in Soho market. His boss, Ted Carroll, owned the stall selling vintage '50s and '60s rock 'n' roll and beat music. Having managed Thin Lizzy, Ted had a good understanding of how the music business worked and was planning his own record company, Chiswick Records. The low-budget, rough and ready beat music The 101ers specialised in was exactly what he was looking for. In the summer of '75, Armstrong encountered The 101ers at the Elgin and fell in love with them. "They were pretty anarchic then. Then Ted saw them at Dingwalls a little while later and they'd tightened up into this great unit. Ted came to the stall the next morning - he's not normally that excitable - and says: 'I've just seen this kid, and he's an absolute star."

The 'kid' was Joe Strummer and he would become a star, but not with The 101ers. Although Carroll had his eyes on the group, it would be another year before they'd set foot in a studio and make any recordings. Before signing The 101ers, Carroll and Armstrong spotted another high-energy beat group, The Count Bishops. Originally called Chrome, the group comprised Johnny Guitar, Zenon De Fleur (Zenon Hierowski), Steve Lewins, Paul Balbi and Mike Spenser. They were further proof that something was happening that would shake the music business to its foundations. The Count Bishops played beat and garage/punk classics, loud and fast. Like their rivals Eddie and the Hot Rods and The 101ers, it was dumb, dirty, rough, ready, trashy, dangerous and different.

Like a growing number of groups, the Count Bishops bridged the past and the present, they were, claimed Paul Balbi "more progressive" than the '60s originators and "a little more contemporary". This new generation of beat groups was recreating the kind of atmosphere and excitement that had drawn teenagers to The Rolling Stones, The Yardbirds and The Action a decade earlier. They clearly wanted to recapture the rawness and spontaneity of the '60s, and audiences wanted to experience it, too. "There's always a market for R&B because there are always people, particularly boys, who just wanna go out on a Saturday night and hear some real live headbanging music," Johnny Guitar explained. "The thing is, whether it's cool for them to go and listen to an R&B band in the first place."

Carroll and Armstrong were well ahead of the major record companies when they signed the Count Bishops to Chiswick Records. Journalist Mick Farren hit the nail on the head when he wrote: "We have produced a new strain of executive fat cat who is just as conservative as the old Tin Pan Alley breed." What the music industry needed was a new breed of entrepreneur who was in tune with what was happening on the street and willing to risk a few hundred pounds making a record with a bunch of scruffy outsiders without keeping one eye on the profit and loss sheet. While major record companies continued looking for the new David Bowie or Les McKeown [Bay City Rollers], Carroll and Armstrong went against the grain and issued records that appealed to an audience alienated by BBC play lists and major label ignorance.

The budding record company bosses wasted no time in booking the proto-punk rockers into the less than glamorous Pathway Studio in Islington. An eight-track recording facility, it would become an important Punk/new wave landmark and second home to Nick Lowe during the early months of '76. "We went into Pathway Studios in Islington with the idea of getting down as many tracks as possible. It was 'we'll bring the amps, you guys bring the beer'," Johnny Guitar told *Sounds*. The tracks recorded there ended up on the now legendary *Speedball*. This EP was the first Chiswick release and sold out almost immediately.

Although Chiswick wasn't the first independent British record company, it led the way for other independents and caught the zeitgeist well before Robinson and Jakeman had the wherewithal to form Stiff Records. Because Chiswick Records had to manufacture records from scratch, it took almost four months from the time the group walked into Pathway and the EP being released. The process was a steep learning curve but proved that anyone could do it. Armstrong later admitted: "We were discovering that getting a record out wasn't the arcane, magical thing - it was pretty easy to get a record pressed - not rocket science. And that was the beauty of the 45 rpm format, of the record industry in those days - you could go out and do it with very little capital."

Future Chiswick Records recording stars The 101ers were used to working with very little capital, but thanks to their residency at the Elgin and a full gig sheet the group was at last making a living from rock 'n' roll and creating a buzz, albeit a small one, in the pages of the music weeklies. It was, however, little reward for over a year's hard graft. As Strummer explained to Paolo Hewitt: "That little cutting from the *Melody Maker* I was telling you about, that was the summit of a year's sweat. That was like the ultimate. That little cutting."

Actually, Carroll and Armstrong were interested, but were busy organising the Count Bishops' debut EP. There were also plenty of pub landlords interested and in August The 101ers debuted at a former country and western club, the Nashville Rooms. That it turned its back on country music for something altogether more risky says much about how the pub circuit was changing. The 101ers might have been playing boozers, but they certainly didn't consider themselves part of that scene. "I think we thought we were doing our own thing," remembers Timperley. "It wasn't as if we were aspiring to become part of a thing that was there already. Obviously, objectively, we were, because we were playing these pubs, but we didn't aspire to being part of that group. And I think increasingly through 1975 and the beginning of 1976, there was a notion that, 'There would be something better!'"

By now The 101ers were a tight four-piece combo comprising Strummer, Timperley, Mole and Dudanski. Timperley had caused a minor crisis when he considered leaving the group for what Strummer called a "lame brained singer songwriter." Strummer was eager to find a replacement and told Allan Jones of the *Melody Maker* in July what he was looking for: "We want a guitarist for a beat group, we don't want any bloody acid casualties thinking they're going to join the Grateful Dead." These were exactly the kind of sentiments that inspired Punk Rock, of course. The minor crisis was averted when Timperley decided to stay. When Strummer described his dream guitarist he could have been describing Higgs and Gray from Eddie and the Hot Rods. In October, Strummer got to experience the Hot Rods first hand when they supported The 101ers for the first of several gigs at the Nashville Rooms. Howard Thompson, recently employed by Island Records as an A&R manager, attended the gig and thought the Hot Rods had something. Thompson later recalled his initial encounter with the group. "Along with their own songs like 'All I Need Is Money', 'Double Checkin' Woman', 'Get Across To You', 'Horseplay' and 'On The Run', they'd carefully choose covers like '96 Tears', 'Wooly Bully', 'The Kids Are Alright', 'Shake' and 'It Came Out Of The Sky', then they'd play everything as if they were being chased by the cops."

The Hot Rods were initially more interested in scoring free drinks from Thompson than discussing the possibility of recording for Island Records, not that he could have offered them a contract even if he wanted. This wasn't some Hollywood fantasy. Because he was new to the business, Thompson had to get the okay from his boss before signing the group. "I had no real reference point as to what the hell I was doing," he said. "I didn't know if they were going to sell records. All I knew was I liked' em. A lot. They played the kind of music I grew up with but gave it a rawer edge and a life-or-death intensity that was hard to ignore. Their shows were thrilling. Back in the office (in the basement of 22 St Peter's Square, Hammersmith) I told Richard Williams that I'd seen something that I really liked and asked if he would come along and give a second opinion. Uh ... and a green light." A few weeks later Thompson took Williams to see Eddie and the Hot Rods at the Red Cow. Impressed by what he saw, Williams gave Thompson the green light and told him to offer them a deal.

20
Something's Going To Happen In The Winter

According to Chris Welch, 1975 was a year in which "the rock experience was reshuffled, re-examined and utilised afresh. A decade of musical output was in many cases put through the sausage machine and came out shrink-wrapped as product." Dr Feelgood had done their bit to remodel, remake and redefine rock 'n' roll, but unlike the Bay City Rollers, Queen or the Glitter Band they avoided becoming just another rock 'n' roll product. They'd kicked against the pricks and achieved more in six months than the combined might of London's pub rock coterie had in the previous three years.

By October they'd stormed the country promoting their second album, *Malpractice*, to ecstatic audiences and glowing reviews. Recording sessions began with Vic Maile producing before the group decamped to Olympic Studios to continue work on the album themselves. "[We'd] come to decide that we had fixed ideas about what we wanted to do and had enough experience to know how to go about doing it." explained Johnson. *Malpractice* was more polished than their debut but had enough rough edges to avoid accusations of selling out. With support from a sold out tour, it reached a respectable 17 in the album charts. The 'Malpractice' tour took the group around the country for most of October and the first week of November. Thanks to the reputation they'd established on the 'Naughty Rhythms' tour, Dr Feelgood had progressed from the university circuit to playing larger halls in the nation's major cities. The Feelgoods were an unstoppable force and weren't going to take nonsense from anybody, especially the rowdy football fans that came to see them. Reporting on the first night of the tour, which kicked off at the Hemel Hempstead Pavilion, Geoff Brown noted how Brilleaux dominated the audience: "Lee has stepped briskly to the front of the stage and he's standing cockily, his chest forward in punkish pride, his legs astride in defiant stance."

The tour was a major undertaking with several dates being recorded either for the BBC or a planned live album that would send the band to the top of the album charts. Their hometown gig at the Southend-on-Sea Kursaal on 8 November was not only recorded but filmed, primarily to promote their next single, 'Back In The Night'. Andy Childs accompanied Dr Feelgood on tour and was impressed with the work of the backroom boys to make the venture a success. "The amount of work that they [Chris Fenwick and tour manager Jake Jakeman put in can't really be measured, but suffice to say that the tour proceeded without a hitch." The right management team was vital to the Feelgoods' success. Andrew Lauder, their A&R manager, noted: "They're the people you're working with all the time. It's got to be a good relationship otherwise you're going to have a lot of problems, regardless of the group."

Chris Fenwick had done a great job but the Feelgoods quickly discovered that playing outside the London pub circuit was just like starting over from scratch. Speaking to the *Melody Maker*; Johnson explained: "You'd start doing 'Riot' which would be greeted with a response in London and everyone's kinda sitting there (Wilko does his remarkable zombie impersonation), but start playing 'Roxette' and people know it." Dr Feelgood were in the process of crossing over. Seasoned fans rubbed shoulders at the bar with recent converts and their thuggish male following was tempered by the kind of kids who got their kicks from the Top Twenty. CBS Records executive, Dan Loggins, told the *Melody Maker*, "To my neighbour Dr Feelgood represents what the Stones represented to me when I was 16." To state the obvious, Dr Feelgood offered something the Bay City Rollers didn't. When the screams and tartan faded, all the Rollers left behind was a hollow experience. For teenagers like Dan Loggins' neighbour, Dr Feelgood represented an honest reality that didn't depend on artifice. All that glam rock did, in both its uptown (Bowie/Roxy Music) and downtown (Bay City Rollers/Mud) forms, was mask reality with glitter and greasepaint.

Dr Feelgood, Eddie and the Hot Rods, Kilburn and the High Roads and The 101ers recycled the urban blues and R&B of Chicago and Memphis. Music rooted in oppression, poverty and the reality of the street; it was old school punk given a British twist. These groups represented a grass roots movement that threatened to splinter the mainstream as a weed has the power to crack a paving slab. Dr Feelgood's 'All Through The City' was a more accurate representation of Britain circa 1975 than Roxy Music's dream world. The Feelgoods' musical simplicity and scruffy attire was something anyone could relate and aspire to.

The seeds of the new wave insurgency had been sown and were germinating. One person who knew better than most that something exciting was in the air was Dave Robinson. On the lookout for new talent for the record company he was planning, Robinson encouraged Ian Dury out of semi-retirement. "After the Kilburns had broken up, Dave Robinson rolled up to me and said 'Let's put a band together.' It was called the Kilburns, though it was purely and simply a different band, so we could get gigs," said Dury. The new version of the Kilburns comprised Dury, Rod Melvin, Ted Speight, John Earle, George Dionsiev and Malcolm Mortimore. Chas de Whalley saw them at the Hope and Anchor in December and was impressed by what he saw. "Dury showed that 'artistically' he is, perhaps, finally getting it together."

Dury and the Kilburns had lost none of their ability to impress audiences and critics alike, but de Whalley still thought they lacked focus. If the new line-up wasn't as visually engaging as it had been, it was still impressive musically and it gave Dury the confidence boost he needed to get back on the road. "I had been feeling pretty low and had been off the road for a year, but luckily Speight was back on guitar, my mate from school. We found John Earle who was a great saxophone player, so it was very high quality musicianship, although it never quite had the glamour of the old Kilburns," Dury recalled.

The group's new set included old favourites and a brace of new Dury-Melvin songs. Yet while it included the hit-in-waiting 'What a Waste', de Whalley couldn't see a commercial future for the band. "Dury isn't the guy for a slick back-up band ... which means, ultimately, he can't be groomed for 'stardom', and is destined to remain a cult." True, with the Kilburns behind him, Dury never would amount to much, and with the exception of 'What a Waste' he still lacked the songs good enough to propel him into the charts, but it was the juxtaposition of Dury's barrow-boy crudeness with the Blockheads smooth funk attack that lit the fuse. No matter how good the Kilburns were they were no match for the Blockheads. Neither did he have the right manager. "I asked Dave Robinson, after three years of being on the road and grasping and all that stuff, I shall be round the bend. When that happens, will you be able to look after me? Will you be able to help me? Will you be of any use to me when I crack up? He said, 'No, I won't. I'll take you down the road to Blackhill," Dury professed.

Blackhill Enterprises was based on the top floor of 32 Alexander Street. Having managed both Syd Barrett and the disorganised Mighty Baby, if anybody could handle Dury, they could. However, Dury's hippie phobia kicked in and despite Robinson's assertion that they were the best people for the job, he wasn't convinced. It wasn't until he met them face to face that his initial scepticism left him when he realised they'd look after him should he crack up. "Peter is a very nice man, very kind man, and I love him to death," Dury said. "We don't always get on to well, because his job is, in a way, to look after my weaknesses. He's managing me, he's managing the things I can't do for myself. That's what managers do."

In early '76, the Kilburns went through another minor but significant line-up change when Rod Melvin left. Chas Jankel replaced him and completely transformed Dury's song writing and fortunes. "The guitar player from Ian & The Kilburns went into the shop [Maurice Plaquat's music shop in Shepherd's Bush] and said their keyboard player had just left," recalled Jankel. "So I got a call saying they were playing at the Nashville. I went down there and watched in awe as they played their set. It was more like a circus than music. Cabaret, but very dark cabaret. Ian was wearing a Tommy Cooper fez, the guitarist looked like Frank Zappa. It was very offbeat. I was hypnotised. After it was over, I walked like a zombie towards the stage and followed the band to where they'd gone. They're all sweating from having finished playing and there was one person facing the door: Ian. He saw me coming and said, 'Ere mate, do I know you? Well fack off then!' And I stood there like a rabbit dazzled by headlights. Then I backed off and the guitar player said, 'You're not Chaz Jankel are you? Oh, sorry about that.' Anyway, I got the gig."

In the following six months, Jankel influenced the group's musical direction and wrote a cache of near-perfect songs that fused Dury's lyrical verve with an infectious funk groove. Jankel had an instinctive rhythmic sensibility that matched Dury's perfectly - Dury was, after all, a frustrated drummer. Inspired by Lee Dorsey's 'Get Out of My Life, Woman' he was bitten by the backbeat bug at an early age. "I remember thinking, 'Wow, this is really groovy'. And I noticed there was a whole lot of emphasis on the backbeat and the snare. That was what really opened my mind to Afro-American music. After that, I started searching it out and it didn't take long before I came across Sly and the Family Stone. They really changed my life. If there was ever one band that was simply awe-inspiring, they were it," he said.

The Kilburns kept going for several months but were going nowhere fast. Jankel could see that all they were doing was treading water and one day suggested Dury break up the group and start again. "I felt there was something ambitionless about the group. Ian was ready for a change," claimed Jankel. "One day, I whispered into his ear: how about disbanding the group, or why don't we write some songs and he said, yeah, that's a great idea. So we knocked the band on the head and started writing." Dury issued a press release stating that he'd been told by doctors that if he continued performing he'd damage his health. In reality, it was all smoke and mirrors. Dury wanted to concentrate on writing and he couldn't do that and perform at the same time. "I wanted to stop and do some writing, plot out something a bit more strong," he confessed. Ian Dury and the Kilburns played their last gig on 17 June 1976 at Walthamstow Town Hall supported by the Sex Pistols and The Stranglers. Things were moving fast and the time had come for Dury to consider his next move. When he re-emerged, a year later, the musical landscape was unrecognizable, but so was he.

21

Letsgetabitarockin'

The British have always been at their best when their backs are against the wall. For many groups working the pub rock circuit that feeling of defiant bullishness must have hung in the air like the scent of stale tobacco. Progress seemed treacle slow. In November '75, The 101ers recorded half a dozen songs at Jackson's studio in Rickmansworth with Vic Maile producing. The session didn't go well and nothing from it would see the light of day while the group was still active. Their hopes had been raised and cruelly dashed, but despite a sense of stagnation they attempted to stay positive. But come the new year they sacked their bassist because of his pessimism. "I think I was an expectant sort of scapegoat," Mole said. "I think everybody was pissed off that we weren't going anywhere, that there wasn't any success happening."

This kind of victimisation usually precedes some kind of major schism in a group, and that's exactly what was about to happen. The omens weren't good but, despite the internal friction, there was plenty of work to keep them busy. That was part of the problem. Any hope of escaping the endless one-nighters looked remote. "I started to lose my mind. I would go around the squat saying, 'We're invisible, we should change our name to the Invisibles,'" recalled Strummer. The 101ers weren't as invisible as Strummer implies. They were getting reviewed in the national press and had a record company, albeit a tiny independent, interested. The arrival of their new bassist, Dan Kelleher, revitalised the group. He co-wrote several new songs with Strummer, one of which, 'Five Star Rock 'n' Roll Petrol', would grace the B-side of their debut single.

With Chiswick Records pushing for a 45, The 101ers headed to Pathway Studios with Roger Armstrong. Over the course of two sessions, they recorded more than enough songs to fill an EP, but only 'Keys To Your Heart' was deemed good enough to make its way onto vinyl. It took a third session at the BBC's Maida Vale studios to yield the record's eventual B-side. Chiswick Records was still little more than a vanity label, an adjunct to Carroll and Armstrong's main business of selling second-hand records. As they were still finding their way through the business of making records, it was several months before The 101ers actually had anything to show for their labours.

With a large and successful independent record company behind them, Eddie and the Hot Rods were better positioned and moving fast. Having failed to successfully capture The 101ers on tape, Maile entered the studio with the Hot Rods in late December to produce their first single. His session with the Rods was more successful and two songs, 'Writing On The Wall' and 'Cruisin' In the Lincoln', were issued as a single in January '76. To celebrate their deal with Island Records, Eddie and the Hot Rods played a showcase at the Marquee on 12 February with the Sex Pistols supporting. Although the Pistols had begun playing college gigs, they were faced with the same options as any other new band and had to play the same pubs and clubs as the pub rock groups they wanted gone. The Sex Pistols appearance at the Marquee was their first high profile London gig, and it established a standard for almost every gig that followed. Somebody forgot to turn on the stage monitors, which pissed off the Pistols to the extent that John Lydon put his microphone stand through them. This didn't sit well with the Hot Rods, who, through no fault of their own, now had to play without monitors. Backstage tensions intensified when Masters took matters into his own hands: "I gave him [Lydon] a little kiddy slap. Nothing hefty. So he starts whingeing like a little girl, and told McLaren, and McLaren sent him back with some other guy. I went to give him a slap and he ran away."

The incident led to feuding between the two groups, but if the Sex Pistols had lost the battle of the Marquee, they'd won the war of Punk credibility. Eddie and the Hot Rods represented a return to pre-modern music that reiterated the values and attitudes of '50s rockers and '60s beat groups. They were part of a long line of punks as pop stylists. Neil Spencer's review of the gig for the *NME* didn't actually mention the Rods, only the Pistols and how they were the shape of things to come: a warning shot across the bows for the old wave to be sure. The Pistols were part of a Punk subculture that represented a post-modern take on pop - Punk as art. These two strands often intertwined resulting in a New Wave style that was frequently difficult to unpick and categorise. Groups like Graham Parker and the Rumour, Elvis Costello and the Attractions, Eddie and the Hot Rods were neither punk nor pop, but occupied a tangled middle ground that existed somewhere between the two. Even if they weren't New Wave it was easy to label them as such.

If punk as pop combo The 101ers were still feeling invisible, that was about to change. On 3 April it was The 101ers turn to experience the Sex Pistols as support group. The 101ers, Chiswick Records and the Sex Pistols joined forces for a gig at the Nashville Rooms. The Pistols looked magnificent in their designer Punk clobber, but, as far as Geoff Hutt who reviewed the gig for the *NME* was concerned, they stank of artifice. Sure, Lydon had attitude, but it looked too rehearsed, too considered. The Pistols, he thought, were trying too hard, and surely real Punks don't try at all. The 101ers, however, made it look easy. But their time was drawing to a close. They were, after all, still playing 'Back In The U.S.S.R.' and lengthy workouts of 'Gloria'. The Sex Pistols were the way, and Joe Strummer knew it. Where once he'd championed the old wave, a few months after seeing the Sex Pistols he'd be yelling 'No Elvis, no Beatles or Rolling Stones' to anybody who'd listen.

Twenty days later they repeated the exercise. This time the Pistols were the undisputed winners, not because they were better than The 101ers, they weren't, but because Vivienne Westwood contrived some light entertainment violence to liven things up a bit. The Pistols were having an off night, so Westwood slapped a girl who had taken her chair whilst she was at the bar at which point Lydon leapt from the stage to join McLaren in a brawl with the hapless girl's boyfriend. The press went to town and Punk Rock with a capital 'P' was born.

The 101ers weren't quite finished, but the writing was on the wall. The group recruited Martin Stone from Chilli Willi and the Red Hot Peppers to deputise for Clive Timperley and played a handful of gigs throughout May and early June. While their repertoire remained unchanged their image began to reflect the coming punk look. "By the end The 101ers were wearing drainpipe trousers. And this might not seem significant to many people. But in a world of flares, drainpipe trousers were the equivalent of shaving your head and painting it orange - it really stuck out," Strummer explained.

Shops like Sex and Boy may have introduced the torn tee-shirt, bondage trousers and safety pin to fashion conscious kids, but Dr Feelgood and Kilburn and the High Roads had helped define the new visual styling long before the Pistols made it the vogue. Peter York's account of changing tastes among London's in-crowd, *Style Wars*, noted: "You only had to talk about a social worker or an ethnic print dress ... to get a laugh. Styles got really tight and aggressive, all the big floppy shambolic post-hippie styles started to disappear from 1975 on ..."

By the time Chiswick Records managed to pull everything together and issue The 101ers debut single, it was too late. On 30 June, the night before 'Keys To Your Heart' was issued, Strummer called time on the group. As far as he was concerned The 101ers were last year's model and The Clash were the future of rock 'n' roll. The 101ers had been formed with one simple aim in mind - to make money. The Clash, however, were on a Bernie Rhodes inspired mission. It's that attitude that divides the punk groups from their new wave brothers. Richard Dudanski and Joe Strummer explained their differences to Paolo Hewitt. Dudanski liked the Pistols' music but "I didn't like the way it was manipulated, basically by McLaren. Just the way he'd set up a scene and they'd get the attention." Strummer: "I saw it not only as a 'good group,' but as a new attitude." It was possible to share Strummer's attitude and operate outside of McLaren's circle of punks. Graham Parker, Elvis Costello and Nick Lowe weren't on a cultural crusade but they did want to shake up the system. As far as they were concerned, the emergence of punk gave them a platform from where they could wreak revenge on the music business. "We wanted heads to roll; they'd been feeding at the trough - and I include the Hairy blooming Cornflake [a.k.a. Radio 1 DJ Dave Lee Travis] and other ghastly people who looked down their noses at us - and now we were going to beat them out of the way. And we did. I can't tell you how proud I am to be part of their demise!" railed Nick Lowe.

As the long hot summer of '76 set in, Eddie and the Hot Rods continued their relentless schedule with a 22 date tour supporting the Kursaal Flyers.

During the tour they decided that Lew Lewis had become too unpredictable and he'd have to go - he'd resurface a few months later with a solo release on United Artists ('Out For A Lark') and later Stiff Records ('Boogie On The Street'). "We had to draw the line. Lew was a real good part of the band, but he was a hard man to control," explained Steve Nicol. With or without Lewis they still hadn't hit their stride. Having failed with one of their own songs they tried again with a live favourite, Sam the Sham's 'Wooly Bully'. Although it was supported by another tour, it too failed to chart.

On 9 July, Sire Records issued the Ramones debut single 'Blitzkrieg Bop'. At the time it sounded impossibly fast, that is unless you'd heard the Hot Rods. If you liked your music fast, loud and live there was only one place to be on the night of 9 July - the Marquee Club in Wardour Street. The Hot Rods had set a new attendance record there before having it snatched from them by AC/DC. The place was packed to the rafters, the group was on fire and a mobile recording studio was on hand to catch the action. The resulting *Live at the Marquee* EP featured '96 Tears', 'Get Out Of Denver', 'Gloria' and 'Satisfaction'. Pretty much your standard pub rock fare and not a million miles from the kind of songs The 101ers had been peddling. The EP was itself a throwback to the '60s when the four-track extended play format was second only to its big brother, the 7-inch 45. It was to have been Island Records first, but was pipped at the post by an EP by Bryan Ferry. It was, Howard Thompson told the *Melody Maker*, "simply a gesture for the fans, because, although none of the tracks were written by the Rods themselves, they were the most requested live cuts."

Despite Eddie and the Hot Rods' impressive following, the single received no Radio One daytime airplay. With DJs like the 'Hairy Cornflake' dominating daytime radio, the BBC was desperately out of touch with what was happening just a stone's throw away from Broadcasting House. Thankfully, not everyone at the Beeb was off the pace - John Peel and his producer John Walters did know what was happening. Peel had started playing 'punk' records on his evening show in May - the Ramones 'Judy Is A Punk' being the first. He'd also aired The 101ers 'Keys To Your Heart' and songs from Jonathan Richman's *Rock 'n' Roll With The Modern Lovers* album. But the majority of the records he played were still by established acts like Eric Clapton, Soft Machine and Roxy Music. By the time the Hot Rods *Marquee* EP came out he was playing more new bands - the Hot Rods in particular. For Peel, this kind of music represented a return to the pre-modern sounds he'd loved as a teenager. "I do seem to remember saying in the mid-seventies, prior to punk, that I would like to see a return to the discipline that was imposed by the 2¼-minute long song - Jerry Lee Lewis was the example I used at the time - that when you get to the studio you'd got two minutes and fifteen seconds in which you'd got to say everything you'd got to say, possibly in your life; and that seemed to me to concentrate the mind wonderfully, and produce quite extraordinary passionate records," Peel explained.

Peel wasn't alone, several others shared the same opinion, Dave Robinson among them. He recalls: "John Peel is the reason why an awful lot of everything that happened in England happened at that time. He is the musical guru at the end of the day. Punk wouldn't have happened without John Peel either. Malcolm McLaren had some vague thing to do with it, but I'd put John Peel down as the major reason." Add a select handful of DJs, an enthusiastic music press and some smart marketing and for groups like the Hot Rods anything was possible. Thompson, again: "We were really astonished that it [*Live at the Marquee*] got into the chart at 56 last week," he said. "The fact that we've hit the chart without Radio One daytime play is interesting." The EP caught the mood of the time and with a large and loyal following developed by unrelenting gigging, it catapulted the group into the lower reaches of the charts.

One sign of the times was the deletion of Masters' cry of 'Are you ready to rock?' from commercial copies of the EP - it wasn't removed from promotional copies. Perhaps somebody at Island Records thought the appeal from Masters too 'rockist'! With rock coming under attack from punk, any references to rocking out had to be removed. But as far as Thompson was concerned, Eddie and the Hot Rods were happy to play the rock card. "The Rods could be termed punk, but they are not a 'Punk Rock Band.'" The band felt a certain reticence to throw their lot in with the Pistols and their ilk given their spat at the Marquee. Punks or not, Island Records were keen to capitalise on their success and finally sanctioned an album. The album's title track, 'Teenage Depression' was issued as a single in October. Despite attempts to distance themselves from Punk, Caroline Coon's review in the *Melody Maker* described them as "the first of the new-wave punk band[s] to trail-blaze into the national chart and they are a fine measure of the storm brewing on the horizon." Prescient words indeed.

22
If It Ain't Stiff

When Dr Feelgood eventually tasted success it wasn't as sweet as they'd imagined. Having reached the top (the only band to outperform them in 1975 was The Who) at least one member of the group was having a crisis of conscience. But the Feelgoods were moving too fast for anyone to jump ship. With two critically acclaimed albums to their credit, Chris Fenwick decided to up the ante by attempting to break the band in America. The boys weren't short of offers either, including one from the mighty Robert Plant who wanted to sign them to Zeppelin's Swan Song label, but Fenwick decided to broker a deal with the bigger and more powerful Columbia Records.

To cement the deal, Dr Feelgood agreed to play at the company's annual convention in San Diego and were accompanied by road manager Andrew 'Jake' Jakeman (who had now adopted the moniker Jake Riviera) and equipment handler Nick Lowe (masquerading as Dale Liberator). These kind of corporate bashes were synonymous with extravagance and excess, but this one was something else. The junket was held at the luxurious Rivermont Hotel and to ensure its employees knew exactly what they could expect, Columbia Records placed a sign in each hotel room that read: "Columbia Records Convention, January 1976 - Total Unlimited Credit". So, if a sales rep wanted to emulate one of the acts whose wares he hawked by chucking his television out of the window he knew his employer would pick up the tab. And to make sure the convention really went with a swing, 20 hookers were flown in from LA. In return for Columbia Records' generosity all Dr Feelgood had to do was perform a brief 25-minute set: piece of piss, eh?

Two months previously, United Artists had held a similarly lavish reception to launch the Feelgoods' 'Malpractice Tour'. Johnson wasn't impressed by either the reception or the "whole star thing" it represented. The fact that the group missed an important sound check really riled the guitarist. In addition he wasn't best pleased about playing to a corporate audience who couldn't give a shit which band was playing. Speaking to the *NME*, Johnson said: "If that is the way big business is done and the way stardom is achieved, then forget it. I don't want to have anything to do with it, because it's 'orrible.'"

The Feelgoods took their frustrations out on the road manager, Jake Riviera. The trip to San Diego was proving memorable but for all the wrong reasons. Riviera was sacked as road manager, an event witnessed by Cal Worthington for *ZigZag*. "Chris Fenwick was continually trying to paper over the cracks in their friendship, but the matter came to a head when the Figure took a swing at Jake after Wllko discovered that his wah-wah pedal, through some oversight, had not been packed with the rest of the gear." Riviera's dismissal was only temporary and he was soon back road-managing the crabby Canvey Islanders. But by now the rift between Johnson and the rest of the group had become as wide and deep as the Thames Estuary. Johnson was no longer socialising with his band mates, preferring instead to stay in his hotel room and write songs. But when they did meet on-stage, ironically, the tension led to some of the most dynamic performances of their career. Michael Barackman reviewed their gig at the Starwood club in Los Angeles for *Rolling Stone* and described them as "frenzied" and "intense". Reviewing their Long Island gig for the *Village Voice*, Frank Rose mused "with intelligent support and hard touring they could become as big a teenage sensation here as Kiss, Aerosmith or Led Zeppelin." God forbid!

Dr Feelgood were poised to take America by storm but, if anything, Johnson found the prospect even more damning than ever. Booked to support Kiss on some stadium gigs in the south, Dr Feelgood witnessed the worst effects of rock star arrogance at first hand. Yankees Kiss didn't extend the kind of down home hospitality associated with the southern states of America to the Feelgoods, in fact they were downright ungracious and expected their guests to use the front of house toilets as a dressing room while they caked on their slap backstage. Quite rightly, Dr Feelgood cancelled the gigs and headed home. It was just another example of spoiled rock star behaviour that rattled Johnson's cage. Speaking to the *NME* he said: "We're not expecting to be treated like stars, to have a star on the door or anything like. But just a reasonable effort."

To get away from the grouchy Feelgoods, Riviera spent his free time nosing out rare vinyl in seedy second hand shops. Noticing the plethora of local independent record companies, he experienced a Eureka moment. "I was working with Dr Feelgood, and I wanted to leave that group," he said, "I'd seen the small record labels in America and wanted to emulate something similar in England." Dave Robinson had been thinking along similar lines since setting up a recording studio at the Hope and Anchor. Robinson was dating Irene Campbell, who shared a flat with Riviera. It was on one of his many visits to see Irene that he got to hear of Riviera's plans. Never one to miss an opportunity, he suggested they form a record company together. "He [Riviera] managed other pub bands, and he was around and I just thought it was an idea," explained Robinson. "He was always very clever with the quip and the energy levels, so I thought the two if us would be better than one. We joined together to be managers to begin with, the record label was going to be kind of a hobby."

Riviera had already got the ball rolling with some funding from Fenwick, Brilleaux and Johnson, who all divvied up cash to get the company off the ground. "Lee Brilleaux said to me, 'You're starting your own label? How much is that going to cost then?' I said, 'It's going to be like £400 to get it going.' He just whipped out his cheque book [and] wrote out a cheque, God bless him," recalled Riviera. His original idea was to issue an EP by Spick Ace and

The Blue Sharks (a group that comprised Dr Feelgood, Nick Lowe and Martin Stone) via the Skydog label. However, contractual problems put an end to that plan.

Even with financial help from Dr Feelgood, £400 wasn't going to last very long. They'd need more capital than that to keep it going, which is where Robinson came in. Robinson's main business was artist management and, unlike Jakeman, his acts actually made money. "Stiff wouldn't have happened at all if I hadn't had a management company," Robinson maintains. "I managed Graham Parker and various other people, so the income from that is what launched Stiff. This idea that the Feelgoods rolled up with all the money; the money actually came from a company called Avancedale, which was my management company. That £400 happened but we never cashed it. [Avancedale] that's what kept us going, paid the phones, paid the office." So the new wave myth that Brilleaux's £400 started Stiff Records is exploded. Still, a generous gesture by him nonetheless.

Robinson was renting the ground floor of 32 Alexander Street from Blackhill Enterprises, and it was from here that the two managers plotted their revenge on the major record companies. Their label would be called Stiff Records, record business slang for a flop, and initially available via mail order, select shops or directly from Alexander Street. To get the label off the ground they planned to exploit the hours of recordings Robinson had made at the Hope and Anchor. Speaking to *Music Week*, Riviera explained Stiff Records' manifesto: "We are dedicated to releasing three-chord songs, lasting three minutes, as well as collector item discs and possible chart records." The initial business proposition was simple: to release product from pub rock acts who had played the Hope and Anchor but were now contracted to other labels. Although Paul Riley was given the job of compiling Robinson's Hope and Anchor tapes into a double album it was quietly dropped because of contractual problems and never saw the light of day. (The closest Stiff Records came to a pub rock album was the *A Bunch Of Stiff Records* compilation.) A sister label, Stiff Groovediggers, that was intended to specialise in reissuing out of print singles was also mooted, but it too came to nothing.

With the Spick Ace and The Blue Sharks EP also shelved, Stiff Records issued a brace of Nick Lowe demos as its first single. "We had two tracks which was 'Heart Of The City' and 'So It Goes' by Nick Lowe that were paid for by Peter Barnes, Nick's publisher. That always was the first single and it used up nearly all of the £400," Riviera explained. Having managed Lowe and employed him to produce Graham Parker's debut album, Robinson was happy to go along with Riviera's idea. "He was looking after Nick so that was the hook up from the Brinsleys, and I thought Nick was always good. Nick was a really good songwriter and I didn't think he'd lost it really."

Since the demise of Brinsley Schwarz in early '75, Lowe had been struggling to disentangle himself from his contract with United Artists. Unwilling to release Brinsley Schwarz when they were offered a better deal with Island

Records, United Artists fought equally hard to keep Lowe on its books. But Lowe and Riviera had a cunning plan. "I was still signed to United Artists in those days, and they were very decent. They let the rest of the group go, but kept me because I was the songwriter," explained Lowe. "So I really had to get out of that deal. But I had to be very subtle. Jake had this idea. I had this selection of real pop songs, and he said, 'Why don't you make a Bay City Rollers fan record? Take it into United Artists and they're bound to think it's horrible.' So I said, 'perfect'. This was the first record I'd ever produced. I had mixed feelings about it, I was kind of proud of it, even though it was so utterly ghastly, it had been done so carefully. Anyway, I took it in and played it, and the tape finished, and there was this silence, and those there said, 'Fantastic! Fantastic, Nick! How much more of this stuff can you give us?'"

Issued using the pseudonym the Tartan Horde, 'Bay City Rollers We Love You' / 'Rollers Show' did nothing in Britain, but went to number 1 in Japan. Riviera's cunning plan had backfired. However, Lowe's next single for United Artists did the trick. 'Let's Go To The Disco' / 'Everybody Dance' was issued under another pseudonym, The Disco Brothers. Unlike Lowe's previous single, it flopped everywhere, including Japan, and this time United Artists let him go. A free agent, Lowe was all set to record for Stiff Records, but United Artists' Japanese office wasn't quite finished with his Tartan Horde scam. 'Rollers Show' / 'Allorolla' was issued to cash in on the Bay City Rollers' continued popularity, but a proposed album of Roller tribute songs failed to appear (for which we must be eternally thankful).

Although he was free of United Artists, Lowe still wasn't ready to make his debut for Stiff Records. In early '76 he issued a cover of Dr Feelgood's 'Keep It Out of Sight' / 'Truth Drug' for the Dutch based Dynamite Records. The company was formed in 1972 by Pieter Meulenbroeks, who shared similar tastes to Ted Carroll, Dave Robinson and Jake Riviera. Dynamite Records would license several singles from Chiswick Records and Stiff Records, but without the same level of success. With little publicity outside of Holland, Lowe's sole release for the company went unnoticed in his homeland, but his profile was about to receive a massive boost thanks to his association with Stiff Records.

With Lowe freed from United Artists' clutches, Stiff Records was ready to issue his debut for the label. 'So It Goes' / 'Heart Of The City' was issued with the jokey catalogue number BUY1 on 13 August 1976. Although Stiff Records was an independent it was nevertheless supported, albeit unofficially, by the same major record company that Lowe had worked so hard to escape. Robinson and Riviera had a very good relationship with United Artists, thanks to their long standing association with Andrew Lauder. "We did a deal whereby we'd press up their first single for them, which was by Nick Lowe," explained Lauder. "They'd sell it by mail order, and then, as soon as they paid us for that, we'd press a second record." Because United Artists was part of the EMI group of companies, it got 30 days credit before having to invoice Stiff for pressing the records. Riviera had plenty of time to sell his stock from the back of his car or by mail order with the added benefit of not paying manufacturing costs up front.

Like the pub rock circuit from which it sprang, Stiff Records was envisioned as a springboard for up and coming talent and established artists alike. A single on the independent label could, it was hoped, lead to bigger and better deals with the majors which was why artists were signed for one-off deals, which Riviera thought was actually more interesting. "There is something of their early days, which are often the most interesting days of bands on record," Riviera rightly observed. Unlike Oval Records which was distributed by Virgin Records, and Chiswick Records which was distributed by President Records, Stiff Records didn't have a distributor. Initially, its records were available by mail order from Alexander Street or from a select handful of shops that included Rock On, Virgin and the recently opened Rough Trade shop. "W. H. Smith and Boots don't want to know about Stiff Records, and Stiff doesn't really want to know about them, so that's fine." Riviera explained. Working like this meant Stiff Records were never going to sell huge quantities of vinyl, but it cut out the middleman and gave them an advantage that neither Oval Records nor Chiswick Records had; they'd have to wait weeks or months to receive payment from their distributors and give them a percentage for their services. By avoiding these delays and costs, Stiff Records was able to react a lot quicker than the major record companies and even their independent rivals.

As important as it was to get their records into the right shops, that was only part of the sales and promotion equation. Airplay on national radio was vitally important to success and Stiff Records' timing couldn't have been better. John Peel's Punk epiphany meant he was playing exactly the kind of records that Stiff Records planned to issue. Robinson asserts that without airplay on the John Peel show 'So It Goes' and Stiff Records wouldn't have been nearly as successful: "John Peel liked the Nick Lowe record and started playing it, that's pretty much it. We could have put out several records that didn't get anywhere, who knows what would have happened?"

Peel played 'So It Goes' every night of the week beginning 23 August exposing it to a national audience. It was also helped by glowing reviews from the national music weeklies. *Sounds* and *Melody Maker* each made the B-side 'Heart of the City' single of the week. Caroline Coon described it as: "Thin Lizzy via Brinsley Schwarz, thanks to Dave Edmunds and Hank Marvin, through Joe Strummer and around Richard Hell, all laced together with Nick's fine style."

Lowe had distilled 20 years of rock 'n' roll and come up with a two-minute pop song that captured the sound, spirit and essence of the times. Although he was far too old to be a Punk, that didn't stop him from jumping on the band-wagon. "I can write in any style. Peters and Lee, for instance," he told Coon. "But all my friends have turned into punks overnight and I'm a great band-wagon climber." Not everybody felt the same way as Lowe. Lee Brilleaux was of the opposite opinion. "I don't admire it when people make out that they're punks and they've got two A levels," he told *Melody Maker*.

What had once been un-commercial was now commercial, and Dr Feelgood were about to peak with the release of *Stupidity*, the band's first live album. Johnson had his finger on the nation's sub-cultural pulse and knew exactly how the album should sound. United Artists, however, had learned nothing. Johnson takes up the story: "He wanted us to do overdubs on it and clean it all up. And I started to say 'No!' If you're making a live record that's the way it should be. If you want to make a smooth record, do it in a studio. It got really eyeball to eyeball with me and the A&R guy. But I didn't waver. And the guy who was engineering told me that he'd said 'we're going to let Wilko have his way on this, and the record is going to die a death, and then he'll have to do as he's told.'" Wrong! This was the first ever live album to make number one in the album charts in its first week of release; Wilko was vindicated.

Issued in October, the first 20,000 copies of *Stupidity* came with a free 7-inch single, and propelled the Feelgoods to the heady heights of the top of the charts for the first and only time. Its success was, perhaps, symptomatic of the changes taking place among kids bored with the top twenty diet force-fed them by the Hairy Cornflake and wonderful Radio One. Besides Johnson, only Riviera and Robinson appeared to have grasped what was happening and all they had to go on was a full contact book, a handful of good ideas and the audacity to take on the major record companies and win. You wouldn't bet against them, would you?

23
Here Comes The Weekend

For the previous six years Dave Edmunds had spent every waking hour recording either himself or others at Rockfield Studios. On the rare occasions when he issued one of his own recordings it was invariably a hit. It was also written by somebody else and probably predated the '60s beat boom. Edmunds had a knack of making note-perfect reproductions of records from the golden age of rock 'n' roll that sounded as new as they did old. More at home in the studio than onstage, he'd all but turned his back on performing, the thought of which filled him with dread. Having down played his solo career for too long, by the mid-'70s he'd come to realise that if he wanted a career he'd better do something about it, and fast. Leaving the Monmouth countryside and Rockfield Studios behind him, he headed for the bright lights of London.

Edmunds was still in the suffocating grip of addiction to Mandrax and booze as well as trying to cope with a difficult divorce. In short he was a mess and in no fit state to think about rebuilding his career. "All my friends - like Terry Williams, [Man's drummer] and Kingsley [Ward] - were just waiting to receive a phone-call saying that I was dead," he said. Whilst producing the *New Favourites* album for Brinsley Schwarz, he'd become friends with Nick Lowe, to whom he now turned to help him through his darker moments. "When he moved up to London I was really the only person he knew," explains Lowe. "He was going through a bad time then - trouble with his wife, drugs, etc.: messy stuff - and I used to go over to his place and keep him company. One thing led to another: he recorded one of my songs ('She's My Baby' on *Subtle as a Flying Mallet*) and I'd go down to the studio with him and just sit there."

Apart from going down the pub or hanging out in the studio neither had considered working together until Jake Riviera suggested they form a group. The ideal low-key opportunity presented itself when Dave Robinson began putting together the Save the Hope and Anchor benefit. Riviera suggested they do the gig just to test the water. Lowe and Edmunds teamed up with Paul Riley, bassist from Chilli Willi, and drummer George Butler for the one-off performance and were joined by Sean Tyla and Ian Dury for a couple of songs. The Hope and Anchor gig convinced Edmunds that the time had come to concentrate on his career rather than hide behind a mixing desk. "If anything has held me back, it's been the fact that I've always been far too busy trying to finish other artists' albums instead of concentrating on my own," Edmunds came to realise.

From 1968 to 1973, Edmunds had produced scores of albums for others and produced four hit singles for himself - all cover versions of old rock 'n' roll songs. The two solo albums he'd issued were also peppered with his favourite songs by some of the best songwriters of his generation. But as every group with one eye on success knows only too well, it's impossible to sustain a long term career on cover versions alone. Edmunds had convinced himself that he couldn't write, but thanks to Lowe that was about to change. Edmunds knew he'd run into trouble if he kept doing cover versions. Thanks to Lowe, his new songs still had the feel of classic '50s rockers but with a modern twist. More importantly they were his and as far as he was concerned it was all rock 'n' roll regardless of who wrote it or when.

The reason his songs sounded familiar was due to his new song writing partner, Nick Lowe. The ex-Brinsleys' bassist and recent solo recording artist had a profound effect on Edmunds and his work. When Edmunds began work on his *Get It* album, it was Lowe that he turned to for assistance. They kicked round some ideas and within twenty minutes had a song. "You don't know what a breakthrough that was for me - this was my first real song that I've ever written in my life," Edmunds gleefully recalls. Lowe and Edmunds' contrasting personalities, ideas and approach to music complemented one another perfectly. Edmunds was the pre-modern disciple of Spector and Wilson who spent hours studying the slapback echo on old Presley 45s. Lowe was the post-modern prankster who absorbed influences like a sponge, mixing them up to the point where the past and present collapsed like some kind of black hole. More often than not it was Lowe who'd come up with an idea and Edmunds who finished it. "Dave is a good songwriter," he explained. "But what he's not good at is having that original burst, the original idea."

The song that had taken them all of 20 minutes to write was 'Here Comes The Weekend', an up-tempo beat number modelled on the Everly Brothers but remade for the '70s. Not only was it written quickly, but it was recorded quickly, too. If previously Edmunds had spent days noodling over a hot mixing desk to make his records, he was in for another surprise when he decided to make a demo of the song with Lowe and his drinking buddies Paul Riley [Roogalator] and Steve Goulding [Graham Parker and the Rumour]. "It's turned out so well that the demo we cut that afternoon for £45 ended up as the finished master," marvelled Edmunds.

'Here Comes The Weekend' was issued around the same time as Lowe's 'So It Goes'. Edmunds, however, had recently signed with Led Zeppelin's Swan Song label, which had the kind of financial punch that Stiff Records could only dream of. Ever since The Beatles formed their Apple empire several Big Time Charlie groups had set up record labels. Most were little more than distribution deals that kept them tied to major record companies. Although Led Zeppelin might have suggested otherwise, their Swan Song label was no different. However, their label manager, Alan Callan, saw it differently: "My view of Swan Song was that it was uniquely positioned in that, whilst other artists had set up record companies, the artists' own flow of income was mainly responsible for the outcome of the label. With Swan Song that was not the case. Atlantic were perfectly happy for the label to become a successful label in its own right and take the risks. I thought we have to be careful. We've brought in Bad Company and Dave Edmunds, who were going to be successful, but we were going to struggle with the Pretty Things and Maggie Bell who hadn't done anything for years."

Edmunds' ties to Swan Song Records paid dividends. His albums for them sold more copies than those he'd recorded for Regal Zonophone and RCA combined. And thanks to label mates Bad Company, his profile in America went up a notch when he toured with them in early '77. But it also had its disadvantages. Unlike Robinson and Riviera, who had plenty of time to plan their artists' next career move, Peter Grant was preoccupied with the real money makers, Led Zeppelin, and simply didn't have the time to lavish on anyone else. He also found Edmunds' on-off manager, Jake Riviera, difficult to deal with. "Dave Edmunds and people like that - I just didn't have time to oversee," he wrote in his biography. "Dave had Jake Riviera as a manager anyway, which brought its own set of problems."

Riviera was the first proper manager Edmunds had. "I've never had a manager - I've always been wary of them," he explained. "Jake came along [...] with all these insane ideas and I thought he was crazy, but 98% of the time he's right and ahead of everyone else. He's probably the sharpest creative brain in the music business today," Had it been left to Lowe and Edmunds they would have been content to develop their studio tans and go down the pub. But their manager had other plans and was, insists Edmunds, the driving force behind Rockpile. "Now Terry Williams is free because Man have split up, Billy Bremner's free because Neil Innes' band have split, Nick's around, ready and willing - so let's do it'," Riviera insisted. With Riviera also booking the studio time, Edmunds had no more excuses not to stake his claim for the main chance.

Man had finally decided to call it a day at the end of '76. Internal fractures and stressful tours of America and Europe played a part in their demise, but it was the rise of punk rock that drove the final nail in their coffin (the band reformed in 1983 when the ghosts of punk and new wave had been well and truly exorcised). Edmunds had known Williams for years and shared a stage with him at Man's 1972 Christmas party at the Patti Pavilion, Swansea when they performed a version of Chuck Berry's 'Run Rudolf Run' with Plum Crazy. Williams was also known to Lowe who was impressed with his attitude as much as his drumming. "The thing about Terry Williams is that he's the non-drummer's drummer," he said. "When drummers get together, they're the most boring people on earth. It's like 'What kind of heads do you use, man,' right? I've seen drummers come up to Terry and [say] 'What kind've drums have you got?' and he'll say 'Silver ones.' Terry doesn't have a bee in his bonnet, he'll just do his drumming. He hasn't got any kind of big deal, well YOU-come-over-here-and-try-to-do-it attitude, and drummers are notorious for having chips on their shoulders."

If Terry Williams was a non-drummer's drummer, Billy Bremner was a guitarist's guitarist. Over the years, the affable Scotsman had played with everybody from Lulu to the Walker Brothers and eventually found himself playing the circuit with Neil Innes's Fatso. "I met them [Edmunds and Lowe] when they came to see me play with Neil Innes and Fatso at the Nashville Rooms in London," recalled Bremner. "They asked me then to make up the final spot in Rockpile."

Rockpile would have a shaky start in life. Contractual problems aside, nobody was sure whether or not it was a proper group or just a backing band for whoever needed it most. Initially, Edmunds thought it was going to be a real band of brothers, but that's not how Lowe saw it. As far as he was concerned, it was something fun to do between Brinsley Schwarz and starting his solo career proper. After a few false starts, even Edmunds had to admit that Rockpile was little more than a group that either he or Lowe could tour with. "It wasn't intended to be an ongoing thing," he said. "It was put together for whoever needs it. Last year I needed it, this year Nick needs it."

As the old wave ebbed and the new wave surged, Edmunds and Lowe found themselves surfing its crest. Before it was analysed, categorised and authenticated by the nation's music journalists, new wave was an unwritten book. In August, Marc Zermati organised the first European Punk rock Festival at Montde-Marsan in the south of France. Witnessed by 2,000 curious French concert goers, it was a microcosm of a much larger musical exchange being played out across Britain's pubs, clubs and music press. Of the British groups that appeared, only The Damned could be described as Punk with a capital 'P'. The rest, The Count Bishops, The Gorillas, Roogalator, Eddie and the Hot Rods, Sean Tyla and Nick Lowe's Blue Girls were all refugees from the pub rock circuit. While they could all be said to bridge the gap between old and new, that they could take part in a 'Punk Rock Festival' reveals just how fluid the scene was. Roger Armstrong, who attended the festival suggests: "It was a funny old time, everything was getting invented - including people - and Montde-Marsan was the first big event that attracted attention to the word "Punk". It was about the handover to the new generation."

It wasn't as straightforward a handover as Armstrong suggests. In visual terms it was more like a Venn diagram with both old and new sharing similar musical and cultural sites from which each could appropriate and create new and different styles. If Lowe could quote from Jonathan Richman's 'Roadrunner', there was nothing to stop The Damned from quoting Chuck Berry in 'I Feel Alright'. Punk may have declared 1976 year zero, but its leaders all shared dirty little secrets. Captain Sensible liked nothing better than to listen to 20-minute improvisations by Egg. Mick Jones of The Clash had been in the Mott the Hoople fan club, and uber Punk Sid Vicious had a soft spot for Jim Reeves. Music wasn't contracting, it was expanding into new as yet undefined areas. Anything was possible, and for those with an enquiring mind the possibilities were endless and the potential limitless.

Mont-de-Marsan was only one example of the shared musical landscape that existed. On 5 September, old guard and young Turks collided at the Roundhouse when The Kursaal Flyers, Crazy Cavan and Joe Strummer's new group, The Clash, shared a Sunday night bill. Old habits die hard and the audience seems to have been made up of the old hippie crowd that preferred to enjoy its music sitting cross-legged on the floor rather than dancing the night away like the younger crowd that flocked to see Dr Feelgood and Eddie and the Hot Rods. This didn't go down well with Strummer. Reviewing the gig for the *Melody Maker*, Chas de Whalley wrote: "The more they sat down, the more Strummer screamed at them to stand up."

Strummer had something to prove. The Clash were out to shake things up, but their firebrand rock 'n' roll rhetoric didn't rest well with an audience that wanted to be entertained, not engage in cultural dissent. Not that anybody had figured out how to dance to The Clash or the Sex Pistols, yet. Nor was anybody prepared for the rush of raw power they projected. Punk was still a minority interest, enjoyed by a small and knowing clique looking to escape the boredom of the suburbs. One way to escape the uniform grey wasteland of urban conformity was to head to the 100 Club in the heart of the city and experience its Punk Rock Festival. The event generated double-page spreads in the music press, but it was attended by fewer than 500 like-minded outsiders and music business voyeurs. For the 500 neophytes that attended, it might have felt like something was happening, but for most readers of the music weeklies it was still an unknown, unheard phenomenon. When The Clash supported The Kursaal Flyers they might as well have been pissing in the wind. The night belonged to the headliners who were about to reach the pinnacle of their career.

Despite Polydor Records promised unprecedented promotion for UK Records acts, The Kursaal Flyers second album, *The Great Artiste*, wasn't the success they'd hoped for. The group continued to impress in concert, but thus far their albums had been critically and commercially disappointing. Being signed to a small label might have seemed advantageous, but as the group discovered, the major record companies still had the upper hand. "The reason we signed to a small company was so we wouldn't be competing with fifty other acts for their attention," lead singer Paul Shuttleworth said. "In retrospect, though, a small record company is looked after by a large company, so you're working for a large company anyway, but you're twice removed. Your own record company hasn't really got enough power to support you in the way a record company should support acts."

Moving to CBS Records in the spring of '76, the Kursaals underwent a change in attitude to record production. Their third album, *Golden Mile*, was produced by Mike Batt, the brains behind the Wombles string of hit singles and albums. Who cared if he was best known for producing novelty records by oversized, fluffy children's television characters, if Batt could work his magic on The Kursaal Flyers it would only be for the better. "We went to Mike and said, 'Everybody who's worked with us before has tried to capture that raw, live thing. But we don't want to be raw, we want to be produced,"

Shuttleworth explained. While everybody else was emphasizing the rough edges and cranking up their amplifiers, The Kursaal Flyers wanted pop sophistication. "'Little Does She Know' [has become a hit because] although the songs have always been there, the recordings haven't," explained Shuttleworth. "The performance on vinyl hasn't come across. But this sounds like a proper record."

While the rest of the group sought a more polished production, Douglas wanted to keep the rough edges Batt was employed to remove. "I think the idea basically, was that we wanted to be produced, I've got no disagreement with that ... we just differ on the results," he said. "We need a producer, because producing by committee is not the way to do things; but it's frustrating because when you write a tune, you know how you want it to be, and when you're in the studio you're going to push for it to go that way. When someone else comes in and tries to put their interpretation on it, there's going to be friction." Douglas clashed with Batt while recording the album but, as far as Birch was concerned, the long dreamt of hit single was the opportunity they'd been waiting for. "I always thought it was easy to get a run (of hits) once you get a start. Maybe it's not. We'll see. We're writing singles anyway." To coincide with the release of 'Little Does She Know', The Kursaal Flyers embarked on the biggest tour of their career. As it progressed the single steadily climbed the charts and landed them an appearance on *Top Of The Pops*. However, Douglas could see the writing on the wall. Punk was about to turn the music business upside down, and he felt the Kursaals' brand of pop was nearing its expiry date. Douglas jumped ship to join Eddie and the Hot Rods, because, he claimed: "It was a meeting ground between the way I play - melodically - and the way the band play - intensely energetic and powerful. They needed what I had to give and I needed what they already had." Douglas' defection to Eddie and the Hot Rods marked the beginning of the end for the Kursaals, who never recovered from his departure.

24

I'm Not Interested That You're Interested

Apart from supporting Dr Feelgood at the Marquee, Flip City had failed to make any impact on the pub rock circuit. The reason for this was, according to Graham Parker, because they were so laidback they were practically horizontal. "They didn't have my aggression or energy," he said, "they didn't have what I was putting out, which was, I'm going to show you fuckers that you don't sit cross-legged on the floor! A year later everyone was on stage giving it stick." Parker shared an approach to performance with Strummer and other new wave upstarts, but Costello had yet to find his new wave mojo. Gigs were so thin on the ground they were reduced to playing house parties. But thanks to their feisty manager, Ken Smith, one such booking led to some free time at the BBC's Maida Vale studio. Following in The 101ers footsteps - they'd also recorded at the hallowed BBC studio - Flip City recorded three MacManus compositions 'Exile's Road, 'Baseball Heroes' (re-worked as 'Miracle Man') and 'Radio Soul' (re-worked as 'Radio Radio').

Armed with the group's new demo tape, Smith headed to the Hope and Anchor to bend Dave Robinson's ear and secure them a gig at the pub rock Mecca. "I booked Flip City because I liked their manager Ken - very eager, very keen - but the band couldn't play at all," recalls Robinson. "They never actually played as a unit ever, and you didn't have to play that great in those days for people to feel it was alright." As unimpressed as he was, Robinson agreed to record them at the venue's studio. Over three sessions they cut a batch of MacManus originals and a handful of covers that included Dylan's 'Knocking On Heaven's Door' and Hank Williams' 'You Win Again'. Despite his reservations, Robinson was impressed by their reading of Russell Smith's 'Third Rate Romance' and considered releasing it as a single. The Amazing Rhythm Aces' version was getting heavy airplay on London's commercial radio stations and the savvy Irishman thought he could capitalise on its success by rush releasing Flip City's version. It was the kind of thinking that had driven British record companies in the '50s. Take an American hit, find a group, any group, it didn't really matter, get them to record a note perfect copy as quickly and cheaply as possible and piggyback on the success of the original. Robinson's idea was as limp as Flip City's recording and reveals that he'd yet to think of a way to subvert the music business. Besides he was too preoccupied with another Hope and Anchor contender, Graham Parker, to worry about Flip City.

As exciting as recording at the Hope and Anchor was, MacManus had lost faith in Flip City. Their brand of lightweight country-rock was becoming as unfashionable as their check shirts and flares; it was time for a little reinvention (Ironically when MacManus recorded his debut album, *My Aim Is True*, he was backed by super slick country-rock combo, Clover). Remodelling himself as D. P. Costello he went solo. A smattering of gigs at the Half Moon in Putney did little to further his career, but undeterred he recorded a set of new demos and hawked them round the major labels looking for a deal. The tape reveals that not only had Costello not found his new wave mojo, he was still struggling to find his own voice. Songs like 'Jump Up' and 'Wave A White Flag' were obviously influenced by American singer-songwriters like Randy Newman and James Taylor and way out of step with what was happening on the King's Road. Costello sent his tape to influential broadcaster Charlie Gillett who played it on his radio show. "I really, really liked it. I played it and I didn't get a peep from listeners. I did not get any reaction from listeners," recalled Gillett. "I thought his voice was great, the words were clever, I couldn't understand that I didn't get any feedback about it, because on other occasions I played Graham Parker on my show and whoosh, he got signed up on the basis of one play. The same [happened] later on with Dire Straits."

The expected rush of record company interest having failed to materialise, MacManus approached Gillett about recording for Oval Records. "He was very appreciative of the fact that I played him, and he came to see us. He said, 'I'd love to be on Oval'. We said, 'We can't put you out sounding like this, we need a band'. We didn't have one. It was frustrating to us and on completely good terms [he] understood the situation. I went to Columbia Records, CBS as it was called then, there was an A&R man who was himself American, I played it to him and said, 'I'm convinced whatever people think of this in England, in America they will love this guy'. He didn't get it. I said, 'He's going to be big and you're going to want to sign him in America and you're going to regret it'. He said, 'When he is big we will sign him in America'. And that's what happened."

Costello later put the constant rejections down to "lack of imagination on the part of the people at most of the other labels. "They can't hear something unless it's put on a plate for them. I didn't think it was all that different; maybe they did. I think it was their ears that were at fault, not mine, and fortunately that's the way I kept thinking about it." The only company to offer Costello a deal was Richard Branson's Virgin Records. Having almost signed Kilburn and the High Roads, it was willing to take a chance with unorthodox talent and expressed an interest in signing Costello. But as inexperienced as he was, even Costello recognised a bum deal when it stared him in the face, and declined their offer. An avid reader of the music weeklies, Costello's eyes lit up when he spotted an article about a new independent record company looking to sign new talent. With nothing to lose, he decided to deliver a copy of his demo tape to their office and at the same time pick up a copy of its first release Nick Lowe's 'So It Goes'. "I read about Stiff Records opening for business," he explained. "I told my boss that I had to go home 'sick' and travelled on the Tube a few stops to the Stiff Records office. A charming girl opened the door and politely received my hand-written tape box and that was that. No big interview, no audition, no cigar-chomping mogul."

Costello was known to both Robinson and Riviera but had failed to make an impression on either. Robinson claims that before co-founding Stiff Records he'd already drawn up a list of potential signings that included Costello, but with only the Flip City demo tape to go on he'd been unable to persuade Riviera. If Riviera hadn't been impressed with Costello when he was one fifth of Flip City, that changed when he heard his solo demo tape. "Elvis's tape was actually the very first tape we received at Stiff. It was so weird because I immediately put it on and thought, 'God, this is fuckin' good,'" he enthused.

Costello's transformation was so dramatic that Robinson didn't twig that he'd already recorded him. "He was quite surprised when I turned out to be the same person," says Costello. "When I submitted the tapes to Stiff, he didn't realise that it was the same person who'd done the earlier tape because I used another name then. It turned out he already had over an hour of me on tape and didn't know it." The confusion concerning Costello mattered little, Robinson and Riviera were of one mind and agreed to sign the computer operator. What they couldn't decide on was whether or not to sign him as a song writer or recording artist. As usual Riviera had the last word. "He [Costello] had one song called 'Mystery Dance', which Jake thought would be great for Dave Edmunds, who at that time I'd just started to work with," explained Lowe. "Jake and I listened to the tape together and Jake said, 'No! We won't sign him as a writer, we'll sign him as an actual performer.'"

Besides Costello, the only musical talent Stiff Records could draw on was a bunch of pub rock losers and hippie has-beens. Lowe's 'So It Goes' was followed by 'Between The Lines' by counterculture darlings The Pink Fairies. The group had reformed in 1975 to play a one-off concert at the Roundhouse, which was successful enough to persuade them to have another crack at the big time. Martin Stone was recruited to complete the line-up and, being good friends with Riviera, suggested that Stiff Records might like to issue a couple of songs they'd recently recorded. "[The Pink Fairies] were kind of at the end of their run," explains Robinson. "But they had a track and people who had tracks kept trotting in and you'd think, yeah, why not? Also you thought, you're not a major record company, what is the criteria of what makes it or doesn't make it? If you liked it or you liked the band, and you thought they needed a bit of space you did it."

'Between The Lines' had all the hallmarks of Stiff Records off-kilter approach to marketing. The single was issued in a picture sleeve, a rarity at the time and the company's first, that stated it was a Bacon Records release. From its earliest offerings, Stiff cultivated an offbeat sense of humour and tapped into the developing record collecting scene. Its records were marketed as 'limited editions' (in reality they sold in larger numbers than most mainstream releases) something that the major record companies hadn't cottoned onto. "Collecting records was always retrospective," says Roger Armstrong. "No-one bought new obscure sixties garage records because they thought in five years' time I'll get a tenner for this. There was no real awareness of that. But punk was like that, possibly because the people involved in the scene were buying records in shops like ours ..."

The way independents like Stiff and Chiswick marketed their releases forced major record companies to re-think the way they operated. Within months all of the major record companies were issuing limited edition records pressed on coloured vinyl with picture sleeves. Buying records became fun again and multi-format releases were developed to feed a growing cult of record collecting.

Snappy marketing ideas aside, Stiff Records still faced the problem of getting its records to a wider audience. There was no national mechanism for distributing records outside of the major label set up. All Stiff Records had was a mail order list, a small network of shops and independent distributors like Bizarre and Scotia. Because it didn't have national distribution its releases had to be hunted down and sought out from back street shops on the seedier side of town. But that was part of the mystique it wanted to cultivate. The whole point was that its records weren't part of the mainstream, nor were they available in mainstream outlets. Speaking to *International Times*, Dave Robinson suggested that initially he was content with this arrangement: "Quite a few people are interested but we haven't been able to get the distribution that we'd like to have to keep the things as it is - they all want to start viewing it as a business as usual. They want us to put out more commercial products." 'Product' wasn't a word that was bandied around Stiff Records small office, nor was it much liked by the staff of a new record shop situated near Ladbroke Grove that would play a small but important part in distributing early Stiff releases, and a significant role in shaping the future independent record scene. Geoff Travis started the Rough Trade record shop after returning to London from America, where he amassed a huge record collection used to stock his shop. A hip version of Rock On, it shared Stiff Records devil may care approach and was committed to making alternative music by up and coming groups and labels available to a wider audience. Unlike Rock On, which encouraged vinyl fetishism, Rough Trade took the opposite approach.

The Desperate Bicycles may be credited with kick-starting the do-it-yourself/start-your-own-record label revolution, but Stiff Records was among the first to dispel the myth that only major record companies had the wherewithal and infrastructure to make and distribute records. It had, after all, made much of the fact that it started with a £400 loan. All you needed was a few hours in a cheap recording studio and £150 to press 1,000 singles. If you were very lucky John Peel might play your record on his nightly radio show and shops like Rough Trade and Small Wonder would be only too happy to sell it for you.

Stiff proved it was possible for anyone with a few hundred pounds to make a record but, unlike Rough Trade, it wasn't driven by politics. Stiff Records worked against the grain. A reaction to the unresponsive, lumbering, inflexible, creatively bankrupt majors, it was flexible, open and approachable. In November '76, the *NME* reported Riviera as saying: "There has been a gap between the million quid advance and scuffling about in a cellar. There has to be a middle ground. I believe Stiff is it." Stiff Records didn't play by the rules and had shown it could sell records by groups that the majors would have struggled with. When quizzed by *International Times* about sales figures, Robinson claimed: "Nick Lowe - I think we're pretty close to 10,000. Pink Fairies - we've done about 4,000. Roogalator have done about 3,000 which is all we've pressed, so we're pretty much out of stock on that. That's a different deal to the others. Basically we said we'd do 3,000 of that which we did. That was it, a kind of one-off thing. Tyla's done about 3,500 maybe 4,000. Lew Lewis has done about 5,000."

For a company without a decent distribution deal, these were impressive sales figures. But Stiff couldn't hope to beat the majors at their own game without decent distribution. Nevertheless, Robinson and Riviera had the advantage of being able to act quickly and, sensing the coming musical storm, signed the label's first punk group, The Damned. Chiswick Records had considered signing the group and had financed their first demos but were beaten to the punch by Stiff. "We missed The Damned," recalled Armstrong, "we'd gone to see them early, one of the first Nashville gigs. Jake and Ted and me were all standing at the back after it finished, and we all looked at each other and said, 'That was great, somebody's got to sign them.' It was terrible, but it was great. I went on holiday shortly after that and when I came back I found that Jake had snapped The Damned up and was putting them in to do an album."

Produced by Nick Lowe at Pathway Studio, 'New Rose' held the distinction of being the first Punk record issued by a British record company. Thanks to Stiff Records, The Damned had usurped the Sex Pistols as leaders of the Punk revolution, much to Malcolm McLaren's chagrin. But there was a downside; Stiff Records became the unwitting victim of its own success. "'New Rose' was so popular that the mail order system couldn't cope", recalled Lauder. Something had to be done because it wasn't the first time Stiff Records had lost out on sales of a hot record. "We can easily sell 5,000 EPs in advance, yet only have sufficient funds to place an initial pressing order of 2,000," Riviera explained.

Stiff desperately needed national distribution but the only way to get it was by getting into bed with a major. But because Stiff wasn't playing by the rules, none of the major record companies could figure out how to deal with them. "They're not sure what we're up to and how we can keep selling thousands of records by people they've never heard of or that they wouldn't want to record," said Robinson. United Artists took the plunge and stepped in to distribute 'New

Rose' making it the first punk single with national exposure. But it was only a stop gap solution, Stiff still had to find a long term answer to its supply chain problem. Without an injection of cash and a deal with a major, Stiff wouldn't have a future. The only record company with the nerve to offer a distribution deal was itself an independent. In early '77 Island Records bit the bullet and signed a two year manufacturing and distribution contract with Stiff Records. "This deal has required considerable Dutch Courage on our part," claimed Island Records' Tim Clark. "I only hope it works." It wouldn't. Riviera's response was designed to keep Island on its toes and was typically cavalier: "I am extremely pleased with this arrangement as it allows Stiff to infiltrate the upper echelons of the record industry and still have the autonomy to double-cross unsuspecting musicians."

25
Surfing On A New Wave

In the months following the break-up of Ducks Deluxe, Tyla found himself adrift like so much rock 'n' roll flotsam and jetsam on the waters of a stormy musical sea, with little idea of what his next step would be, beyond that he wanted to call the shots rather than having the management-by-committee situation that being in a group so often entails. In true Tyla style though: "I got it really wrong from the start, because I was never sure of what it was going to be," Tyla admits with commendable honesty.

The Hope and Anchor was still attracting pub rock down-and-outs like moths to a flame, and with little else to do Tyla booked himself into Dave Robinson's studio to record some demos with what was fast becoming The Rumour. Robinson was on the lookout for someone to front this pub rock super group and asked Tyla if he was interested. Although he didn't know what he wanted, Tyla knew The Rumour weren't nearly rough, dirty or raucous enough for his brand of rock' n' roll and told Robinson to keep looking. With hindsight this appears another case of Tyla shooting himself in the foot, but we'll never know if Sean Tyla and the Rumour would have had the same appeal as Graham Parker and the Rumour.

Instead he teamed up with his brother Garry, Help Yourself guitarist Richard Treece and drummer Phil Nedin, to form The Tyla Gang. To get the ball rolling he self-financed some recordings at Rockfield Studios. Holed up in the Welsh countryside, Treece excelled himself and played some blistering guitar on 'Texas Chainsaw Massacre Boogie'. Tyla was blown away by his playing, but when Treece tried to replicate his guitar pyrotechnics on stage he fell apart. When Chas de Whalley reviewed their first chaotic gig at the Newlands Tavern he wasn't impressed. "Admittedly this was their first public appearance and allowances have to be made, but there were cracks and flaws tonight that no amount of onstage confidence can eradicate," he observed. It was time to make some changes. Treece was ousted and replaced by an ex-member of Man, Alan 'Tweke' Lewis. "With Tweke on board the band got really hot," said Tyla. "We got so tight, I was sweating buckets trying to keep in the game! We started gigging a bit around the pubs and the whole thing began to feel very good Indeed." Next to go was Tyla's brother who swapped rock 'n' roll for a steady job in Civvy Street.

Tyla was the kind of guy who needed his ego checked and massaged, a difficult balancing act. Without a manager to play Sigmund Freud, Tyla was nothing. "My sole motivation comes from people's belief in me, because it's a catalyst," he told the *NME*. "But the most important thing is that I have to believe them." Despite doing the rounds he couldn't find a label that was prepared to make the leap of faith and believe in him. "Island offered us a deal and then reneged," he recalls, "Chrysalis listened to the tapes four times and still turned us down and A&M wanted to hear a complete finished album! I could see the same old pattern beginning to emerge and I had to sort it out - we needed a manager."

Tyla had simply been looking in the wrong place. Tired of hawking his demos round uninterested record companies, he turned to the world's most flexible record label to kick start his career. Robinson and Riviera were beginning to build a small empire on the failed careers of pub rock has-beens and Tyla was a prime candidate for their recently launched label. Impressed with the demos he'd recorded at Rockfield Studios, they cut a deal and issued 'Styrofoam' and 'Texas Chainsaw Massacre Boogie' as a double 'B' side single - a real artistic breakthrough. At the same time Tyla became an Advancedale-managed artist. With a hip management team and the world's coolest record label behind him, things were starting to look up. However, with Tyla, life is never that simple. Stiff wanted to follow the single with an album and sent The Tyla Gang back to Rockfield Studios to make it, but there was a caveat from Riviera who asked Tyla to "complete it in five days and keep costs below £1,600, citing as an example The Damned, who did theirs in two days for four hundred," Tyla explains. The sessions didn't go well, and according to Tyla they "sounded like shit". The proposed album never materialised, though one track, 'The Young Lords', did surface on the *A Bunch Of Stiffs* album.

Like his former band mate, Nick Garvey found life after Ducks Deluxe tough. Exchanging his bass for a cement mixer, and the snug of the Torrington for a cold, wet building site, he soon drifted back to the pub rock circuit. Garvey recruited Richard Wernham and Robert Gotobed to form The Snakes and worked up a set of rough and ready rock 'n' roll. "We used to just play Chuck Berry songs and the like, no originals," he recalled. We were not, strictly speaking, a hot commercial property." They were so un-commercial that initially they didn't even bother with a bass player. The Snakes was simply a fun way to make a few bob and pull a few birds. With no thoughts of turning professional they would have drifted in pub rock purgatory for as long as the fun lasted. That was until an old friend of Garvey's persuaded them otherwise. Richard Ogden, former press officer at United Artists, thought they had potential and offered to become their manager. Ogden put the group on a small retainer and began planning their rise to stardom.

Although they were a dyed in the wool covers band, Garvey had a stash of songs he'd written with Andy McMaster that Ogden used to secure a one-off deal with the Dutch Dynamite label. But in keeping with their credo of only playing covers these were disregarded in favour of the Flamin' Groovies' 'Teenage Head' and the old R&B favourite 'Lights Out'. Garvey preferred interpreting other people's songs rather than performing his own because: "I could never hit upon a style or an attitude though that said anything at all while at the same time allowing me to feel comfortable performing it." Garvey rediscovered his song writing prowess when he teamed up with his former band mate Andy McMaster, who'd recently secured a deal with a music publisher. The magic was still there, as was the Ducks' edgy attitude, only now they were stylistically simpatico with the emergent new wave scene. "Well, me and Nick just started writing songs together and were really surprised at how good they were, so we thought we'd better put a group together to play them," explained McMaster. "They were pop songs with good melodies, but real hard-edged ..."

In November '76 they headed to Pathway Studios to record some demos. "We demoed four new songs at Pathway with Andy on the bass, me on guitar and a Welsh drummer called [Phil] Nedin, from Sean's band, whom we exhausted; we played a lot faster than he was used to, they were exciting tracks," explained Garvey. Previously Garvey had played bass, but now decided he felt more comfortable playing guitar. Like many bassists he'd been coerced into the role because nobody else wanted the job. "When Nick played bass with Ducks Deluxe, I never saw him play bass except at gigs, at home, it was always guitar," McMaster explained. Because the new group was going to be guitar based, McMaster's keyboard skills were put on hold while he took bass lessons from Garvey. "I didn't know what the instrument was like at all, so I thought I'd like to try it," he explained.

Finding a drummer with enough stamina for the job was easy; Garvey simply called Richard Wernham, who in typical punk style decided to call himself Ricky Slaughter. Finding a second guitarist was slightly more difficult. Their initial choice was Rob Hendry, who appeared with The Motors when they made their debut on 4 March '77 at Stevenage College. Five dates in London (including the Marquee) followed and on 22 March the group recorded three tracks for a John Peel session. Ogden was using all his music business connections to promote the group and just two months from making their debut The Motors signed with Virgin Records. However, Hendry wasn't long for the group and was replaced by Bram Tchaikovsky (real name Peter Bramall), who had auditioned for the band in the time honoured way of responding to an ad in *Melody Maker*. "It happened right away," he recalled. "Once I heard it, I knew it was the band for me. It moved, it was earthshaking!"

Live dates with The Heavy Metal Kids preceded recording sessions with producer Robert John 'Mutt' Lange. Garvey, however, was unhappy with Lange's production, much preferring the Pathway demos. "Menacing it was," he said. "A clean crystal clear sort of sound, instead of just plain fast, which is what we actually degenerated to in the end." Looking back, McMaster claimed that the music was shaped as much by record company pressure as by the pervading musical environment. "We signed a recording contract and we started doing it for real," he said. "We had deadlines to meet and that changes the music."

26
Sneakin' Suspicion

With a number one album and a sell-out tour to their credit, Dr Feelgood should have been happy campers. But the pressure of life in the fast lane was pulling them apart rather than drawing them together. Johnson was feeling the pressure most of all; his teetotal ways and loner insularity never sat comfortably with either the rock 'n' roll lifestyle or the Feelgoods' hard drinking image. Flung into the deep end, without a thought of how they'd cope with fame and wealth, tensions within the group had been building for some time. The final straw, at least as far as Johnson was concerned, came during sessions for their fourth studio album, *Sneakin' Suspicion*. Bert de Couteaux was brought in to produce, partly at the suggestion of their American record company, to buff up their sound. Brilleaux liked what de Couteaux had done with Albert King and thought he could do something similar for Dr Feelgood. "I suppose it had a lot to do with sounding more 'professional'. If only to show everyone we weren't just a bunch of ol' skifflers."

Although Johnson went along with the idea, his vision for *Sneakin Suspicion* was very different. "More ethnic, more raw than it was, in order to gain greater freedom that way, like Beefheart: just get totally crazy within this thing that we could do," he told the *NME*. According to Brilleaux the sessions began as amicably as they had always done: "That's why Johnson's departure was such a bolt out of the blue ...." Brilleaux must have been putting on a brave face though as all the signs of Johnson's growing unease had been visible for some time; his dislike of lavish parties, a perceived lack of respect for their fans, disgust at conspicuous corporate over-indulgence, and the thought of having to tour America - a country he abhorred - combined with the pressures of writing more songs all added to his unhappiness. Speaking to the *Melody Maker* just before recording *Sneakin' Suspicion*, Johnson put his misery down to the group's success and yearned for a Paradise Lost: "Sometimes you want to go back to the pubs. These big gigs get a bit much after a while. There's a danger you'll lose the atmosphere."

If Brilleaux noticed this change in the group he wasn't saying. Neither did he experience the same pressures as his partner. He didn't have to worry about writing hits, and if things became too much he could always relax with a drink or two. Johnson's indulgence, speed, didn't relax him - it had the opposite effect. Once they entered the studio, the pressure was piled on and Johnson was persuaded to try a song he'd never intended to record with Dr Feelgood. "I had written this other song ['Paradise'] ages before, which I never intended for the Feelgoods to record," he said. "Tim Hinkley, who had come down to play keyboards on the LP, had heard it and suggested that we try it. I said I'd not really thought about it. Anyway, I rearranged it a bit, and we'd laid down a backing track, and one evening Lee came to my room and said, 'Wilk, I can't do that song, I just can't'. So, I said, 'OK if you can't, that's the end of it." Unhappy with Johnson's take on The Byrds' 'Triad', a song that resulted in its author, David Crosby, being sacked, Brilleaux pressed Johnson to record 'Lucky Seven', a song written by their old mate Lew Lewis. Wilko's response was emphatic: "If that record goes on the album, I'll leave the band. I don't want to be heavy about it. but that's the way it is. It isn't Dr Feelgood."

When asked, Johnson maintained that his departure had everything to do with an unbridgeable fissure within the group and nothing to do with disputes over songs. "It was nothing to do with that. That was just some bullshit," Johnson explained. "There had been a lot of tension that had built up. I was teetotal then, and they used to like a drink. Lemmy from Motorhead used to say it never worked 'cos you're a speed freak and they're all drunks."

Johnson used the argument as an excuse to throw another wobbler - his biggest yet. "It was miserable at the end when it sank in that they didn't want me," he recalled. "People were looking at me as if I was weird. I remember being so fucked up and lonely in this hotel in Paris and not being able to say anything, staring at my plate and then realising that everybody was looking at me, standing up, walking out and thinking, I've done it again, another wobbler. I hate to think of all my wobblers, my moods, my isolation. I used to act heavy and be an intolerable twat when all I really wanted to do was ask for help. But I made it impossible for anyone to reach out to me. I wasn't wronged, it just got to the point where people couldn't stand me."

Sneakin' Suspicion was issued a few weeks after the debut album by Joe Strummer's new group, The Clash. The Feelgoods had been wrong footed, de Couteaux made them sound as safe and predictable as the mainstream pop they'd fought to undermine. It was a production too far and left the group sounding distanced from the scene it influenced. Johnson had been right in wanting to make it rawer. Dr Feelgood had lost the authentic punk posture that had made them so popular. Although the album sounded like it had been recorded by a group of impostors, it still managed to squeeze its way into the top ten. Naturally, CBS Records in America loved it, it was, however, the last Dr Feelgood album the company would issue. That particular territory was now closed, forever.

Johnson's departure forced Brilleaux into some serious soul searching and briefly considered his position in the group. "Maybe it's time to leave the business ... with a bit of dignity, y'know, but then I thought - I like this. I want to carry on." It wasn't going to be impossible to keep the group going without Johnson, but it was going to be difficult to recruit another guitarist with his originality. Henry McCullough and Tim Hinkley were recruited as temporary replacements for a short European tour. This could have turned into a permanent arrangement, the option was certainly considered, but the pair weren't quite right in terms of feel. "We were lookin' for somebody that was goin' to join us as a part of Dr Feelgood and somebody as hungry as us."

Brilleaux told *Melody Maker*.

Auditions for Johnson's permanent replacement were held at Feelgood House on Canvey Island where they found a 23-year-old guitarist, John 'Gypie' Mayo, who was every bit as hungry as they were. While Dr Feelgood were breaking in their new axeman, Johnson set about assembling his new group. Initial reports suggested that he was rehearsing with ex-Chilli Willi bassplayer Paul Riley and ex-T.Rex drummer Davey Lutton. However, Lutton was quickly replaced by another ex-member of Chilli Willi, Pete Thomas, who'd recently returned from California. History would record that none of the aforementioned would form Johnson's new group, The Solid Senders. When the group did appear towards the end of the year, Johnson confirmed its line-up to the *NME*. "There's John Potter on piano, Steve Lewins who used to be in The Count Bishops on bass and Alan Platt from Salt on drums."

Having previously shown nothing but contempt for punk rock, Brilleaux realised that *Sneakin' Suspicion* had been a mistake. What was needed was a return to the raw R&B that originally defined the group. Who better to produce them than their one-time equipment handler and now in-demand producer, Nick Lowe? If Lowe had spent the preceding year doing odd jobs for the Feelgoods and answering the telephone at Stiff Records, the previous six months had been a whirlwind of activity. His one-off performance with Dave Edmunds at the Hope and Anchor had led to the formation of Rockpile with Billy Bremner (guitar) and Terry Williams (drums).

The group made its debut supporting Man at the Roundhouse in December '76 followed by some low-key appearances on the pub circuit. Lowe had also been busy recording a follow up to 'So It Goes' with Edmunds, Steve Goulding of the Rumour (drums) and Roger Bechirian (keyboards) that would form the irreverently titled *Bowi* EP. (David Bowie had recently issued his *Low* album, so obviously Riviera and Lowe had to make a jokey reference to the thin white duke's inability to spell Nick's surname. Barney Bubbles even went as far as to have Lowe photographed against a similar burnt orange background to that used on the Bowie album).

However, before Lowe had a chance to promote his new EP, it was time to put the new Feelgoods' album into pre-production. Lowe decamped to Feelgood House to knock the album into shape before heading to his home from home, Pathway Studios. The new Dr Feelgood album would be a return to the rough and ready minimalism of the group's first album. Simplicity was the key and as Lowe preferred feel over perfection, he did his usual trick and fired them up with copious amounts of alcohol. "He was a real one-take merchant like they say," recalled Brilleaux. "Just bash it down and tart it up later. That really is his motto." Issued in September '77, *Be Seeing You* was up against some pretty strong competition. According to Mick Farren, Dr Feelgood now occupied an uneasy middle ground that was as unsatisfying as a Chinese meal. "They still play basic, ballsy R&B. But once you've said that, you've said it all - and in the long run that's hardly good enough."

Dr Feelgood found it difficult to progress beyond the basic R&B template and never would. What you saw was what you got. The shock of the new had long worn off and with the advent of Punk, Dr Feelgood seemed as cosy as the snug at the Hope and Anchor. Farren concluded his review by suggesting that the Feelgoods had lost their way and were becoming conservative compared to the anarchic zeitgeist that was prevalent in late 1970s music: "Conservatism (with a small c) may be okay if you're a merchant banker. If you're a rock and roll band it's the path to stagnation."

27
Cider Bottles At Dawn

In the few months since it started trading, Stiff Records had established the kind of reputation on which empires are built. It led where others followed, had a knack for spotting new and exciting talent and could shift vinyl by no-hopers like it was going out of fashion. To be a Stiff recording artist was to be different, challenging and exciting. What Stiff Records lacked in financial clout it made up for in flair, imagination and talent. Its distribution deal with Island Records gave it the kind of national coverage other independents could only dream of. Everything was in place for Stiff to produce its first chart hero. Charlie Gillett knew Elvis Costello was a star in waiting, but he had to pass because he didn't have a group to back him; Riviera and Robinson did - Clover. A group of country-rock loving hippies from Mill Valley, California, which featured the soon-to-be-famous Huey Lewis, they were the quintessence of everything about to be washed away by the new wave. Advancedale brought them over to England, signed them to Vertigo Records and put them to work. They gigged constantly, recorded a Nick Lowe produced single, 'Chicken Funk', an album, *Unavailable*, produced by John 'Mutt' Lange, and backed Twiggy on her album, *Please Get My Name Right*. As soon as they finished recording with the world's first supermodel they began working with this year's model, Elvis Costello.

Before Riviera and Robinson committed what little dosh they had to recording an album with the unproven singer-songwriter, they spent £50 on two songs, 'Radio Sweetheart' and 'Mystery Dance', recorded with John McFee, Mickey Shine and Nick Lowe. The results confirmed what they'd believed all along, this man had talent; but for once they were stumped with what to do with it. "At one point it was seriously suggested that I share a debut album with Wreckless Eric, supposedly in the style of the Chuck meets Bo release on Chess," recalled Costello. "I just happened to visit Pathway on the day of Wreckless' first session. While Mr Lowe took him round to the pub to build up his courage, I cut enough new demos to make nonsense of this idea." Presenting his managers with embryonic versions of 'Welcome To The Working Week', 'Miracle Man' and 'Waiting For The End Of The World', there was little they could do but agree to finance a full album.

With Clover in tow, minus Alex Call and Huey Lewis, Costello found himself "pinned behind an acoustic baffle with my amp and a vocal mike" in what resembled a cold, damp telephone box. Time spent rehearsing with Clover at Hedley Grange paid dividends and under Lowe's direction they completed the album in six four-hour sessions. Lowe got results by stoking up the group and capturing the excitement on tape. "When I think about how Nick produced this record I have a mental picture of a big cloud of Senior Service smoke and his arms waving wildly about the tiny control booth," recalled Costello. "He was emotional, hilarious, incredibly enthusiastic and generous, though I certainly wouldn't have embarrassed him by saying any of this at the time."

Recording the album was the easy part, selling it was going to be altogether more challenging. *My Aim Is True* might have been packed full of great songs but it didn't sound like the future. Compared to the raucous blasts of teen angst that were beginning to find release on vinyl, *My Aim Is True* sounded tame and restrained. If Costello was a vengeful, bitter and twisted young man, he didn't sound it with Clover backing him. Riviera was going to have to work overtime to make him a star. His secret weapon was the talented graphic artist Barney Bubbles. Pooling their ideas, they set about creating an image for the singer that was provocative, shocking and guaranteed to grab the nation's jaded journalists' attention.

Phase one was to re-name their protege; D. P. Costello being not nearly rock 'n' roll enough. Taking a leaf from Larry Parnes' book and the Punk fad for silly names, Riviera proclaimed that from now on D. P. Costello would be known as 'Elvis Costello'. "I thought D. P. Costello sounded like Billy J. Kramer, so that was out," recalled Riviera. "I also got him to wear horn-rims. The idea was that he would be like Buddy Holly on acid." Robinson and Riviera claimed that Costello was more than happy to go along with the idea, but Costello suggests otherwise. "I didn't feel I had any say in it really, it felt like it was happening to me. Was it a good idea? Probably not? Do I care? No. There were crazier things going on around me, I got off pretty lightly. (The early marketing) all felt like a huge prank, which it still does. It seemed so ludicrous - I'm not even a big Elvis Presley fan."

If Nick Lowe could quote from rock 'n' roll's back pages when writing pop songs, why not adopt the same approach to creating an artist's persona. It was a daring idea; Elvis Presley was, after all, the originator, the one who'd kick-started the rock 'n' roll revolution, the undisputed king. Without the changes being wrought by the Punk revolt the idea could easily have backfired. Six months earlier and Riviera's wheeze might have positioned Costello as a novelty act. Timing was everything and once again Riviera's was spot on. It was flawlessly in keeping with the times. Joe Strummer had seen the future too and there was no place for Presley, The Beatles or The Rolling Stones in his vision of 1977. Like Strummer's protest song, the new moniker was a poke at the bloated corpse that Presley, rock 'n' roll and the music business had become. It also had the effect of erasing Costello's recent past and presented him a new as a mysterious outsider whose ideas and attitudes sat somewhat uneasily with those of his snottynosed contemporaries. The brief was to package Costello's first single with the minimum of information to add to his air of mystery, and should curious journalists ask any awkward questions there'd be no answers forthcoming from Stiff Records.

Issued in March 1977, 'Less Than Zero' was a critical success but an unmitigated flop. Its theme of hypocrisy and institutionalised racism captured the zeitgeist and was as pointed as anything Lydon or Strummer were writing. Like all great artists, Costello was perfectly in tune with his times and had a knack of expressing himself with a contemporary turn of phrase. It was this as much as anything else that captivated Robinson. "I like folk music, I suppose, and that's really what the search was for. I thought The Beatles were folk music. People who were writing about the social place they were in. That I think was true and it's really down to songwriters," he explained.

Costello was one of those songwriters, but if his single had a failing it was that it sounded like a more sophisticated version of Flip City. Clover's slick Californian musicianship didn't dovetail with the sentiment Costello was attempting to convey. Even when it was performed with the Attractions it sounded a little pedestrian. Had the single been supported by a national tour and received some decent airplay it might have fared better, but without either it sank without trace. Never was a single more aptly titled.

With only ten singles under its belt, Stiff Records had managed to create a formidable reputation as the new wave label. Although none of its early singles made it into the charts, the disappointing response to Costello's debut single must have been cause for concern. Robinson and Riviera knew it was going to take more than a few snappy slogans and John Peel to turn their bunch of pub rock rejects into stars. But with a lot of hard work, strategic marketing, good press, and a little luck, their dream would become a reality.

Issued on 27 May, Costello's second single, 'Alison', sold no better than his first. A bittersweet ballad, it was wildly out of step with what was happening at the Vortex and the Roxy and completely wrong footed the public and music press alike. By now Punk had really taken off with The Stranglers' debut album sitting in the top five, The Clash at 12 and The Jam at 20. The revolution wasn't quite as comprehensive as the music weeklies suggested because there was still plenty of room for Genesis, Wings and Fleetwood Mac in the charts.

If Robinson and Riviera wanted to position their protege within the Punk milieu then 'Alison' wasn't going to do it. According to Robinson, a lot of thought and energy went into every single Stiff issued. "It's not a question of putting out singles because that's what the act's contract states - we wouldn't be able to survive in that area," he explained. "We have to believe in a record and a lot of research goes on before we make a judgement." If 'Alison' didn't happen for Costello as Robinson and Riviera planned, it was, however, proof that he was a remarkable talent capable of punching well above his weight. 'Alison' was a surprisingly mature song for one so young and quickly established itself as a classic. Like most of what appeared on *My Aim Is True*, it was written in the summer of '76, late at night after Costello had clocked off work. Like Lowe, Costello wasn't afraid to borrow from his favourite songwriters, but he was a little more subtle with his references. "I had based the chorus of 'Alison' on the Detroit Spinners' 'Ghetto Child'," he confessed, "but I don't think I mentioned this at the session." It was during this session that Lowe knew he was working with somebody special. "For someone as young as he was to be so clear and in control of what he was trying to portray and get across was maturity beyond his years. Understated and very soulful. I'm not ashamed to admit that I cried."

To coincide with the release of 'Alison', Costello supported Graham Parker and the Rumour at the Nashville Rooms. Even if the few hundred people who saw the shows had rushed out and bought the single, it would have made little difference to its chance of chart success. Hit or miss, 'Alison' convinced Robinson and Riviera that the time was right to release *My Aim Is True*. The first artist to sign to Stiff Records - everyone else remained free agents or had signed one-off deals - Costello received an advance of £150, a weekly pay cheque matching his wages at Elizabeth Arden, a new cassette tape recorder and a Vox battery powered practice amp. Not even The Damned got a battery powered practice amp! Plans were also drawn up to fit him out with a group, a tour, a third single and a high profile advertising campaign to promote his album.

Pete Thomas re-acquainted himself with his former manager when The Damned hit Los Angeles during their American tour. Riviera convinced Thomas that he should return to London, it, rather than Los Angeles, being where the action was. Flown back to London at the expense of Virgin Records on the pretext that he was going to join Wilko Johnson's new band, Thomas was poached for Costello. "It seemed like a good time to be in England," he recalled, "so I went back and auditioned for EC with the other two Attractions who had answered ads in the *Melody Maker*." The other two were Bruce Thomas (no relation) and Steve Nason.

Bruce Thomas had been knocking around the music business for years and was in fact a seasoned musician, having played bass with Quiver long before it teamed up with the Sutherland Brothers and found success. Thomas prepared for the audition by learning both Costello singles before heading to a seedy rehearsal room in Putney to meet the surly singer. "I went to the audition and sort of pretended I was learning them for the first time. So I looked like I was really competent," he explained. However, the apparent ease with which he picked up songs didn't impress Costello, who had some concerns about the bass player's age and musical tastes. But fate was on his side. Pete Thomas was a long-time fan of Quiver and persuaded Costello to employ the former hippie bassist. "In the end, he [Pete Thomas] probably swung it for me - he was probably so determined to play with me he overrode Elvis's desire not to have me," says Bruce Thomas. Steve Nason, renamed Nieve once he joined the Attractions, had attended the Royal College of Music, had no experience of playing in a group, but knew his way round a keyboard and had attitude: he was hired on the spot.

Christened The Attractions they made their debut backing Costello at a private function at Island Records the day after Stiff issued '(The Angels Want To Wear My) Red Shoes' as a 45. Nick Kent witnessed the gig and began the process of kingmaking. His review made bold claims suggesting that Costello was rock 'n' roll's latest and greatest saviour. If 'Alison' had misdirected the music press, it was obvious from Kent's review that Costello was much more than some kind of new wave answer to Eric Carmen. Kent's closing sentence said it all: "When all the self-conscious new-wavers are drowning, Elvis will be on top. No shit."

Elvis Costello and the Attractions made their public debut in Penzance, far from the prying eyes of London's journalists. Unknown to them, they were about to enter the eye of the new wave hurricane. Robinson, Riviera and Island Records' marketing department were working overtime to ensure their success. Three days after playing in the extreme South-West of the country, Costello, minus the Attractions, made his television debut performing 'Alison' on Granada Television's *Granada Reports*. The appearance coincided with the release of his debut album. Everything and everyone was focused on turning this £1000 investment into a goldmine.

Costello appeared on the cover of *My Aim Is True* grasping his new Fender Jazzmaster guitar for all he was worth. His exaggerated knock-kneed pose, a grotesque parody of the kind of rock 'n' roll cliche that had been handed down by everybody from Eddie Cochran to Pete Townshend, was another example of Riviera inspired japery that was entirely misread by everybody who saw it. Photographed by Keith Morris, Costello was inspired to throw exaggerated rock 'n' roll shapes by Barney Bubbles, who was directing the photo shoot from behind the camera. "People wanted to believe that this was some sort of very aggressive image, but if you look at the outtakes, I'm laughing in almost all the shots," Costello recalled. "There was just something inherently ludicrous about that pose to me, because it was the opposite of what I felt like. I didn't feel like a rock 'n' roll star. I was just some guy working in an office who'd written some songs. And the fact that I had this absurd name and was posing like a rock 'n' roller with these splayed legs - it was a satire."

It might have been a spoof, but it was a perfect image that caught the public imagination and made for a great advertising campaign. Double-page spreads were booked for all the weekly music papers. Each featured part of a "cut out and keep" poster based on Morris' photograph. The idea was that fans would have to buy all the papers to collect the set. It was all part of Stiff's ongoing strategy to tap into the developing cult of record collecting and to make music fun again. "It was to attract attention and amuse journalists," says Robinson. "You've got to remember there were four papers on the streets weekly, they all needed stuff in them so it was a golden time for people like us, who were thinking on our feet and were getting a bit excited and were having a few drinks every night." Riviera had run a similar campaign to promote Chilli Willi and the Red Hot Peppers' second album, but at the time nobody had the imagination to see its possibilities. The whole point of the exercise was to engage, intrigue and make people aware of the record. The difference with *My Aim Is True* was that Riviera was the boss now and could pretty much do what he liked. The campaign might have been risky and expensive but as far as Riviera was concerned it was the logical extension of the campaign he'd run with Chilli Willi a few years earlier. "We wanted to really engage with fans and, since there were so many papers, why not come up with a collectable series?" he reasoned.

A series of collectable posters wasn't enough; Stiff also manufactured a series of collectable album covers. Its first such effort was The Damned's debut album, initial copies of which featured a photograph of Island Records recording artists Eddie and the Hot Rots in place of The Damned. "It was fun wasn't it," says Robinson. "It was an actual mistake which we then turned to our advantage." If the Hot Rods cover was indeed a 'mistake', the Costello cover was a carefully contrived conceit. The back cover had a photograph of Costello surrounded by a typical Bubbles trademark, a wash of fluorescent colour. Bubbles was a stickler for detail and often visited the printers to ensure it met his exacting standards. Riviera accompanied him one day and discovered that the colour could be changed at no extra cost. "We ended up doing at least 50 versions. I remember Barney came in with a colour code pamphlet for bathroom tiles, and we instructed the printer to change the ink on every batch of 5,000 according to the colour on it," explained Riviera.

Few people would have bought every variant of the Costello cover, but the music business was taking note of what Stiff was doing and had begun to flood the market with similarly marketed limited editions. "People are beginning to appreciate what we're doing and there have been some direct lifts of Stiff's marketing approach," Riviera told the *Melody Maker* in August '77. No sooner had Stiff put the fun back into rock 'n' roll than the music press cried hype. Multi-formats devalued music, it was argued; people were buying records not because of the quality of the music, but for the colour of the vinyl or for the pretty picture sleeve. Max Bell claimed: "The recent push on 'fun promotion' means you're now a collector whether you like it or not. Or rather, you aren't a collector at all, you're a glorified consumer."

The downside might have been that a few people bought the records simply because they were pressed on coloured vinyl, but at least they bought them and might even have enjoyed them had they bothered to listen. The other reason for the sudden rush of limited editions was the high initial chart placing they created. The major record companies weren't slow to catch on and Roger Armstrong of Rock On/Chiswick Records could see that, despite what Chiswick and Stiff had achieved, the majors still held the upper-hand: "Selling records is about mechanisms and efficiency. Getting records into the shops is more important than promotion because singles are already artefacts; they serve as their own band promotion," he claimed.

Stiff Records knew the importance of getting records into shops, that was why it was distributed by Island Records and employed a plugger to service national and commercial radio stations. Ironically, Costello's '(The Angels Want To Wear My) Red Shoes' wasn't pressed on coloured vinyl, didn't have a picture sleeve nor was it a limited edition. Nevertheless, this 'radical' marketing strategy did the trick and the single sold well enough to get Elvis Costello and the Attractions their first national television appearance on *Top Of The Pops*. Although the single failed to chart, their appearance on the BBC's flagship pop programme helped promote the album which sold a reported 11,000 copies in its first 3 days and eventually reached a respectable number 14 in the album charts.

If Riviera claimed publicly that he could do without the major record companies, in private he knew that he couldn't survive without them. He'd experienced major record company power at first hand when he accompanied Dr Feelgood to the Columbia conference in San Diego. Riviera and Robinson might have been happy selling records from the back of a car; they may even have given the impression that they couldn't give two hoots about the major record companies, but they both knew the only way to the top was to get into bed with them. Naturally, Riviera wasn't going to do anything as boring as make an appointment or go cap in hand to some cigar chomping executive. He planned something altogether more entertaining than that. Targeting one of the biggest and most powerful record companies in the world, Riviera planned to highjack Columbia Records annual convention, which was to be held at London's Hilton hotel, with a little street theatre. Two Stiff Records employees were dispatched to the Hilton with placards reading 'Welcome To England, The Home Of Stiff Records', and to liven things up a bit, Costello would perform a solo set right outside the hotel entrance.

Costello cranked up his tiny battery amplifier and powered his way through 'Welcome To The Working Week', 'Waiting For The End Of The World' and 'Mystery Dance' drawing a crowd of bemused tourists, Columbia Records' kingpins and the local police. Walter Yetnikoff, head of Columbia/CBS Records, caught only a few seconds of Costello's act before racing into the hotel to order some more hookers for a poolside meeting. Journalist Lisa Robinson tried to persuade him to stop and listen by telling him Costello was a star in waiting, but Yetnikoff recalls dismissing her pleas with: "Fine, I'll let my A&R men sign him." Yetnikoff was one of the most powerful men in the music business and he knew it. A self-confessed hedonist, he was Mr Excess and exactly the kind of major label bigwig Riviera loved to wind up. But he was also the kind of person you didn't want to piss off. Riviera and Robinson would have to walk a fine line or risk losing everything. The pair began negotiations with Columbia Records to secure a production-distribution deal for Stiff Records in America that would transform the company from a small independent with attitude into a multinational with proper budgets and real clout. However, Riviera was about to throw a spanner in the works that would scupper the Columbia deal but secure Lowe and Costello a contract with the label.

Riviera had grown tired of the day-to-day frustrations of running a record company and wanted out. "We were kind of pirates, people with huge egos, so it wasn't going to work with Dave and I banging heads all the time, so it was much better to let him get on with it," recalled Riviera. Robinson was completely thrown by Riviera's news which threatened to undermine everything he'd work for. "It was a total shock, totally out of the blue, when we were in the middle of negotiating a very, very decent deal, it was going to set us up for the next five years, we were making a deal with CBS as was and Sony as is now, and they were really hot to trot, they really liked Elvis, they liked Nick."

As far as Riviera was concerned Stiff Records had served its purpose. It had launched the careers of Lowe and Costello and now it was time to move on. Commenting on his decision to dissolve his partnership with Robinson, Riviera told *Billboard*: "Ever since hearing 'Anarchy In The UK' by Johnny Rotten and his Sex Pistols, I have come to realise that the only validity in life is to build to destroy." Riviera hadn't destroyed Stiff, but he had taken it to the edge. Dividing the spoils of their partnership, Robinson kept The Damned, Clover and Graham Parker and the Rumour for Advancedale and retained control of Stiff Records. Riviera took Costello, Lowe and the Yachts for Riviera Global Management and signed them to Columbia Records for America and to Andrew Lauder's new Warner Brothers-backed company Radar Records for Britain.

Robinson's luck continued to hold. Stiff Records was hot property and although Riviera had scuppered the Columbia deal, Arista Records were also hot to trot. Arista Records snatched the deal to distribute Stiff Records in America partly through fear and one-upmanship. Andrew King explained why: "In America, big deals come out of the barrel of a smoking gun. It's no good having great records, you have to have great records and a gun. Deals get done out of fear. People like Arista don't do deals because they think your stuff is wonderful, they do deals because they are frightened that somebody else is going to do the deal. It is all done on terror."

Once again, Stiff came out on top. The deal generated some much needed income, helped launch the company in America and set it up to benefit from a bigger and better deal with Columbia Records further down the line. Although Arista pumped a small fortune into a high profile marketing campaign and a tour to promote Ian Dury and The Blockheads, neither *New Boots And Panties!!* nor *Live Stiffs Live* sold well. A pragmatic Paul Conroy told *Rolling Stone* that American kids would have to wake up and broaden their tastes. Journey and REO Speedwagon were out and Elvis Costello and Ian Dury were in. He also noted that Stiff Records would have a real problem with the American press, because unlike England where they could pull a publicity stunt one day and it would be in the papers the next that wouldn't happen in America because it didn't have music weeklies. Finally, there was radio. Most stations in America only played Top Forty records and didn't give new bands a chance to be heard or develop.

All Stiff Records had to do was bring about a complete change in attitudes to dominate the American music scene: an impossible task. Even if American kids woke up to what was happening in England and Europe, it would have to be on a scale equivalent to Beatlemania. Stiff Records had some good acts, but nothing to rival The Beatles in terms of talent or marketability. The lack of a weekly music press in America didn't help either. With only monthly publications to promote its records, and with little support from Top Forty radio stations, Stiff would struggle to get itself noticed, let alone effect change on the kind of scale it needed to succeed. When Stiff Records did eventually secure a distribution deal with Columbia Records for America, a defiant Robinson said: "We have been waiting nine months for this deal and this completes our world domination." Far from achieving world domination, under the Columbia/Epic umbrella, Stiff's only real success was with an artist who wasn't even signed to the company in Britain, Ian Gomm. His sole top twenty hit, 'Hold On', was the only single issued by Stiff/Epic to chart in America.

28
Old Wave, New Wave, No Wave

Since releasing their debut album, Graham Parker and the Rumour had gigged constantly, opened for Ace and Kokomo, recorded a follow up album, *Heat Treatment*, and undertaken their first American tour. Parker's razor-sharp songs, combined with the Rumour's ferocious energy levels, established them as one of the most exciting acts in the country. Constantly pushing to increase his profile, and with his heart set on chart success, Parker suggested they record a cover of an old Trammps song. "Graham wanted to cover this song called 'Hold Back the Night,'" explained Belmont, "and it was a really good idea as it turned out, and we did three other tracks on [the EP]." It was a nod to his past, performed with a perfect combination of respect and bravado. "That's the stuff I'm really influenced by, early soul and blues, Wilson Picket for instance is a great fave of mine," Parker told *Nuggets*. "The same stuff that Van Morrison likes, and I'm influenced by him a hell of a lot. All of us in the band having the same attitudes towards music has helped to give us such a good feel on record and on stage."

It was an attitude that was becoming increasingly prevalent. Even the Americans were beginning to pick up on it. Writing in *Rolling Stone*, Greil Marcus claimed that Parker's arrival in America signalled a massive change in attitude which would wipe away all the wimpy rock that had prevailed until his arrival. So enthused was Marcus by Parker's music that he believed it would "cut a swath through most everything around it". Parker was surfing a new wave that was about to swamp everything in its path. A combination of strong song writing skills aligned with a rambunctious attitude to performance kept him afloat on what was becoming a very choppy musical sea. "There was a crossover," maintains Belmont. "We used to get a lot of punky looking people at our gigs. Although we didn't sound like a lot of those bands, we did have the same kind of energy level that they had when we played. There was nothing laid back about Graham Parker and the Rumour. Even though we were probably more seasoned players than the kids in those punk bands, we weren't unacceptable to a lot of those audiences. You could definitely tell that things were changing, which was no bad thing. There were less and less of those awful serious bands. Although there were still a lot of them around and particularly in America. America is so vast, in the middle they were still living back in 1973. Bands like Journey and Styx, these awful, awful bands, who we also played with by the way."

Winning over audiences on the East and West coasts would be relatively simple thanks to strong airplay, but replicating that success in middle America was going to require a lot of hard work. Arriving at a gig after having covered hundreds of miles, bored, tired and hungry, they couldn't afford to give anything less than their best. Through sheer power of performance, Graham Parker and the Rumour sliced through the flabby corporate rock that was still de rigueur and effected a genuine reawakening that alerted dozing middle America to the coming storm of British groups that followed.

One of the first British new wave groups to follow Parker and the Rumour was Eddie and the Hot Rods. Previous to the arrival of Graeme Douglas, the Rods relied on Higgs and Hollis for original material. With the ex-Flyer among their ranks - albeit without the blessing of CBS Records - Eddie and the Hot Rods finally acquired a writer with the melodic edge to take them to the next level. "It was an ideal situation. They needed what I had to give and I needed what they had already." Douglas explained. Douglas' innate sense of melody would smooth over the group's rough edges and make it more accessible to a wider audience. But with punk stealing all the headlines it was felt that the group needed a quick make-over. With the music weeklies full of spotty faced punk rockers, Eddie and the Hot Rods were beginning to look long in the tooth. In an attempt to distance itself from the old wave, Eddie and the Hot Rods decided to re-brand themselves as The Rods. Stiff Records had done it with Costello and would do so again with Ian Dury. If it worked for them, surely it would work for Eddie and the Hot Rods. It did.

The first single issued under the new snappy moniker was the Douglas-Hollis penned 'Do Anything You Want To Do'. Inspired by Aleister Crowley's maxim "Do what thou wilt shall be the whole of the law", it neatly encapsulated punk's nihilistic streak and the Rods' own attitude. If the music press had greeted their previous singles with waning interest, the release of 'Do Anything You Want To Do' was met with unreserved enthusiasm. Making single of the week in several music papers, it matched the mood of the time perfectly. Writing in *Sounds*, Alan Lewis said: "I suspect that this record will reach the widest audience so far: slowed-down and tuneful enough to get pop air play, hard and fast enough for the street." *NME* scribe, Tony Parsons went further: "Their best single so far, superior even to the *Live Marquee* EP recorded in the halcyon daze of last summer."

With plenty of backing from the press, the single was marketed by Island Records taking a leaf out of Stiff Records' book and issuing it with a picture sleeve and as a limited edition 12-inch single. The cover depicted the late occultist Aleister Crowley with a pair of Mickey Mouse ears plonked on his head. It didn't go down too well with his supporters, who apparently put a hex on The Rods. "In retrospect it wasn't the best of ideas to mess about with Aleister Crowley," said Paul Gray. "It wasn't long before the letters started coming from his followers, saying we were playing with fire and threatening dire retributions on us all. At the time it was unnerving and we tried to laugh it off, but uncannily enough we suffered more than our fair share of tragedies soon after." Crowley's influence obviously didn't reach as far as the pop charts. Despite the evil eye the single worked its way into the top ten. It was The Rods' finest moment. Booked to appear at the Reading Rock festival, the single's success pushed them up the running order to second on the bill behind the very 'eavy, very humble Uriah Heep.

If the summer of '76 had been one of the hottest on record, the summer of '77 was one of the wettest. Naturally, the heaviest downpours occurred days before the Reading Rock Festival opened for business, with the effect that the site became a sea of mud. The festival all but ignored what was happening on the street. If you were looking for some sunshine and punk action you'd have been better off travelling to Mont-de-Marsan in France, where, according to Sean Tyla, The Tyla Gang blew The Clash, The Damned and The Jam clean off the stage. Not only did stay-at-home rock fans have to wade through conditions akin to the Somme, there were turgid sets from The Enid, Hawkwind and Widowmaker to endure.

There were also more contemporary sounds on offer from Ultravox and The Motors. To capitalise on The Motors' appearance at the festival, Virgin Records scheduled the release of their debut single for the following month. The Motors had been building a respectable following that helped push the highoctane Robert John 'Mutt' Lange produced 'Dancing The Night Away' to number 42 in the charts. Saturday night headliners Graham Parker and the Rumour had also benefited from Lange's magic touch. Having produced their hit 'Hold Back The Night', he turned his attention to producing The Rumour's debut album, Max. It revealed a funkier side to the group and proved popular in America, managing a 10 week run in the *Billboard* charts peaking at 125. It was, no doubt, helped by another lengthy tour of America that Graham Parker and the Rumour undertook supporting Thin Lizzy.

Lizzy were riding high on the back of 'The Boys Are Back In Town' and promoting their new album, *Bad Reputation*. Despite the two group's different approaches to music, they complemented one another in concert and got on well together off stage, too. The fact that Thin Lizzy were at their peak encouraged Graham Parker and the Rumour to give their all. "That one was when we really started to kind of go for it," recalled Belmont. "Thin Lizzy were very good at that time, very hot and they had 'The Boys Are Back In Town'. We got on very well with them and it was really good fun. [We went down] pretty good because we were shit hot, even then we knew our stuff, we had our shit together. We were building up our own audience as well, we would be doing big club gigs, headlining big several hundred capacity club gigs, as well as the kind of theatre gigs with Thin Lizzy. It was a very busy year."

Graham Parker and the Rumour had a new album, *Stick To Me*, to promote. Originally produced by Bob Potter at Island Studios, the album had to be re-recorded from scratch because of a fault with the master tape. "The whole album had to be scrapped because the master tape was leaking oxide or something," recalled Parker. "The producer, again, didn't seem to spot it. We saw this black stuff coming off the tapes but he didn't notice it. When we came to mix it, it was un-mixable. The hi-hat was leaking through all the tracks. It was a nightmare, because we had a tour coming up."

Parker's original vision was for the album to have a big production. "It had lots of strings, horns, extra backing vocalists, it was quite a big production," recalled Belmont. With an American tour booked but no album to promote, there was no other option than to re-record the album as quickly as possible. "We went back into the studio with Nick Lowe, because we needed to record this album quite quickly," explained Belmont, "and if you wanted to do that you got Nick in and we did it in a week. Not only that, but it was a week in which Nick spent a lot of the time having a drink and telling jokes. He didn't seem to do a lot of work but we got it done."

Nick Lowe might have saved their bacon, but his earthy production wasn't what Parker had wanted. Neither did it go down well with American critics, most of whom weren't ready for Lowe's bash it down and tart it up later production style. "It's a very intense, grungy-sounding record," says Parker, "but I kind of like it now for that reason. But in those days, of course, the American press panned it. They thought I should sound like Boston or Journey or something. They thought I should have a slicker sound."

Much to Parker's frustration, *Stick To Me* didn't perform any better in America than the Rumours' *Max,* only managing 124 on the *Billboard* charts. The previous year, Parker had been riding on the crest of a new wave, but with the rise of punk he'd lost momentum. Rather than surfing the new wave he now looked to be in danger of being wiped out by it. "In 1976, I was being touted as somebody special and different, and I was," Parker recalled. "I was the angry young man du jour. A year later, I wasn't. Fair enough." Parker found himself burdened with an image problem. Writing in *Time,* Jay Cocks hit the nail squarely on the head when he posed the question, "Graham Parker's music is 1) new wave, 2) old wave, 3) no wave, 4) punk rock,) 5) pub rock, 6) none of these, 7) all of these." It was a predicament that would haunt Parker for the rest of his career. "My image is very vague," he admitted. "That makes it difficult for audiences to fully latch onto me and critics to know where to put me."

Parker wasn't the only one feeling frustrated; The Rods had temporarily abandoned Britain for America, but weren't enjoying the experience. The tour kicked off in New York City just as Graham Parker and the Rumour headed home. Still buzzing from the success of 'Do Anything You Want To Do' and with the Steve Lillywhite-produced *Life On The Line* album to promote, The Rods weren't happy at being cast adrift in a foreign land. Their album got good reviews in the British press and, thanks to the recent hit single, Island Records had finally got behind them and was marketing the album for all it was worth. Released late in the year, *Life On The Line* eventually peaked at number 27. It might have climbed higher had the group been available to promote it. Nevertheless, it was a remarkable improvement on their debut. Lillywhite shared Lowe's approach to record production and appeared to have picked up some of his tricks while engineering for him at Graham Parker and the Rumour's Marble Arch session. "He didn't take any notice of the VU meters - they got taped up so you couldn't look at them," explained Masters. "And he got things out of a band that other producers couldn't get out of them. He'd rather use one good take than chop together six fair ones. He used to get you vibed up."

Faced with the realities of a seven week winter tour of North America, The Rods were feeling anything but 'vibed up'. According to press reports their opening salvo of gigs at Max's Kansas City in New York were well attended, but reaction to them was unenthusiastic. It was like starting from scratch and very disheartening. Speaking to *Trouser Press*, Dave Higgs said: "Well, the kids just sat there. They didn't stand up or move or anything. The first night we thought, 'Oh, another night. We'll play better tomorrow.' But after about a week of playing here, we decided it was the audience that was the problem, not us." With their album languishing at number 174 on the American charts, and with seven weeks hard slog behind them they were understandably feeling tired and frustrated. Rather than break America, it looked like America had broken them. "All my illusions about rock and roll in America have been shattered," Higgs continued. "I don't think America would know a good rock and roll band unless they advertised it on TV."

The Rods had fallen for the American dream in exactly the same way their predecessors had 20 years earlier. The difference was that The Rods actually got to experience the reality at first hand rather than through Hollywood's glitzy filter. Everything they'd learnt about America from listening to records or watching films was proved to be false. Not only were the audiences distant, none of the groups they got to see could hold a candle to their British counterparts. In fact, Douglas was so disillusioned by the experience he claimed American groups were "rotten". "I'm glad we came over here," he said. "Because now I'm sure what I always thought was true. And that's that the best rock and roll bands came from England."

They'd established a presence in America but, like Dr Feelgood before them, it marked the beginning of the end. Returning to Britain just before Christmas, they were offered another American tour, this time with Elvis Costello, starting in January. Another two months in America was too much to contemplate, but not everyone in the group was against the idea. "It was our first chance to have a month off since mid '75, and it was the first major rift within the band," says Gray. "Whilst most of us wanted to do it as it would have given us a chance to build our following more, Dave especially was growing tired of the constant touring and particularly disliked America. He refused to go." Instead of touring America with Elvis Costello and the Attractions, The Rods decided to stay at home and embarked on their longest tour yet, with Radio Stars and Squeeze supporting. Twelve months earlier the press had been ready to write them off. Thanks to the addition of Graeme Douglas, a hit single and a lot of hard work, that had changed. Dreams of making it in America had come to nothing, but the prodigal sons had returned home fired up and eager to build on an already formidable reputation. The Rods seemed unstoppable. Only bad luck or Aleister Crowley could stop them now, and Crowley was dead.

Sean Tyla was also down on his luck. No sooner had he got it together with the Tyla Gang than everything fell apart, again. However, the release of 'Styrofoam' had given him a real confidence boost and he was soon back on his feet again. "This time I'm going to do it from the most left-field angle I can think of, I'm going to get hold of a load of definite mysteries - and I did," he told the *NME*. The Tyla Gang Mk II came together by chance. With time on his hands, Tyla found himself at the Tunnel rehearsal studio in Southwark which was owned by Robin Greatrex. "I knew he was getting into management so I called by one day," Tyla recalled. "As I got into the place, this huge wave of guitar music hit my ears. It was awesome!" Tyla had stumbled upon his dream guitarist, Bruce Irvine. The new lineup was completed by ex-Winkies drummer, Michael Desmarais, and bassist Brian Turrington. "Michael and Brian were recruited because Robin had managed them in the past. They were a unit and though neither one of them were the type of musician I had in mind originally the music began to work," he explained.

Heading back to the pub rock circuit, the Tyla Gang began building a formidable reputation that quickly led to a tour supporting AC/DC. At last someone was listening and a couple of major record companies put in offers but, having experienced more than his share of major label bullshit, Tyla signed with a newly formed independent. Fred Cantrell, General Manager at Island Records had recently signed Stiff Records to a distribution deal and decided the time was right to throw in his lot with American independent Beserkley Records and run its British operation. "The Beserkley deal started out in the pool room at Island Records," recalled Tyla. "Island Music were still hanging in with me financially and suggested I talk to the record division's General Manager, Fred Cantrell. I didn't know it then, but that meeting would start the craziest roller-coaster ride of my life!"

With the right management and record company behind him, Tyla was ready to take on the world. Unfortunately, the world wasn't ready for Tyla. The Tyla Gang's debut album, *Yachtless*, was released to rave reviews, but despite constant touring, sales were disappointing. Tyla's hopes of cracking America were dashed by Beserkley Records' distribution, which was nonexistent. The company was, quite rightly, focusing its attentions on Europe. When it eventually secured American distribution it was with the GRT Record Group, whose biggest act thus far was ancient bandleader Lawrence Welk! Even with strong European distribution, the Tyla Gang weren't out of the woods yet. The influential British music press tended to overlook their hard-rocking ways in favour of what was happening down the Vortex. Unlike the equally rowdy Motors, the Tyla Gang never would crossover into the mainstream. Not heavy enough for fans of the Pat Travers Band, AC/DC and Rush, all of whom they supported, and not pop enough for the fickle mainstream, the Tyla Gang was doomed to wander rock's purgatory with little hope of redemption.

29
The Tommy Cooper Dialectic

Like madcap alchemists in a backstreet laboratory, Robinson and Riviera had turned oddball talent into gold. Having initially drawn on a cabal of failed pub rockers, by the early summer of 1977 Stiff Records had embraced the emergent punk and new wave scenes and issued singles by The Damned, The Adverts and Elvis Costello. But true to form they still found the time, money and energy to release quirky, off-kilter records by artists that other record companies wouldn't have touched with a bargepole.

On 1 April - a telling date if ever there was one - Stiff Records issued a single by the aged comedian and actor, Max Wall. 'England's Glory', written by Ian Dury and Rod Melvin, had been a staple of The Kilburns' set and earmarked by their one-time manager Dave Robinson as a possible single. (A live recording of the Kilburns performing 'England's Glory' was later issued on the B-side of a special edition of 'Sex And Drugs And Rock 'n' Roll' that was given away at the *NME*'s 1977 Christmas party.) The proposed Kilburns' single didn't happen, but Robinson still thought the song had legs. If Dury wouldn't play ball then Robinson would have to find somebody who would. British comedy heavyweights Ronnie Barker and Warren Mitchell were approached, but neither showed any interest. Max Wall, on the other hand, loved the idea and was booked to record it with the usual Stiff crew. (Dave Edmunds produced and Nick Lowe played bass).

As charming as Wall's reading of 'England's Glory' was, Robinson's faith in the song wasn't matched by sales. It sold so few copies it had to be given away with the compilation album *Hits Greatest Stiffs* simply to make space in Stiff Records' cramped office. It was, however, the acorn from which a mighty oak would grow. Robinson knew how to influence Dury and by persuading one of his heroes to record the song he sent a powerful message to both Dury and his managers.

Since disbanding the Kilburns, Dury and Jankel had written oodles of Mockney quatrains for the Upminster kid's debut solo album. The funk-loving Jankel had a knack of writing melodies and grooves that supported Dury's tales of London's low life perfectly. Together they were unstoppable. "Having met Chaz, it was pretty obvious we could write well together. All the time I was interested in making music you could dance to that had jazz and funky influences," explained Dury. "I didn't want slavish adherence like the Average White Band, who were almost copyists, although they were bloody good. I wanted to use that funk edge and be English as well. Chaz thought along the same lines and he was a genius."

With funding from Blackhill Enterprises they booked into Livingstone

Studios to cut some demos with Kuma Harada (bass) and Peter Van Hooke (drums). Among the songs they recorded was an early version of 'Wake Up And Make Love With Me'. It would turn out to be a real eye opener because it revealed faults with both Dury's lyric and delivery. "I got it home, and it was done with me with an American accent," Dury recalled. "When I listened to it back, I was feeling ill; I was going, 'who's this jerk?' Then I saw Gordon Nelki, Charlie Gillett's partner, and he said, 'Oh, doing the old Barry White are ya?' And I went, 'Oh no, am I? I went home and I thought I've got to do this another way. And I lived with it, with really acute embarrassment at who I was trying to be. So I changed the lyric to make it funny, the only thing I could think of was laughing, I couldn't come steaming in on a cloud of angel dust, so I did it again in English.'

When Dury re-wrote and re-recorded the song two things happened. He discovered that he was as much an actor as he was a vocalist and he found his voice. It wasn't a pretty voice, nor could it be called a singer's voice, but it was a voice ripe with character. Dury's was a voice as English as fish and chips, as sharp as a flick knife and as greasy as a mechanic's hand shake. It was rich with poetic allusions and as foul-mouthed as a costermonger. It could drip with tenderness or be ragged with rage. It was a voice that knew what it was to be excluded and how to express itself in compelling, shocking, and daring ways.

Nine months later, Dury and Jankel booked into Alvic Studios to record some songs Dury had written with an American journalist, Steve Nugent. It was here that they were introduced to the future Blockheads' rhythm section. Norman Watt-Roy and Charlie Charles were exactly what Dury and Jankel had been searching for. "Once we had Charlie and Norman in the band, I knew we had a good firm," recalled Dury. "The first things we recorded with them were 'Sex And Drugs And Rock 'n' Roll' and 'Blockheads.'" Dury had tried to persuade Jankel to set the lyrics to 'Sex And Drugs And Rock 'n' Roll' to music but Jankel thought the subject old hat. Nevertheless, every time he went to Dury's flat he found the lyric at the top of the pile of papers awaiting his attention. Jankel's indifference was reflected in his inability to set the lyric to music, and it wasn't until Dury sang him the song's main riff that he was inspired to finish the tune. Unknown to Jankel, Dury had 'borrowed' the riff from an obscure jazz album by Ornette Colemen. "When me and Jankel wrote this song we stole the riff from a Charlie Haden bass solo on a 1960 Ornette Coleman album called *Change Of The Century*," Dury confessed. "I met Charlie Haden later and he told me that he'd nicked the riff too, from a Cajun folk tune!"

Moving to Workhouse Studios, the embryonic Blockheads began work on what would become *New Boots and Panties!!*. Recorded during studio downtime, the album was a remarkable mix of Dury's disparate influences, Jankel's funk sensibility and outstanding musicianship. It is the rare example of an album that caught the zeitgeist and yet remains apart from it. It wasn't punk, but it had a punkish attitude, nor was it in any conventional sense pop, but it had a pop sensibility. It wasn't R&B, but that didn't mean you couldn't dance to it. *New Boots and Panties!!* was a unique synthesis of styles that blurred boundaries. It's the kind of album that comes along once in a lifetime and changes the musical landscape forever.

Robinson was one of the first people to hear the album and expressed an interest in issuing it on Stiff Records, but Dury's manager Peter Jenner had other plans. "When the tracks started trickling downstairs, I thought this is pretty good, there's some good stuff here," recalled Robinson. "At that point Jenner was telling me he had important meetings, and I said, 'Fine, if nothing comes up, Peter, you know where we are." Jenner took the album to every major record company he could think of, but was met by a wall of indifference. "As they say, the record industry is run by shoe salesmen and drug addicts!," explained Dury. "So in the end I said, well there's a record company downstairs, why not give it to Stiff.'" Stiff Records definitely wasn't run by 'shoe salesmen and drug addicts', it was run by rock 'n' roll insurgents fuelled by cheap cider and a determination to beat the major record companies at their own game. Robinson had already shown his commitment to Dury by releasing 'England's Glory'; licensing *New Boots And Panties!!* from Blackhill Enterprises was further evidence of his belief in the twice failed pub rocker. It was a gamble - but everything Stiff Records did was a gamble - that would save both parties from creative and financial ruin.

Naturally, Stiff wanted a single and what better choice than the song dismissed by Jankel as cliched - 'Sex And Drugs And Rock 'n' Roll'. Released on 26 August, it made single of the week in several music papers. Reviewing it in the *NME*, Tony Parson said: "[It] proves conclusively that Ian Dury is writing the soundtrack for a generation, which thankfully ain't really got sweet FA to do with being *Blank*." With the exception of the two Johns (Peel and Walters) the nation's airwaves were still controlled by joyless, reactionary prudes who thought the song eminently debased. "It was banned by the BBC when we released it as a single," explained a stoical Dury, "but it sold about 18,000 copies. With this song I was trying to suggest there was more to life than either of those three - sex, drugs and rock 'n' roll, or pulling a lever all day in a factory." If the BBC wouldn't play the kind of records Stiff issued then the only way to get its artists heard was to take them on tour. With this in mind, Robinson and Riviera planned to take a reworked version of the 'Naughty Rhythms Tour' on the road in the hope that it would turn one or more of its acts into stars. However, ten days before the tour was due to open in High Wycombe, Riviera told Robinson he was leaving and taking Lowe, Costello and The Yachts with him. Riviera and his acts would meet their commitments and complete the tour but the battle lines had been drawn. Robinson's acts - Ian Dury, Wreckless Eric and Larry Wallis - would face off Riviera's - Nick Lowe and Elvis Costello - as the tour made its debauched way around the nation's town halls and universities.

The 'Stiffs Greatest Stiffs - Live' package tour would follow the 'Naughty Rhythms Tour' template. All four acts - Larry Wallis performed his two songs with Nick Lowe's band Last Chicken In The Shop - would play 20 minute sets in rotating order. "The revolving bill was part of the pitch," recalled Robinson. It was typical Stiff bravado. It believed, or would have the public believe, that all of the acts were potential headliners. Of course they were, otherwise Stiff wouldn't have signed them, would it? But as with the 'Naughty Rhythms Tour', Riviera's plan fell at the first hurdle. No sooner had rehearsals begun than it became blindingly obvious that certain acts either didn't have enough material (Nick Lowe) or were woefully under-rehearsed (Wreckless Eric). "It was obvious it wasn't going to work, so it became two revolving bills," recalled Robinson.

Lowe was suffering from a loss of confidence and struggling to get his career off the ground. Having teamed up with Dave Edmunds to form Rockpile he had possibly the best rock 'n' roll group in the country at his disposal. But Lowe was too busy playing mind games to take anything seriously. In May, Rockpile had joined Bad Company on an American tour organised by Edmunds' record company, Swan Song. It wasn't a happy experience. Rockpile were unceremoniously chucked off the tour and replaced by The Outlaws. Edmunds claimed it was because Bad Company weren't selling out dates and that several had been cancelled. "Apparently, they've never gone down that well in the south and there were some big dates coming up down there, and to play it safe they brought in The Outlaws," he told the *NME*. However, rumour had it that Bad Company weren't happy following Rockpile's furious rock 'n' roll onslaught, although both Edmunds and Lowe were quick to dispel any such ideas, even though they clearly weren't founder members of the Bad Company fan club when they described the 'supergroup' as "exciting as a sack of old rotting spuds. It's so absolutely brainless that it's not worth ... I mean, it's hardly worth even possessing an opinion about Bad Company really."

Bad Company were the wrong company to be keeping. They were exactly the kind of group Lowe and Riviera wanted gone and Lowe's critique was typically on message and bitingly humorous. The pop pranksters woes were further exacerbated when Bad Company's label boss, Peter Grant, became Edmunds' manager. Grant claimed there weren't any ill feelings and even offered Lowe a recording contract, but in reality he found Riviera impossible to deal with. The heavyweight Led Zeppelin manager wasn't the kind of person to play games - this was business, there was no place for Riviera's brand of rock'n'roll insurgency. Despite his growing discontent, Lowe agreed to appear on *Top Of The Pops* with Rockpile to promote Edmunds' latest hit, 'I Knew The Bride (When She Used To Rock 'n' Roll)'. Yet behind the apparent carefree demeanour, Lowe was not a happy bunny. Speaking to the *NME* in March '78, Costello said: "Nick was going through this incredible period of misery and depression as a result of the whole Rockpile episode with Swan

Song and all that." Lowe quit Rockpile because he claimed it didn't meet his musical requirements. He wanted to draw on a pool of musicians to indulge his desire to be everything from a pure pop prankster to post-punk avatar. "[With Rockpile] only one facet of what I do was being involved really," he explained.

Lowe was undoubtedly multi-faceted, but one thing he wasn't good at was timing. With only weeks to go before a lengthy national tour, Lowe found himself without a record company or a group. He was, however, incredibly lucky to have the support of the two Dave's - Robinson and Edmunds. Although they'd been stabbed in the back by Lowe and his manager, they both had the good grace to give him a second chance. Nevertheless, Edmunds couldn't fathom why Lowe left the group. "What I can't understand is why Nick walked out on Rockpile," he said. "Not even me so much ... but he honestly had the best."

Who knows what Lowe was thinking; no sooner had he dumped Rockpile than he was out on the road with what was basically Rockpile and friends. His new group, which began life as The Nick Lowe All-Stars before becoming Nick Lowe's Led Zeppelin - a dig at Grant and Co. if ever there was one - and finally Nick Lowe's Last Chicken In The Shop, featured Williams and Edmunds augmented by Larry Wallis, Pete Thomas and Penny Tobin. Billy Bremner probably decided against the tour because of Lowe's attitude to Rockpile. "He [Lowe] said something to Billy ... something like 'Oh well, I won't be doing this for long' which really hurt Billy who's always been totally committed to the concept of Rockpile," explained Edmunds. Lowe's lack of commitment to either Rockpile or his career was evident throughout the tour. Everything, including his backing group, was a big joke. Here was Dave Edmunds, one of the country's best guitarists playing drums and, to double the irony, Lowe employed Pete Thomas, a drummer at the top of his game, to play guitar. Riviera and Lowe must have split their sides at that wizard wheeze.

Wreckless Eric and the New Rockets, which comprised Eric (vocals and guitar), Dury (drums), Denise Roudette (bass) and Davey Payne (saxophone) were no better equipped, having only played two gigs prior to starting the tour. "We did Birmingham and Essex University with The Damned," Wreckless told the *Melody Maker* on the opening night of the tour. "Birmingham was wet. So were The Damned. And in Essex the audience didn't know what to make of us." Put simply, Wreckless Eric and the New Rockets weren't nearly rock 'n' roll enough to close the show, so any idea of a fully rotating bill was quietly dropped. "The idea that we would rotate [groups], the first couple of nights that's the way it went, you know, we might open," explained Costello. "And of course, the nights that particularly Eric closed was a disaster. They quickly worked out that it just didn't work to rotate the entire bill, so they ended up rotating the opening acts and rotating the headliner after a couple of nights." This meant that the order had to be either Wreckless-Lowe-Dury-Costello or Lowe- Wreckless-Costello- Dury.

Having overheard Robinson and Riviera planning the tour, Dury made sure he was part of it. But he didn't have a group to tour with. "Then they asked us to tour so we asked Charley Charles and Norman Watt-Roy and they said yes, but only if they could bring the rest of their band, because they'd been playing for Loving Awareness," Jankel explained: "The other members of the band were Micky Gallagher and Johnny Tunbull, so they came and then Ian brought in Davey Payne who played sax in Kilburn and the High Roads." At 35, Dury was already an old man in pop terms. This was his last chance and he wasn't going to let anything or anyone get in his way. Already bitter at having his thunder stolen by a bunch of punk upstarts, he pulled out all the stops and spent hours honing his set with the Blockheads while his rivals were down drinking at the bar. "Ian is a very considered person, very conceptual," explained Jenner. "He would know what games he was playing. Anything that happened would not have been accidental. Ian saw the tour as an opportunity to upstage Elvis. He knew he was always going to win."

Dury used the rotating bill to his advantage. Playing drums with Wreckless Eric was taking it out of him to the extent that he required a break after each performance. That meant Dury and the Blockheads ended up closing the show more often than Costello and the Attractions. When 'Sex And Drugs And Rock 'n' Roll' became the tour anthem, Costello had to admit defeat and settle for second best. But Dury did more than simply outflank Costello, he used every trick he'd learned in the previous six years to create a spellbinding visual analogue to his knock-'em-dead stage show. He was unbelievably charismatic; the ultimate edgy outsider, he exuded an aura of menacing backstreet thuggery that was only partly ameliorated by the hokey vaudevillian theatricals he employed between songs. But scratch the surface and there was a tangible vulnerability to Dury's performance that was all too human. It wasn't simply his fragile physicality, an effect of his polio; his inarticulate stuttered introductions made public what was hidden away in institutions like Chailey Heritage Craft School. He deliberately exaggerated his disability to confront his audience with its own doubts, prejudices and aspirations.

Costello quickly realised that Dury wasn't going to be a pushover. "I think Ian was definitely the more competitive," he said. "He really knew this was the moment. He'd had one career where it hadn't really connected and he knew his moment was there." Costello didn't help himself by steadfastly refusing to play any songs from his new album. This was, he claimed, to get his manager "at it". "I knew we'd get some stick," he said. "I don't care. I don't want to get boring. You've got to keep everyone at it." Keeping everybody 'at it' didn't necessarily mean keeping everybody happy. But Costello wasn't going to come out on top by simply playing *My Aim Is True* from beginning to end. It wasn't just about who had the best album or who performed the best set, this was a clash of egos. The winner would be the one with the biggest appetite for success and that was without question Dury. Costello later confessed: "I didn't really know what I wanted. I was drunk out of my mind most of the time, and just everything was going very fast. And all I wanted to do was play as fast as possible and get to the pub."

Like Wilko Johnson, Costello was a bit of a loner who found rock 'n' roll excess distasteful. Touring with a bus full of hedonists wasn't his idea of a good time, and as the tour drew ever closer to its conclusion he was compelled to express his feelings in song. The result was 'Pump It Up' in which Costello painted a bleak picture of life on the road and the ease with which sex, drugs and rock 'n' roll could seduce even the most righteous of individuals. 'Pump It Up' would become a hit for another record company, but Stiff was about to issue another Costello classic that would propel him into the top 20.

On 14 October Stiff issued 'Watching The Detectives' to coincide with the tour. The additional publicity worked and the single became a highlight for all concerned. When it peaked at number 15 in the charts, it became Stiff Records' greatest hit. Riviera and Robinson's faith in the geeky computer programmer was validated and Costello had found his form. "'Detectives' was very important because it was the first song that proved to me that I could write in a whole new style," he said. Part of the record's success was down to the unique sound its producer, Nick Lowe, coaxed from a ramshackle 8-track studio situated in Islington, London. Taking the opposite approach to Edmunds' everything but the kitchen sink style, Lowe fashioned a remarkably stark sounding record from the most minimal of musical elements. Featuring Steve Goulding on drums and Andrew Bodnar on bass, it was the first hit, discounting the Tartan Horde, he'd ever produced and he remains justifiably proud of it. "The one I have the most affection for - there's loads of them - but the one that always sounds great to me is 'Watching The Detectives', because it's got such a peculiar sort of sound and yet it really comes across great on the radio."

Rather than join in the drunken revels and celebrate the release of his finest 3 minutes and 43 seconds thus far issued on record, Costello maintained his offish party pooper stance. But there were plenty of others on the tour bus whose sole intention was complete and utter bacchanalian self-indulgence. To keep themselves amused most of Lowe's touring band formed the 24 Hour Club to while away the long hours after shows. "We had a deal," explained Wallis, "any time of the night or day, if a member of the 24 Hour Club banged on your hotel door, no matter the time of day or night, you had to have an alcoholic drink. We used to get our wages, and if we still had our wages left an hour later we were slipping."

Edmunds was out to have as much fun as humanly possible, and became an enthusiastic member of the club. "Edmunds was getting very drunk," recalled Lowe. "We'd all been doing it, but Dave's hangovers were now so dreadful that he couldn't really perform the next night. I could sense he was gonna blow me out or let me down. I could see it coming." Despite his drinking and drugging, Edmunds acquitted himself well on stage, it was offstage that things got out of hand. When the tour hit Manchester, the 24 Hour Club, minus Lowe, hit the bar. Edmunds, Wallis and Pete Thomas were having a late night tipple when Edmunds decided he simply had to retrieve some valuables from the safe keeping of tour manager Des Brown. Charles Shaar Murray was covering the tour for the *NME* and although he didn't witness what happened he did record that: "During the night, there'd been an altercation, a bit of midnight raving that had gotten out of hand, a prank escalated into a full-scale accident."

Lowe, who was sharing a room with Brown, slept through the entire incident but was caught on film by Nick Abson, who was documenting the tour for a proposed movie, describing the events to his fellow travellers. "Des is carved up," he said, "it looks like Sharon Tate up there, you know blood all over the place. There's a note by [my] bed, 'Nick, you missed the sound of breaking glass, make sure you have your boots on when you get out of bed." When Lowe discovered what had happened, he went ballistic and demanded that Edmunds apologise. Unrepentant, the guitarist was sacked, albeit temporarily, from the tour. It wasn't the only violent incident to happen on the tour, but it was the most disturbing. Every cloud has a silver lining though and it provided Lowe with the inspiration for his biggest hit, 'I Love The Sound Of Breaking Glass', and when he discovered that Edmunds wasn't entirely to blame, he invited the guitarist back to finish the tour.

If drink, drugs and high jinx threatened to derail the tour, the only thing that kept it on track was the music. "The thing that united all of us," Lowe suggested, "even though, say, Dury's music and my music are a totally different thing, is that there is a point where it meets. That's in the attitude, the ideas coming across. The accent isn't on a musical thing - even though Dury's got a shit-hot group backing him - but on the ideas. That's what's exciting, it's the way it's put across." It was attitude and musicianship that made Ian Dury and the Blockheads the undisputed champions. From the very first gig, reviewers made it clear that they were invincible. "The winner [is] Ian Dury with his cocked grin and cheery grunt, helped by his amazingly brilliant band, certainly the best of the night," wrote Tim Lott. Vivien Goldman was just as fulsome in her praise: "Although Ian had lost his voice, he still managed to grip the onlookers by the appropriate areas." Dury's nightly performances helped push *New Boots And Panties!!* to number 5 in the charts, and a run of hit singles helped keep it there for an incredible 90 weeks.

While other tours were simply about promoting an act or album, the 'Stiffs Greatest Stiffs - Live' tour captured the spirit of teen rebellion which was spreading across the country. It was a crucible in which the old and the new came together to negotiate new meanings and agendas. Its cast of boozy, half-cocked entertainers played out themes of urban crisis, tested musical conventions and mixed rock hyperbole with knowing irony night after night. The 'Stiffs Greatest Stiffs - Live' tour didn't mark the beginning of the end of rock 'n' roll, it marked the end of a new rock 'n' roll beginning.

30
Crawling To The U.S.A.

In the ten days between finishing the 'Stiffs Greatest Stiffs - Live' package tour and beginning their first American tour, Elvis Costello and the Attractions began recording the This Year's Model album under the boozy eye of producer Nick Lowe. By this time Lowe's studio of choice was the larger and more impressive Eden Studios in Chiswick. The move marked more than a change in location, it also marked a change in relationship. The geeky young man who'd recorded his debut album in days off from his day job had changed beyond recognition. Lowe might have sat in the producer's chair, but it was Costello who called the shots. "He definitely had the final say, absolutely all the way down the line actually," recalled Lowe. "Slowly I started backing out of my rather heavy handed producer role and basically just sat there while he did the record and approve or raise an eyebrow and give him a sideways look if I didn't think it was going to work."

Even if he was taking a back seat, Lowe was the perfect man for the job. His working methods dovetailed perfectly with Costello's. Like Lowe, Costello wasn't averse to quoting from pop's back pages when he felt like it. "We never made any bones about the fact that we ripped stuff off from other things," he told Peter Doggett. "Sometimes it was done very consciously, and sometimes it was simply me thinking about it and not telling the rest of the band." Besides offering advice, Lowe's main job was to recreate the kind of energy levels the group generated on stage in the sterile environment of a studio. "I thought that was what recording was like," explains Pete Thomas, "but I've never come across anything like it since. It was like a whirlwind in the studio, it was like, 'Go on do it again! Do it faster! Hit the drums as hard as you can! Have another drink! Nick would just work it up into a frenzy through the day until by the time you got the track you were playing stuff you never even thought you could play." Most of what Elvis Costello and the Attractions recorded for *This Year's Model* had been road tested on the Stiffs Greatest Stiffs - Live tour, but any thoughts of completing the album had to be put on hold while they toured America.

America's interest in new wave had been fuelled by floods of British imports, news reports and its own regional music scenes. The combined effect was having a dramatic impact on the slow moving leviathans that controlled the music business. Pockets of new wave resistance were popping up across America and could no longer be ignored. Writing in the January 1978 edition of *Billboard*, the head of Sire Records, Seymour Stein, said: "In North America there are now active and growing scenes in Boston, Detroit, Cleveland/Akron, Los Angeles, Chicago, Seattle, San Francisco and Toronto." They were, he claimed, all directly attributable to New York's punk and London's pub rock scenes. While America would soon experience what the media termed a second British Invasion, this conquest of American hearts and minds has to be put into context. In February '78, Adam White wrote in *Billboard*: "The [British] acts most favoured are those which have made the most commitment to America - financially, geographically and even emotionally ...". White listed some of the British artists that had committed to America, it didn't make good reading. Rod Stewart, Peter Frampton, Electric Light Orchestra, Pink Floyd, Led Zeppelin and the Bee Gees were the acts making big bucks from Uncle Sam. There wasn't a new waver in sight.

The foundations for Costello' s success had been laid by Dr Feelgood, Graham Parker and the Rumour and Eddie and the Hot Rods, all of whom had toured America prior to Elvis Costello and the Attractions heading the second British Invasion. Despite their best efforts, disco, hard rock and middle of the road pop still dominated the charts; it was going to take a combined and sustained offensive to overturn the tyranny of pap that kept American youth sedated. Recalling his first journey across America, Costello couldn't believe how depressingly homogenous radio programming was. "We were driving down the freeways of America and tuning the dial and getting different parts of the same track on different stations. 'Blue Bayou', the Roy Orbison song, was a big hit for Linda Ronstadt, you could hear different sections of the same song. That's how blanket the acceptance of The Eagles, Linda Ronstadt, Fleetwood Mac, Journey, Boston, Foreigner [was]."

However, a creeping realisation that something was happening was making its way through the boardrooms of major record companies. Independent record labels that for decades had serviced minority interests were having break-out hits with new wave groups. Jem Records had cornered the market in new wave imports and had the rights to 50 independent record companies. Afraid that they were missing out, the majors wanted a piece of the action, and according to [Jem boss Marty Scott "[they] have made overtures to Jem as far as getting help in selling the [new wave] product. They feel due to our success, Jem knows the right way to break the retail market."

In Britain, the retail market was such that you could walk into any high street newsagent or branch of Boots the chemist and buy the latest single by the Sex Pistols, The Stranglers or The Clash, but finding singles by The Desperate Bicycles or The Television Personalities might have been trickier. In America, new wave records weren't available in most downtown chain stores, they had to be sought out in backstreet independents. If new wave was going to take off in America it needed mainstream distribution. The major record companies knew it and, despite his hatred of all things corporate, Riviera knew it; that's why he signed Costello and Lowe to the biggest record company of them all.

Punk had a lasting influence on popular music, but with the exception of The Clash, it didn't achieve broad commercial success in America. New wave was just as influential, but because it had the melodic edge it was more palatable to mainstream tastes and therefore had more chance of success. Combining the ferocity of Punk with the melodicism of The Beatles, Elvis Costello and the Attractions were destined to become very big indeed. According to Nick Lowe, Costello crossed over and appealed to hardcore music lovers and pop fans alike. "Elvis' audience, for instance, consists not only of people who are music enthusiasts, but also a lot of young girls who really get off on him like they do with Gary Glitter or did with Marc Bolan: I've never seen that before."

While Columbia Records struggled to persuade radio stations to give Costello airplay, the press was beating a path to his door. There was so much interest in the British punk/new wave scene that public relations guru Toby Mamis told *Billboard*: "We haven't had to hype the groups as much as just expose them." Riviera wasn't going to just expose his boy, that would have been too easy. He did the opposite and refused all interview requests except for a few heavyweight publications like *Time*. Naturally, Costello played his part to perfection. Having railed against his countrymen, he turned on his hosts. "I also hate the Americans because they'd got so much and do so little with it," he said. "People on the West Coast were so nice it was driving me mad. If one more person said, 'Have a nice day,' I thought I might kill him." Only the late American shock rocker GG Allin was mad enough to actually want to kill his audience; all Costello wanted to do was provoke his. It was all a big game intended to generate as much publicity as possible, and it worked. The media loved it but, like Columbia Records' attempts to sweeten his records, it did its best to pour some sugar on his sour image. After all, he hit all the right buttons; he could sing and wrote songs you could whistle. "The songs are angrier than the soft rock that spun out of Southern California onto the record charts this year," *Time* told its readers, "and Costello sings them with a prophet's urgency." Put like that, who'd be afraid of Elvis Costello? But not all press reaction was positive. According to Costello, some Americans found his version of rock 'n' roll totally alien. "The reviews we got from when we first went to America were really funny," he recalled. "They said things like we sounded like we formed on the plane, and they made up these great meaningless cliches like 'they suffer cymbal crashing ineptitude.'"

Inept or not, there were plenty who dug their brand of revamped rock 'n' roll, and by the time the tour ended at the Stone Pony in Asbury Park, Costello and the Attractions were well on the way to becoming the hottest thing in America apart from the Mojave Desert. The following night Costello burnt his final bridge. Booked to appear on *Saturday Night Live*, as a last minute replacement for the Sex Pistols, he was under pressure to promote an album he'd already outgrown. Costello appeared to acquiesce to record company pressure, before pulling the kind of stunt his manager loved. Everything seemed to be going to plan as the group powered through 'Watching The Detectives'. Next up was 'Less Than Zero', but Costello took a leaf out of Jimi Hendrix's book, stopped a few bars into the song then launched into

'Radio, Radio'. "I believed that we were just acting in the spirit of the third word of the show's title," Costello later claimed, "but it was quickly apparent that the producer did not agree. He stood behind the camera making obscene and threatening gestures in my direction. When the number was over, we were chased out of the building and told that we would 'never work on American television again'. Indeed, we did not make another U.S. television appearance until 1980 [two years later]."

His stunt did the trick; it generated acres of press coverage, but was a hollow victory. As much as Riviera, Costello and Lowe wanted to overthrow the established music business, to be successful they had to work with it not against it. Without the financial backing of Columbia Records, the power of commercial radio and television, the influence of the print media and a network of clubs and theatres, their plans for world domination would have come to nothing. With this huge machine behind him, Costello achieved something no other new wave act had; he'd taken America by storm. Within weeks of *My Aim Is True* being issued, it had sold 100,000 copies and climbed to number 32 in the charts.

Returning to England, Costello handed the new wave baton to his former label mate and rival, Ian Dury. Arista Records had picked up *New Boots And Panties!!* for American distribution, which according to Peter Jenner cost them a cool $100,000. Arista spent heavily on advertising the album, but more on buying Ian Dury and the Blockheads tour support with Lou Reed. The former leader of the Velvet Underground was as cantankerous as ever and did everything he could to make his supporting act's life as difficult as possible. For all his punk credibility, he was exactly the kind of spoilt 'star' the new wave railed against. Consequently, when the two rockers met, there was an almighty crashing of egos. "One of the big mistakes we made was going to America to support Lou Reed," Dury told Chris Welch. "Arista thought we'd get an open-minded audience supporting this famous lounge lizard, Lou Reed. But he had a pot belly and trainers and was about as subversive as a packet of crisps."

The tour kicked off on 26 March in Los Angeles. If American audiences found Costello alien, what was it going to make of a middle-aged polio victim who spoke like a character from a Dickens' novel? More often than not, audiences were simply bamboozled; all they wanted was to hear Mr Grumpy Pants grind his way through 'Walk on The Wild Side', but the Blockheads were a force to be reckoned with and they easily won over more receptive audiences with their unique mix of rock and funk. In new wave hotspots like San Francisco, Ian Dury and the Blockheads rather than Reed were the main attraction. "We did seven nights in a club in San Francisco," recalls Dury's handler Fred Rowe, "and on the first night there were about two or three hundred people there, the second night there was about a thousand, and the third night it was pissing down with rain and we got there about three in the afternoon for another check and later I looked out the window and there was a queue three deep. I said, 'Ian, look out the window', he goes, 'yeah, a queue for fucking Lou Reed,' and I said, 'Lou Reed ain't on until ten, that's your queue out there. They don't start queuing at seven o'clock to see Lou Reed at ten, they are here to see you at half past eight.'"

As the tour progressed, audiences blew hot and cold, and by the time they reached the Bottom Line in New York City, Ian Dury and the Blockheads had had enough and Dury vowed never to tour America again. On his return home he told Paul Morley: "I don't want to conquer America at all. I feel like Britain has just conquered me completely. I feel so fucking lovely about Britain. That's made me happy." Perhaps one reason Dury failed to win over large parts of America was because the cultural traffic was all one way. Dury's lyrics were too culturally specific and his use of slang made him as unintelligible as a Martian to American punters. British audiences could engage with Dury's songs because he held up a mirror in which they saw their cultural reflection. American audiences couldn't be expected to have that closeness. They didn't share the experiences nor could they relate to characters like Clever Trevor or Billericay Dickie. When *Billboard* reviewed *New Boots And Panties!!* it suggested that because of "the strange subjects Dury chooses to laud in songs [...] his appeal might be limited." They weren't just whistling Dixie, and certainly not 'Plaistow Patricia' for that matter. American record companies were only too aware of the cultural gap, and when Columbia Records issued Costello's *This Year's Model* they even went so far as to remove '(I Don't Want To Go To) Chelsea' and 'Night Rally' because it considered the lyrical content "too English".

If American audiences found Dury difficult, back home he was fast becoming a star. Midway through his American tour, Stiff Records issued 'What A Waste' as a single in Britain. While the group slogged its way across America, 'What A Waste' began to climb the charts, and by the time the prodigal Dury and the Blockheads returned it was well on its way to the top ten. (It would spend 12 weeks in the charts and peak at number 9.) With Dury finally achieving the commercial success he deserved, Stiff poured everything it had into a witty advertising campaign to promote the only act it had selling records. "We spent a lot of money on Ian Dury, although the record [*New Boots And Panties!!*] had sold about 40,000, and I thought there was a real vibe for Ian, but we were going to have to promote him properly. We had cash in the bank and we booked a series of provocative ads. 'Give up smoking and give us your money' was one of them, and it worked. Suddenly the record started to move by itself," Robinson recalled. Ian Dury and the Blockheads were everywhere, front covers, television appearances and headline tours. The hard part was going to be staying at the top.

Elvis Costello and the Attractions returned to America in late January '78 for another month of club dates. Tour support had been offered to Eddie and the Hot Rods who passed up the opportunity, deciding to promote their new album *Life On The Line* with a British tour instead. Starting in Texas, Costello and the Attractions headed North where they were joined by Nick Lowe and Martin Belmont at the El Mocambo club in Toronto. Lowe and Belmont joined them for the encore, belting out raucous versions of 'Nutted By Reality', 'Shake And Pop', 'Heart Of The City' and 'Breaking Glass' - the latter being Lowe's latest British single. Costello's performance was issued as a promotional album, and Lowe's as a promotional EP. But rather than back what was fast becoming Lowe's first hit single, Columbia Records bafflingly issued 'So It Goes' to a very cool reception.

When Riviera split with Robinson in the late summer of '77, he formed Riviera Global Record Productions and signed Lowe, Costello and The Yachts to a new British company, Radar Records, which was formed by Martin Davis (Managing Director) and Andrew Lauder (Head of A&R), both of whom had worked at United Artists and therefore knew Lowe and Riviera well. Like the other major labels, Warner Brothers wanted a piece of the new wave action and financed Radar Records as an independent satellite label. Robinson and Riviera hadn't brought down the major record companies, but they had changed the way they worked. Blindly following fashion and with a "me too" mentality, every major record company simply had to have its own 'independent' label. But rather than foster new talent as Stiff Records did, all the pseudo-independents did was cherry pick acts that had grown too big for the tiny labels that signed them when nobody else was interested.

Riviera and his artists were only too aware that while Stiff Records had been fun, it lacked financial clout. "The problem with Stiff was when all the bills came in and all the boring stuff; everyone wanted to go down to the gigs and hear the new records and there was no one taking care of the fucking accounts," Lowe recalled. "So we wanted to go with a record company where we could have a certain amount of freedom, but also have the machinery to take care of all that boring stuff and Radar is a happy medium. They've got Warner's clout and in England that's very substantial. Also, they've got Martin and Andrew and they're good guys. They understand me and Elvis and Jake and all our little idiosyncrasies."

With Radar Records up and running, Davis and Lauder jumped at Riviera's offer when it came along. "I took Jake out for a Greek lunch," recalled Lauder, "to tell him I was starting a new label, distributed by Warners. He announced that he was leaving Stiff, taking Elvis Costello and Nick Lowe with him. Were we interested? We didn't have any artists, so of course we were!" Better still, Radar Records licenced most of its artists from other record labels or production companies like Riviera's. This meant that Costello and Lowe retained ownership of their recordings and, once their contracts expired, had the right to licence them to whoever they liked. "He [Riviera] did some things back then that were quite revolutionary which, thankfully, I - and indeed he - is getting the credit for," explained Lowe. "For instance, having the copyright revert back to us, you know. Back in those days, that never happened. You signed to a label and they just signed you off to other people when they'd had enough of you."

Recording costs for Lowe's debut album were kept to a minimum by using the very affordable Pathway Studio and spare time at the end of sessions he was producing for others. "I made that record in down time, really, in between the other things I was doing," he recalled. "It was more of a collection of sweepings from the floor, really, more than an actual project that I'd actually thought about." The first single from the album was the song inspired by Dave Edmunds' night of madness on the Stiffs Greatest Stiffs - Live package tour, '(I Love The Sound Of) Breaking Glass'. Recorded with Andrew Bodnar, Steve Goulding and Bob Andrews from The Rumour, it made number 7 in the British charts. Its minimalist funk groove led some critics to believe that Lowe had pinched it wholesale from Bowie's song of the same name, ironically from the album *Low*. But if Lowe was quoting from Bowie he was quoting ideas rather than riffs. "Basically I'll just lift ideas because I think ideas are the most exciting part of the whole thing," he told the *NME*.

Lowe took basic beat group principles, mixed them with a dash of irony and made 'pure pop for now people', which was the title Columbia Records gave to his album *Jesus Of Cool* in America to avoid pissing off the good folks down in the Bible Belt. What he created was a pop bridge between the past and present. Bypassing the turgid ramblings of progressive rock and the tawdry kitsch of glam, it described a shift in musical ideas that was part of a much larger cultural movement. What's more, it was easy. Anyone with half a brain could play with the symbols, codes and meanings that constitute pop style. "It's good from an audience point of view, because it's easy to listen to but still a bit thought-provoking," Lowe declared. In other words, everyone's a winner - artist and audience.

Far from being 'uncool' new wave was ubercool, and Lowe was the scene's prophet of pop. Reviewing Lowe's album in *Trouser Press*, Tim Windsor noted: "On the surface Nick seems to be playing pleasant tunes, nothing more than the 'pure pop for now people' of the American album's title but before long you realise that he's playing with your mind, turning it inside out and showing you a lot that you might have missed without him." Lowe didn't make the record just to impress his friends, switched on critics and *NME* readers, it spoke to a generation that knew nothing of pop's rich history or the crimes perpetrated against it. What kids wanted was music that said something witty and intelligent in the classic form of the three-minute pop song. New wavers like Lowe made the kind of records the kids wanted to hear: records that captured the excitement and spirit of youth in ways that only the young understand. "It was our turn," Lowe said. "Suddenly it was as if somebody was saying to me, 'OK, you're the new generation, you've learnt your craft, now what have you got.' I was suddenly at the front of the queue and I wanted to make a name for myself."

Lowe's efforts to make that name for himself could at times appear somewhat perplexing, but thanks to some snappy advertising and constant touring things were looking up. "We got the record out and to our amazement it sold very well," a contented Lowe was pleased to report. He'd come a long way since Kippington Lodge.

Riviera was a past master at capturing the public imagination and knew the message had to match the medium. Who better to oversee this side of things than Barney Bubbles? His striking artwork captured Lowe's pick 'n' mix aesthetic in all its mischievous glory. The sleeve featured shots of Lowe adopting different rock personas, and a photograph on the back cover of the American edition made him look for all the world like a warped light-entertainer. The album's apparently blasphemous title - *Jesus Of Cool*- also worked to his advantage. As mentioned, Columbia Records insisted it should be changed for the American market to *Pure Pop For Now People*. Not only did it want the title changed, it also wanted the content and sleeve altered too. Two versions of the same album: how '60s; how post-modern; how could it fail? Riviera couldn't have gilded the lily any better had he tried. But despite a lengthy American tour with Rockpile supporting Costello, the album only managed a disappointing number 127 in the American charts. (It peaked at number 22 in the British equivalent.)

America still had a long way to go to catch up with Britain, but perhaps part of the album's disappointing American sales was due to Rockpile. If ever a group suffered from an identity crisis, it did. The previous year, Edmunds received top billing because he had the album out. Now the group was billed as Nick Lowe's Rockpile with no mention of Edmunds. Recording solo albums with Rockpile didn't work either because Edmunds and Lowe each melded the group's sound to their requirements, thereby diluting its signature sound. The problem was nobody could decide if Rockpile was a stopgap or part of a long term career plan. With Lowe and Edmunds pulling in different directions, Rockpile was a two-headed rock 'n' roll Hydra let loose on an unsuspecting public.

In concert, Rockpile was a living manifestation of the creative experiments Edmunds and Lowe usually reserved for the studio. "We're trying to create a space for ourselves that ... celebrates the beat and the old influences without being just a carbon copy or an instant replay," Edmunds told the *Melody Maker*. Despite the struggle to give Rockpile a coherent identity, according to Edmunds the touring was beginning to pay dividends. "I hope that eventually people will start thinking of us as Rockpile, rather than Dave Edmunds, Nick Lowe, Uncle Tom Cobley and Rockpile," opined Edmunds.

The problem remained that Edmunds and Lowe were signed to different record companies. If they'd shared the same label then promotion could have been more focused and tours arranged to their advantage. As it was, no sooner had Rockpile finished promoting Lowe's album than it was back on the road doing the same for Edmunds' latest, *Trax on Wax 4*. The first album Rockpile recorded as a group, it was Edmunds' first album recorded in its entirety over a 13 day period, rather than over months or years as had previously been the norm. If touring did little to fix the idea of Rockpile in people's minds, it was beginning to have an effect on their solo careers. "To sell records you've got to actually tour. Touring did a lot for me. I had five or six albums that had never sold more than 30,000 copies worldwide. After all the touring we did in 1977 and '78, my last album did a quarter of a million," Edmunds enthused.

Although Rockpile would remain a rock 'n' roll paradox, the relentless touring was beginning to pay dividends. Driven by a couple of mavericks and co-managed by two of the biggest egos in the business, Rockpile was constantly on the cusp of making it. The following year both Edmunds and Lowe scored hit records with 'Girls Talk' and 'Cruel To Be Kind' respectively.

While Rockpile were having a whale of a time riding on the cusp of making it big, Graham Parker was becoming increasingly frustrated by his lack of success in America. He pointed the finger at Mercury Records. The company was already viewed with suspicion by some in the music business because of the way it mishandled The New York Dolls, and now there was a rumour it was doing the same with Graham Parker. American sales of the first two albums were 30,000 and 60,000 copies respectively. Not bad for a new wave act, but not good enough for Parker, who was hungry for success. One might think that Mercury wanted him to be successful too but, as far as Parker was concerned, his inability to break America was entirely due to his record company. "Mercury buried me, that's a fact," he said. "I was before any kind of explosion of new music, and I think I suffered from that, and I suffered from Mercury being incredibly cheap. Mercury didn't spend in any way."

Parker delivered his sign off in two-fingered style, with the bitingly titled 'Mercury Poisoning' and fulfilled his contractual obligations by delivering a live album, *Parkerilla*. Turning his back on Mercury and America, Parker toured Australia, New Zealand and Japan before returning to Europe. With Mercury Records a fading memory, Robinson negotiated a deal with the new wave friendly Arista Records for America, and towards the end of 1978 Graham Parker and the Rumour began recording the critically acclaimed *Squeezing Out Sparks*. With the right support from Arista, the album sold 200,000 copies and peaked at number forty in the *Billboard* charts. The success Parker craved had finally arrived.

31
If We Make It, You've Got It Made

With two of its biggest stars having jumped ship to a major label for more money but less fun, Stiff Records was being kept afloat by Ian Dury and the Blockheads. Dury was about to hit his commercial peak with a brace of singles and a near-chart topping album, but Stiff couldn't rely on the Blockheads forever and needed to develop new talent, pronto. Robinson's fast-track solution was to revamp an idea twice used before; the package tour. "In 1978, Dave decided we had to amp it up another level so we decided to send the people round the country on a train, which was a very clever idea but an enormously expensive one," explained Stiff press officer Nigel Dick. The previous Stiff tour had lost £11,000, recouped by sales of *My Aim Is True* and *New Boots And Panties!!*. The Be Stiff tour of October and November 1978 was an even bigger gamble, forecast to cost £100,000. It was a risk, but one Robinson thought they could manage. "We are on a ledge a lot of the time..." he said, "I think we can manage about three majorish mistakes a year. Big companies can always pull in money from different countries to cover them, but we can't and that is what makes it fascinating."

To offset some of the costs, Robinson secured sponsorship from Polygram, the Bron agency, Ensign Records and the *NME*. The other national music paper promoting the tour, *Sounds*, spent £35,000 on a ten-week campaign that included a free Stiff/*Sounds* album, *Can't Start Dancing*, that featured all the acts plus Ian Dury and the recently signed Rumour. As an added incentive, and to ensure the gigs were well attended, a 6-track album comprising recordings of Devo's 'Be Stiff' by each of the acts was offered to anybody who kept their ticket stub.

The tour was indeed a fascinating prospect and as far as Lene Lovich, she of the unusual vocal tones, was concerned, it was a near perfect solution to breaking new bands. "There was five Stiff acts, plus one extra band who was backing Rachel [Sweet]. All of the artists on this tour were brand new artists who nobody had ever heard of before. Well, I suppose people had heard of Wreckless Eric. But he was the only one really. Everyone else was really new to the music scene and it was a real introduction to the public. We travelled to all sorts of different places that bands don't normally ever go to."

Robinson's fascinating experiment was made all the more interesting by the fact that like the previous Stiff package tour it had a rotating bill. "I think the idea of having six totally different types of acts on a bill was a really interesting one," explained Lovich. "I mean perhaps the audience got worn out by the time the sixth band came on, but it was also good for us as performers because we'd never really been performing our own music before."

With six bands on the bill the tour gave more bands for your buck, but if it didn't turn a profit it'd be Goodnight Vienna for Stiff Records. To ensure its success, Robinson threw everything the company had into promoting the tour, the label and the bands. The Be Stiff campaign was the biggest and most expensive Stiff Records had undertaken. Four days before the tour kicked off in Bristol, Stiff Records issued albums by Jona Lewie, Mickey Jupp, Lene Lovich, Wreckless Eric and Rachel Sweet. Each album was available in three editions, coloured vinyl, black vinyl and picture disc, all designed to appeal to collectors. Browser cards were also issued to record dealers to encourage them to file the albums under Stiff - each album had 'File Under Stiff' printed on the back sleeve - rather than under the artist's name. Any other company would have considered the wheeze commercial suicide, but not Stiff and Robinson had boundless chutzpah. "I knew the tour would be alright. We believed in it, worked very hard and the music was right," Robinson said.

The inescapable fact though is that Robinson was gambling the company's shaky finances on the outcome of an expensive tour by a bunch of losers, unknowns and oddballs. Mickey Jupp was a blues boom veteran and stalwart of the Southend scene. With his group Legend he recorded a brace of albums for Vertigo Records without commercial success. He'd been on Robinson's list of acts to sign to Stiff, but had missed the boat during the label's initial rush to sign every pub rock failure looking for a final hit before last orders were called at the musical bar.

Signing with Stiff, he was teamed up with fellow Southender and Procol Harum founder Gary Brooker to record his *Juppanese* album. "The album started off with Gary [Brooker] producing but Stiff wanted to start again with Nick Lowe and the band Rockpile," Jupp recalled. No sooner had Lowe settled down and opened a bottle of cheap wine than the prickly Jupp took offence at one of Edmunds' jokes and went off in a sulk leaving Stiff with two half-finished albums that it had to stitch together to complete the project. It was an uncompromising attitude that coloured his brief time with the company. He wasn't too happy with the idea of touring either. "At the time I was aged 34 and rated as 'most deserving but least likely to succeed' sort of person. The Stiff tour wasn't much fun as far as I was concerned. I remember playing Newcastle City Hall one night and thinking: 'What the hell am I doing here? Why am I doing this?' I hated it. The whole experience of being on stage just wasn't me." When he was told that the entire enterprise was going to be repeated in New York City, Jupp threw another tantrum and stayed at home. "When it was announced that they were going to New York, I said, 'Bugger that, I'm not going,'" he recalled. His group, The Cable Layers, went without him but failed to impress.

Jona Lewie was another blues boom veteran who'd scored a one-off hit in 1972 with 'Seaside Shuffle' as part of Terry Dactyl and the Dinosaurs. Forming

The Jive Bombers with Martin Stone, who was still looking for a permanent home after Chilli Willi and the Red Hot Peppers, the group was offered a contract with Chiswick Records but turned it down. Stiff Records signed Lewie as a solo artist and issued his debut single for the label, 'The Baby She's On The Street'. It was a resounding flop and his debut album did no better. But Robinson's belief in him did eventually pay dividends with a brace of hits that included 'You'll Always Find Me In The Kitchen At Parties' and the infuriatingly catchy Christmas evergreen 'Stop The Cavalry' - both produced by ex-Brinsley and Rumour man Bob Andrews.

Lene Lovich was discovered by Charlie Gillett. "Fantastic guy - gave breaks to a lot of people like Elvis Costello, Dire Straits. We listened to his show every week on a Sunday on Radio London. We thought 'this guy, he knows everybody. He could help us. He must be able to!' We didn't know at the time but he had been managing Ian Dury and so he already knew the people at Stiff Records." Signed to Gillett's Oval Music company, Lovich was part of a group recording songs that showcased the song writing talents of Jimmy O'Neill. "We recorded various tracks of this songwriter's and we also recorded a song called 'I Think We're Alone Now', which was by Tommy James and The Shondells originally. We took that track to Stiff and Stiff seemed to be very interested in this. I don't know if it was because of the song or my voice, because of the way we'd arranged it, because it was different from the original."

Gillett played the tape to Robinson, who hated everything except for Lovich's recording of 'I Think We're Alone Now'. Robinson insisted on issuing the track as a single and told Gillett to whip up a B-side double quick. In typical Hollywood fashion, Lovich wrote 'Lucky Number' with her partner Les Chappell the night before the session. ('I Think We're Alone Now' b/w 'Lucky Number' was issued via Stiff's mail order outlet in an edition of 5,000.) When Robinson needed a single to coincide with the tour he remixed 'Lucky Number' and issued it as the A-side. "Bob Irwin, the drummer, Les [Chappell] and Lene, went to the studio, speeded it up by a horrifying amount, hit the snare on the second and fourth beat all the way through the song, and then had everybody chant 'number two' at the end and turned this attractive album track into a irresistible single," recalled Gillett. Issued on the back of the Be Stiff tour, 'Lucky Number' surprised everybody when it soared to number 3 in the charts. "We were absolutely amazed. Even the record company didn't know it was going to do that well. It was just a song that had gone down quite well live," explained Lovich.

A veteran of the first Stiff tour, Wreckless Eric had a new album to promote and an advance to re-pay. Despite Stiff Records considerable attempts to make him a star, he was destined to forever remain a cult. Eric, like Jupp, wasn't impressed with the way Stiff handled either the tour or his career. "I hated all that one big happy family thing. How can you have one big happy family when you put five albums out on the same day by different artists and put the chart positions up in the dressing room every night or every week?," he said. Lovich agreed that Stiff piled on the pressure, but suggested that the situation mellowed as the tour progressed. "Things might have been a bit competitive to start with when we didn't know each other. But we soon found out that we're all so different that there was no real jealousy or in-fighting," Lovich recalled.

Stiff Records' approach to its acts was to push them as hard as it could and see how much they'd take. Robinson had witnessed what this had done for Costello and Dury on the first Stiff tour and knew it was a sure-fire way of producing electrifying performances that translated into acres of press coverage and record sales. Nothing comes easy and as far as Stiff was concerned an artist was either on the train or off the rails. Eric's problem was that his career was stuck at the red signal. In fact, he didn't even consider what he was doing in terms of a career. "The whole thing was a laugh that was the great thing about it. We weren't serious about it", he recalls. Either he wanted success, which meant doing what he was told, or he could undermine everything, including his own career, and remain a cult. He chose to remain a cult, which he still is to this day, living in America with American musician wife Amy Rigby.

Besides looking for old and new British talent, Robinson set his sights on America. He'd been alerted to Akron, a new wave hot spot, by local weirdoes Devo, who sent a copy of their debut single, 'Joko Homo', to Stiff Records in the hope of securing a distribution deal. Robinson signed Devo and, convinced that Akron held the solution to all his problems, teamed up with Akron-based songwriter and producer, Liam Sternberg, who had recorded a batch of demos with local teen sensation, Rachel Sweet. "Liam was intent on selling his Akron compilation," recalled Sweet. "He sold the idea to Stiff and he sold them the demo tapes ... The next thing I knew I was getting reviews for an album I didn't know I was on." The resulting *Akron Compilation* was another unmitigated commercial disaster. It did, however, deliver Stiff the sweet 16-year-old Sweet, who achieved moderate but short-lived success with the label.

With no Costello or Dury to battle it out night after night. everything rested on whether or not this troop of rock 'n' roll eccentrics could pull it off. "Everyone realises there's too much as stake and too much to lose if they fuck it up," road manager and M.C. Kosmo Vinyl told the *Melody Maker*. Having a dig at Lowe and Costello, he continued: "No one on this tour has got a Radar Records to go to when it's all over," Robinson knew it was a gamble that had to pay off. "This time the press will be more critical," he told the *NME*, "they're always more critical of Stiff than the majors."

This was actually a back-handed compliment. Nobody gave a toss about CBS, except The Clash and maybe Elvis Costello, and their expectations of them were low, but the kind of people who bought into the Stiff ethos cared passionately about the company. For some, Stiff Records had become more interesting than some of its acts. Its witty marketing made it and the tour the real stars, not the bands. "It was another of Dave's great gags but a gag that was so big that the artists were somehow encompassed by it, they were blinded by it," explained Nigel Dick. "What you saw was the tour rather than the individual artists." Looking back, Lovich agrees that at this time Stiff had become somewhat self-centred: "I don't think Stiff had a lot of respect for artistic ... identity. They just wanted to be successful." When the press reviewed the acts rather than the hype, Robinson's prediction about negative criticism came true. Reviewing the London gig for *Sounds*, Sandy Robertson forecast: "Jona Lewie will get obscurity (undeserved), Mickey Jupp will get obscurity (deserved), Wreckless Eric will get drunk." He was kinder about Sweet's chances - about the only true prediction from his crystal ball gazing - but it was Robinson not Robertson who had the last laugh.

If Jupp and Eric were financial rather than artistic mistakes, that still left Stiff with one 'majorish' mistake in reserve. Not that it had to worry too much about its finances now that Ian Dury had hit his commercial peak. Issued a week after the Be Stiff tour pulled into the sidings for the last time, 'Hit Me With Your Rhythm Stick' topped the charts and sold a million copies. Ian Dury and the Blockheads did more than give Stiff its first number 1 and a nice seasonal financial boost, such was their impact that, according to Charlie Gillett, their success rubbed off on other Stiff acts. "With Lene Lovich [we] were very lucky to be literally the next single after 'Hit Me With Your Rhythm Stick', and radio was like, 'What's next?' And we were it." Actually Rachel Sweet and Wreckless Eric followed Dury with singles, but Lovich had the biggest hit when 'Lucky Number' sold an impressive half million copies.

One and a half million singles sold in the space of a month was a remarkable comeback for a company that at the beginning of the year was literally off the rails. Its success was due to an unfailing belief in its artists, a clever marketing campaign that promoted both the company and its acts and a successful tour, all achieved with little regard for money in the bank. Stiff's attitude had paid big dividends and was rewarded by repeated chart success. The Be Stiff tour made headlines in the national press and helped propel the company to a position where it could compete with the majors on equal terms. It was everything Robinson had dreamt of, but he wasn't about to rest on his laurels. There was still America to break, and that's where the Be Stiff tour headed next.

Landing in Manhattan in mid-December, Stiff's motley crew booked into the Bottom Line from 17 to 20 December to showcase their unique talents. Reviews were mixed with suggestions that Stiff had lost some of its edge, but Scott Isler claimed he'd witnessed the future and hoped that Stiff Records' unique take on rock 'n' roll would refresh an otherwise stagnant American music scene. Besides showcasing Stiff's latest batch of rock 'n' roll wannabes, the gigs were part of a concerted effort to secure an American distribution deal for the label. Having failed to break Ian Dury in America, Arista Records passed on the label's latest batch of quirky albums. Stiff couldn't crack

America without a distributor. Everything rested on Robinson, who worked tirelessly to finalise the deal with Columbia Records that had been wrecked when Riviera left him in the lurch some 18 months earlier.

The Be Stiff showcase worked and by the summer of '79 Stiff Records had a production and distribution deal with Columbia Records. Ian Dury, Lene Lovich and Ian Gomm, who was signed to Albion Records in Britain, had albums issued on the Stiff/Epic label, while Rachel Sweet's record, which was remixed for the American market, was issued by Stiff/Columbia. In early August, Stiff/Epic/Columbia launched four albums in a repeat of the Be Stiff campaign a year earlier. Columbia Records was expecting big things from the deal with one unnamed marketing director claiming: "We plan to move some big numbers on this acquisition and to do that we have to hustle."

Not all of Stiff Records' artists were as fortunate as Sweet and Lovich. Wreckless Eric and Jona Lewie weren't signed to Columbia Records, instead their albums were issued by the recently formed independent Stiff America label. "I think Clive Davies [President of Arista Records] wanted to buy Stiff Records, dump everything and just have Rachel Sweet which I thought was short-sighted really," recalled Eric. "Several other record labels were interested in bits of it, and I think everyone else got a deal with CBS or Epic but no one wanted me, I was a bit much I think. So a man called Allen Fry, who had a company called Arse, a management company that looked after me, Nick Lowe and Elvis Costello, started Stiff America." (Virgin Records and Island Records employed a similar practice when their respective distributors Atlantic and Warners rejected albums considered un-commercial.) Eric was finally rewarded with the first release on Stiff America, *Whole Wide World*, a compilation of his first two albums issued in early November '79.

While Robinson's troop of misfit musicians was enjoying the delights of Manhattan, Rockpile moved into Eden Studios in Chiswick, London, to record a double album's worth of material. Because Edmunds and Lowe had yet to sort out their contractual problems, the finished songs were divided between Lowe and Edmunds and issued as solo albums. (Edmunds' *Repeat When Necessary* and Lowe's *Labour Of Lust*.) A few weeks earlier, on 28 November, Radar Records issued Lowe's sixth solo single, 'American Squirm'. In fact it was a split single, the B-side being a frantic reading of Lowe's old Brinsleys' anthem '(What's So Funny 'Bout) Peace, Love And Understanding' by Elvis Costello and the Attractions hiding under the pseudonym Nick Lowe And His Sound. The most cursory listen should have alerted even the cloth-eared to the fact that it was Costello not Lowe handing lead vocals. Further clues to the identity of the real singer could be found in the picture sleeve which depicted Lowe in large hornrimmed shades clutching one of Costello's Fender Jazzmaster guitars - the one with 'Costello' inlayed along the fret board. The single was a physical manifestation of the odd couple's working relationship and a talisman for the coming year in which both would score the biggest hits of their careers.

The first few days of Rockpile's recording sessions were filmed for a Granada Television documentary, *Born Fighters*, broadcast in November 1979. It revealed just how quickly Rockpile worked in the studio. Lowe's bash it down and tart it up later production style meant that the band laid down a song a day. "It was one, two or three takes. If it was more, we'd say 'dump it, and go on and do something else, we'll come back to it later'. You can hear it in those tracks," Terry Williams told *Rhythm* magazine. This frantic work-rate produced several outtakes including cover versions of the Detroit Spinners 'Living Just A Little' with Bremner on vocals, Dr Feelgood's 'No Mo Do Yakamo', and two Lowe compositions 'Best In The World', also recorded by Dr Feelgood, and 'How Do You Talk To An Angel'.

Arrangements were worked out as they went along to the extent that Edmunds and Lowe were still deciding who should sing on which track right up to the last minute. Edmunds attempted Lowe's 'Endless Grey Ribbon' only to have his vocal replaced by Lowe, who issued it on his album. "I usually get Nick's cast-offs," he divulged, "though not by design. He'll play me something - some half-done song - and forget about it. Six months later I'll say 'What about that one you played me?' and he'll go, 'oh, yeah.' Then I sit down with him, sort it out, and make it work." Edmunds also drew on the song writing skills of Graham Parker, who provided 'Crawling From The Wreckage', and Elvis Costello, who donated 'Girls Talk'.

Costello was on a roll. Having scored a couple of top thirty hits with 'Pump It Up' (number 24) and 'Radio Radio' (number 29), he was about to leap into the top five and rub shoulders with the likes of Blondie, Abba and Queen. While his producer slaved over a hot mixing desk at Eden Studios, Costello and the Attractions were on a whirlwind 27-date tour of Britain to promote his new album, *Armed Forces*, issued on 5th January 1979. A pop masterpiece influenced by Bowie's suite of albums *Station To Station*, *Low*, and *Heroes*, Iggy Pop's *The Idiot* and *Lust For Life*, Kraftwerk's *Autobahn*, early Abba and The Beatles' *Abbey Road* and *Yellow Submarine* albums, it was the sophisticated face of new wave and a remarkable advance on *My Aim Is True*, recorded less than two years earlier. "On the musical side I was real conscious of breaking out. So the second album, *This Year's Model*, is harder than the first. That's also because it was English musicians and they played with a different attitude. The next album, *Armed Forces*, was much sweeter. As it worked out the style in itself and the stance became the straitjacket, not the music," Costello told Bill Flanagan of *Musician* magazine. It was a stance that did him no real harm, at least until he hit America later in the year. After all, he'd set out to be confrontational and playing the bitter and twisted card was all part of Riviera's master plan. As Charles Shaar Murray noted "Listening to Elvis Costello does not make you feel comfortable. If it does, you're listening to it wrong. Start again."

Fuelled by ego, speed and alcohol, Costello and the Attractions were not the most stable group of musicians on the planet at this time, consequently recording sessions could be tense and belligerent affairs. "People would get very intense about one particular thing. For instance, Steve Nieve would walk out of the studio because he thought we were playing a song too fast. Like calling time out in a football game," Costello told *Musician* magazine. It was Lowe's job as producer to keep the wagon rolling and under control. Armed with nothing more than a packet of Senior Service, a bottle of white wine and a handful of gags, Lowe coaxed stellar performances from the band that, according to Costello, "[kept] the heart and pop soul of this record [intact]".

The album's standout pop gem, 'Oliver's Army', was issued as a single and became a surprise hit. Costello had written the song after a trip to Northern Ireland, where he witnessed ridiculously young British soldiers in full battle dress armed with automatic rifles patrolling the streets of Belfast. "The song was based on the premise: 'they always get a working class boy to do the killing'. I don't know who said that; maybe it was me, but it seems true nonetheless. I pretty much had the song sketched out on the plane back to London," Costello recalled. Its dark narrative, which became something of a Costello trademark, was alleviated by Steve Nieve's infectious piano part borrowed from Abba's 'Dancing Queen'. With 'Oliver's Army' Costello learnt that it was better to subvert the system from within rather than battle away at it from beyond the pale. The classic insider as outsider, his songs both celebrated and critiqued the music and culture that he inhabited. Not only was Costello's music uncomfortable, and at times irritating to listen to, at its best it made you think and question things.

Despite selling 500,000 copies, 'Oliver's Army' stalled at number 2 in the charts but ensured that the album, which came in an elaborate Barney Bubbles designed sleeve that owed much to his earlier work for Hawkwind, (think of the *Armed Forces* sleeve as a new wave version of *In Search Of Space* without the acid) sold like hot cakes. [The album peaked at number 2 in Britain and number 10 in America.] The new wave tide was beginning to turn; there was room in the charts for a bunch of angry young men, and they'd proved that they could flog records. It had been a slow revolution that required compromise on both sides, but as the majors acquiesced to their demands the acts began to deliver the goods artistically and commercially. Speaking to the *NME* only two years earlier, a prophetic Matthew Kaufman, head of Berserkley Records, said: "New Wave will be accepted when it becomes palatable - The Byrds made protest folk rock but watered it down for AM consumption without any important social statement left." With 'Oliver's Army', Costello not only made his music palatable, but unlike the Byrds he made needle sharp righteous statements too. In the years that followed he'd refine his song writing skills with songs like 'Ship Building' and 'Pills And Soap' that were memorable not only for what they said but how they said it.

In February, Costello and the Attractions set off on another lengthy American tour to promote what was fast becoming his most successful album thus far. Everything was set for Costello to transcend the new wave scene and become a full blown pop star. However, no sooner did it look like he'd cracked America than his stance almost strait jacketed his career there, forever. Building on the 'We hate Americans, we're only here for your money' routine of the previous year, Costello and Riviera worked overtime to provoke the American media. "We were still doing a bit of myth building, being objectionable and 'New Wave' at the time, annoying people and being generally punkish in our attitude," explained Bruce Thomas. Midway through the tour Costello and the Attractions played the Agora Club in Columbus, Ohio. Arriving at the local Holiday Inn they discovered, to their 'delight', that Stephen Stills and his entourage was booked into the same hotel. Costello was in no mood to talk to anybody, least of all Stills who represented everything he'd worked so hard to undermine. Road weary and more than a little tired and emotional, Costello and the Attractions entered into a conversation about music with the Stills' party. Bruce Thomas again: "What started out as good natured banter, teasing Stephen Stills and so forth, gradually got a slight edge to it and the edge became a bit sharper."

The Attractions idea of a bit of fun quickly got out of hand, according to a report of the incident in *People*: "Costello called James Brown a jive-ass nigger. Next, according to an onlooker, Bonnie [Bramlett] said, 'All right, you son of a bitch, what do you think of Ray Charles?' He said, 'Screw Ray Charles, he's nothing but a blind nigger.'" Speaking to Radio 1 for a documentary some years after the incident, Costello said: "I was completely drunk and I tried to outrage them by making sort of racist remarks. The form that it took was really trying to shock these people by critiquing people who were so beyond criticism that I couldn't believe they couldn't see the irony." Somebody from the Stills' party snitched on Costello to *Rolling Stone* magazine and what had been an ill conceived drunken remark was used to fuel a backlash that took Costello years to recover from. According to Riviera, the American liberal media had been waiting for an excuse to knock Costello, and this momentary stupid lapse of reason was all it needed. "We didn't do encores, we didn't do interviews. We just came, played a show and left your town. The trouble is, when you say to a journalist, 'my artist is too talented to talk to you. Instead of talking to you and your Columbus Gazette newspaper he could be writing a song. Which in the great scheme of things is more important?' They don't like it. In fact they hate it. And they want to knock you off your pedestal."

Forget the media furore that surrounded the Sex Pistols American tour a year previously, it was this drunken encounter between old and new wave that made America really sit up and take notice. Costello had done more than say something offensive, in light of the anti-American sentiments he'd expressed since stepping foot in the country, his remarks about Brown and Charles were taken as an attack on America itself. Consequently his career opportunities were severely curtailed. Radio stations stopped playing his records and his concerts were picketed by Rock Against Racism, an irony not lost on Costello and the Attractions who'd played at a RAR festival in London the previous year. Columbia reportedly considered dropping him, stopped promoting *Armed Forces* and dropped plans to release 'What's So Funny ('Bout Peace, Love and Understanding)' as a single. The Armed Forces tour that began with so much promise ended not with an attack but with a retreat.

Back in Britain, Ian Dury and the Blockheads were preparing their second album, *Do It Yourself*, issued on 18 May 1979. Pieced together from songs leftover from *New Boots And Panties!!* and others worked up at Dury's house in Kent, it offered a dramatic change in sound and subject. Gone was the ferocity and edginess of Dury's debut as well as the colourful characters and much of the Cockney slang. *Do It Yourself* was funky, jazzy and more polished and, like its predecessor, it did not feature a hit single. Neither did Stiff see fit to add Dury's next blockbuster single, 'Reasons To Be Cheerful', to the album as it had added 'Sex And Drugs And Rock 'n' Roll' to *New Boots And Panties!!*. "There was no single. At that time Dury insisted that they didn't appear on albums, which hurt its commercial prospects," says Roblnson.

With no single to promote the album, *Do It Yourself* was helped on its way by a lavish promotional campaign that focused on Barney Bubbles' sleeve design. Inspired by a book of wallpaper samples, Bubbles' design was issued in a number of variations - 27 different versions and counting. "Barney said we should do a few variations, but my idea was that we should do a lot and give each of our licensees around the world their own covers," recalled Robinson. This was another of Robinson's expensive whims and with one eye on the balance sheets he cut a deal with Crown to provide free materials for use by Stiff as part of its promotional campaign. Stiff Records sent out a barrage of promotional material including badges, ties, paint brushes, paint pots and wallpaper to the media and retailers. It even sent its staff to decorate the offices of the music weeklies. Thanks to another imaginative marketing campaign, a large and loyal following and a recent number 1 single, the *Do It Yourself* album climbed to number 2 in the charts. Sales, however, weren't as strong or sustained as *New Boots And Panties!!*. Maybe this was inevitable?

Having helped Costello's flagship album, Lowe now had time to concentrate on his own career. With recording sessions over, Rockpile was booked into its first major British tour. The previous year Rockpile had managed only nine British dates, eight of those in small London venues like Dingwalls and the Nashville Rooms. Their first British tour of universities and Top Rank suites was a big step up but disaster struck when Edmunds burnt his hand on the radiator of his car and the tour was delayed. When Rockpile finally hit the road at Leicester De Montfort Hall on 22 May, everything was set for Lowe and Edmunds to take the charts by storm. Both had recorded radio-friendly singles (Edmunds scored a UK top five single with 'Girls Talk', while Lowe peaked at number 12 on both sides of the Atlantic with an old Brinsleys' song he'd co-written with Ian Gomm, 'Cruel To Be Kind').

Originally recorded for what would have been the Brinsleys' swansong album, 'Cruel To Be Kind' had been kicking around for years before Lowe was persuaded to resurrect it. "I wrote it with one ear on 'The Love I Lost' by Harold Melvin and the Blue Notes," he recalled. "As I reinvented myself as a thrusting New Waver, I was a bit embarrassed by the song, but when Columbia Records hove into view in the shape of Greg Geller, he insisted - to my horror - that I record 'Cruel To Be Kind' on the next album." Lowe can't have been that horrified by the song because it had already appeared on the B-side of his 'Little Hitler' single. Given the Rockpile treatment, it transformed Lowe's career on both sides of the Atlantic. But there was little time to enjoy the fruits of his labours. No sooner had Rockpile finished touring Britain than they were off to America for another two months slog, this time supporting Blondie.

Whether it was fronted by Edmunds or Lowe, Rockpile was beginning to make a name for itself in America. As far as Terry Williams was concerned it was precisely the lack of a front man that ensured the group's success. "We didn't have a Bono or Robert Plant: there was no front man in Rockpile, that's why we were so great at club level in America, the 2-3,000 seater places," he explained. Onstage Rockpile was a band of equals, all of whom could have fronted the band if they'd wanted. (Check out some of the band's live recordings and you'll hear the audience calling for Billy as loudly as for Nick or Dave).

Edmunds' old wave aesthetic combined with Lowe's new wave attitude to create a powerful pop punch that was beginning to find favour in America now that new wave had finally established itself there. "I'll tell you what I think about Rockpile in America," Lowe told *Trouser Press*. "We've been really lucky up to now, especially with the support gigs that we've done. There was Bad Company - and we got thrown off that tour. There was Elvis and Mink De Ville, which was when "New Wave", in inverted commas, came about, and then Van Morrison and Blondie. We've got a great deal of goodwill going on over there for us."

Rockpile was in the process of doing something that most bands only dream of. It was crossing over into the mainstream and on the cusp of making it big. It was the kind of band that appealed to old school rockers, disenfranchised new wavers and pop fans in equal measure. Besides being a cracking live experience, the band's success was due in equal parts to its melodic edge and punkish attitude. Most Americans found it difficult to identify with some of the more extreme new wave/punk bands because they hadn't experienced the punk scene at first hand either in London or New York. All most Americans had was the music which they couldn't relate to and didn't like. "I think with myself, or Elvis, or Parker, or Dury the approach is a lot easier for Americans to understand," explained Lowe. "There's almost an overreaction - they like us too much, because they've been dying to get cracking, but can't really relate to The Damned. I think what people like about Rockpile is the way we put it over, whatever it is we are doing - rock 'n' roll, pop whatever - the attitude more than the actual article."

Like their new wave contemporaries, Rockpile weren't prepared to pander to fashion; it had to be their way or no way. "There's no way we're going to start losing sleep about constructing a record for FM radio," Lowe told Scott Isler, Lowe sounded as defiant and bloody-minded as Costello or Dury. But having said that Rockpile weren't prepared to pay lip service to FM radio, in almost his next breath he claimed that he'd do almost anything to get a hit. "I think I could pretty much debase myself to unplummeted depths to get a hit 45," he said.

Lowe was being disingenuous; he wasn't prepared to debase himself for 15 minutes of fame. Still haunted by the Brinsleys' Fillmore experience, he was wary of what fame might bring. Aided by Edmunds, he was about to undo everything the band had worked so hard to achieve. Like his manager, Lowe had to destroy in order to create. As Nietzsche put it, 'always doth he destroy who hath to be a creator'. With Rockpile's star in the ascendancy and a hit single under his belt, Lowe was revelling in his creativity but staring into the abyss of celebrity. To redeem his past he had to destroy it and was caught in an extended moment of becoming that he found intoxicating. "We had a real fame phobia," he later claimed. "We just didn't want to make it, and the longer we held it off and sort of killed our own career, we had more and more fun. I mean, the best time to be in the music business is that time when you're just about to make it. Not when you do make it, because that's when it gets really boring and dull ..."

Edmunds was equally ambivalent about his place in the band and its future. Ever the reluctant hero, like Lowe he feared becoming a rock superstar. "With Rockpile, I thought I was safe just being a member of a band, not actually fronting it," he told Bill Holdship of *Creem*. What made Rockpile great would lead to its demise. Like it or not, somebody had to stand centre stage, it couldn't continue as a band of sidemen forever.

Once Edmunds' contractual problems were sorted out, Rockpile could finally release an album under its own name. But now that Edmunds and Lowe had to collaborate and define a distinctive style of their own they hit a stumbling block. While Rockpile had been on the cusp of making it, collaboration hadn't been a problem because although they were working together they were moving towards different goals. But as soon as they were no longer solo artists but members of a band, cooperating became an issue: like a couple who happily live together for years only to find it all turns sour when they formalise the relationship and tie the knot. "One minute we were doing 'Knife And Fork', a bluesy, shuffley thing, and the next it was 'Teacher Teacher', which would have been okay if we'd been 17 in frilly shirts. That album was too varied. We were all too polite about each other's contributions. No soul left in it. It was time to change again," explained Williams. Rather than stick to their guns, Lowe and Edmunds did compromise and constructed a record for FM radio. "I would have preferred to pick 'Knife And Fork' [as a single] - which demonstrates what I would like Rockpile to be, though it's not the obvious hit," Edmunds told Dave DiMartino. "But I'd rather have a flop with that one than 'Teacher Teacher'. It's too deliberate an attempt to get a hit."

With Edmunds and Lowe at the helm, Rockpile was beginning to tack wildly from pre-modern rock to post-modern pop. Unable to agree what course the band should take; Edmunds and Lowe lost the plot and the band began to implode. "When we were making our respective solo albums involving Rockpile, [Lowe would] have the final say if it was his album and vice versa," explained Edmunds. "But once we started recording together as a band, we began running into problems. It ended up sounding like half a Dave Edmunds/half a Nick Lowe album, which led me to believe we weren't going in the right direction as a whole."

Lowe couldn't have disagreed more. As far as he was concerned, it was precisely the tension between himself and Edmunds that made Rockpile so good. "I'm not comparing us to The Beatles, but what made The Beatles' albums so good was that they were holding each other in check. I don't like any of their solo albums as much as when they were all together, when they were holding each other in check so to speak," Lowe told Nicky Horne of Capital Radio.

Despite Edmunds' and Lowe's differences, the album did very good business in America, where it peaked at number 27 in the *Billboard* charts. But the band's success was short-lived. Not only were Edmunds and Lowe clashing in the studio, Edmunds was losing respect for Riviera. "I didn't think he was handling things right and I told him so," Edmunds explained, "and he doesn't like people saying things like that to him." The rift between Edmunds and Riviera undoubtedly exacerbated the rift between Edmunds and Lowe. (Riviera remained Lowe's manager until he retired to Eel Pie Island.) The band's continuing identity problem - was it a real band of just there to back Edmunds and Lowe? - an inability to come up with suitable material, and the failure to blend Edmunds' and Lowe's conflicting styles ensured that Rockpile's end was nigh. These boys sure knew how to snatch defeat from the jaws of victory.

On 26, 27, 28 and 29 December 1979 some of new wave's brightest hopes rubbed shoulders with some of rock's elite at a series of charity concerts held to raise money for the people of Kampuchea who had suffered so cruelly under Pol Pot's regime. UN Secretary-General Kurt Waldheim asked Paul McCartney if he'd play a one-off benefit concert which developed into four nights at the Hammersmith Odeon, London. Three of the concerts were headlined by established acts, The Who, Queen and Wings. But the second night saw Ian Dury and the Blockheads top the bill, a sure sign they rubbed shoulders with the best of them. The concerts didn't only showcase Stiffs' greatest hit, they were proof that new wave had crossed over into the mainstream. During their concert on the third night The Who performed 'Music Must Change' from their recent *Who Are You* album. Townshend introduced the song by saying it had a portentous lyric. In fact, the lyric didn't foreshadow a musical uprising because it had already happened. The Clash, Rockpile, Elvis Costello and the Attractions, The Specials and The Pretenders were evidence of that. Townshend only had to look around him; new wave bands outnumbered established acts 2 to 1.

Although it wasn't the Albert Hall, the Hammersmith Odeon was a long way from the Tally Ho. Only a few years earlier some of the bands would have struggled to fill the toilets at the Hammersmith Odeon, let alone sell it out for five consecutive nights as Dury and the Blockheads had earlier in the year. That the concerts featured more new wave whippersnappers than established rock leviathans was proof that the balance of power was shifting. What had started as a backlash against hype had become a howling wind that blew through the moribund corridors of the music business. A handful of bloody-minded musicians and managers created a genre that made rock 'n' roll exciting again. The pub rock scene produced a raft of musicians that dared to be different and provocative. When they re-emerged as thrusting new wavers the mainstream was ready for them and success was theirs for the taking.

Some of them took it, some of them didn't: this book is a testimony to all of them.

"I'll salute the new wave, and I hope nobody escapes"
('I'm So Bored With The U.S.A.' -The Clash)

Where Are They Now?

The 101ers
When The Clash imploded, **Joe Strummer** acted in a couple of films, including Alex Cox's *Straight To Hell*, which also featured The Pogues. He played guitar for the Pogues whilst regular axeman Philip Chevron was ill, and rejoined briefly in 1991 as singer when Shane MacGowan left the band. Strummer also was well received in his role as Johnny in Jim Jarmusch's film *Mystery Train*. In the 1990s he formed the Mescaleros. He had an underlying heart defect (which didn't stop him running the Paris Marathon in 1982) and died in 2002 aged only 50. **Clive Timperley** formed the Passions who had a 1981 hit with 'I'm In Love With A German Film Star' (about Roadent, The Clash and Sex Pistols roadie). **Richard Dudanski** drummed with PiL for a while, but later relocated to Spain to set up a recording studio.

Ace
Post Ace, Paul Carrack joined Roxy Music as keyboards player, subsequently working with Squeeze, Roger Waters and Mike and the Mechanics. He also toured and recorded regularly as a member of Nick Lowe's band and is still in demand as a session musician and songwriter (the Eagles have covered a couple of his tunes). Not bad for someone who could originally only play in the key of C! **Alan "Bam" King** relocated to New Zealand. For **Fran Byrne** see Bees Make Honey.

Barney Bubbles
In addition to art, Bubbles directed several band videos, including the Specials and Elvis Costello. He also redesigned the *NME*'s logo and recorded an album Ersatz with a band including Hawkwind's Nik Turner called the Imperial Pompadours. Bubbles suffered from bi-polar disorder and also had problems with the Inland Revenue. These were probably contributing factors to his suicide in 1983.

Bees Make Honey
Barry Richardson formed the Barry Richardson Band and also Beeline, relocating to Belgium in the 1980s where he sadly died of cancer on Christmas Day 2001. **Fran Byrne** took the drum stool for Ace on leaving the Bees and later joined Frankie Miller's touring band as well as Juice On The Loose. Much in demand as a session musician he has worked with such diverse artists as Chris Jagger and the Pogues. **Deke O'Brien** and **Mick Molloy** went on to join Irish band Nightbus, with O'Brien founding Scoff Records, one of Ireland's most influential labels, as well as producing many acts. **Malcolm Morley** joined the Man Band for one album (Rhinos, Winos and Lunatics) and has had an eclectic career since working in various capacities with artists as diverse as

Ian Gomm and Plummet Airlines (with whom he recorded a tantalising lost album), Wreckless Eric and Donovan. In 2001 he recorded a solo album Aliens and later another Help Yourself record. He still puts in occasional live appearances.

Brinsley Schwarz

Bob Andrews moved to New Orleans in 1992 and has played with many of the great musicians there including his hero Alan Toussaint. When the Brinsleys split, **Ian Gomm**, wife Karen and family moved to Wales where he built a recording studio in which he recorded the Stranglers and Van Der Graaf Generator frontman Peter Hammill, amongst others. He has released 10 solo albums (including the wonderfully titled *Gomm With The Wind*) and 'Cruel To Be Kind', which he co-wrote, was a number one in Spain for teen sensation Naim Thomas. A little known fact is that Gomm also writes football songs using various pseudonyms for various clubs. He released the album *Crazy for You* in 1997, and *Rock 'N' Roll Heart*, featuring Jeff "Stick" Davis and Pat McInerney, in 2002. Gomm released the 2010 album *Only Time Will Tell* with the American singer-songwriter Jeb Loy Nichols for the Relaxa Records label. **Nick Lowe** has kept doing what he does best, writing great songs. He still tours to this day and has worked with outstanding musicians such as Ry Cooder, Jim Keltner and John Hiatt in Little Village, Paul Carrack and Geraint Watkins. He married into country music's aristocracy when he wed Carlene Carter in 1979, the marriage lasting until 1990. He worked with her step-father Johnny Cash, who recorded a chilling version of Lowe's 'The Beast In Me' on his American Recordings album. Lowe lives in Brentford. **Billy Rankin** worked with Ducks Deluxe, Terraplane and Dave Edmunds after leaving the Brinsleys, and has now retired from the music business, briefly resurfacing for Ducks Deluxe's comeback gig at the 100 Club in 2007. **Brinsley Schwarz** himself continued to work with Graham Parker on occasions throughout the 1980s before becoming a highly skilled luthier, making and fixing guitars for many well-known musicians. As of 2012, he was back on tour with Ducks Deluxe, and in 2016 toured with Graham Parker and released his first solo album *Unexpected* on which he wrote all the songs, played all guitars and bass and sang all the vocals. He followed it in 2021 with his second solo album *Tangled*.

Chilli Willi and the Red Hot Peppers

Martin Stone moved to Paris where he is became a very successful book scout tracking down rare books for customers. He died in 2016. **Phil Lithman** worked with the Residents amongst other people, but died of a heart attack in 1987. **Paul Riley** has become a producer/engineer of note, has a record label (Proper Records) and has sometimes played with the Balham Alligators. In addition to playing with Elvis Costello and the Attractions, **Pete Thomas** has worked as a session drummer for Sheryl Crow, Suzanne Vega and many more.

He is also in supergroup Works Process Administration and a local band, Jack Shit, in Los Angeles where he now lives.

Elvis Costello
Costello's career has, of course, gone stellar and he has consistently refused to be pigeonholed into one style. In 1977 it would have been impossible to imagine him working with artists as diverse as Paul McCartney and Tony Bennett or contributing work to two Grateful Dead tribute albums. Perhaps the ultimate affirmation of his superstar status is that he has appeared in an episode of the Simpsons!

The Count Bishops
They abbreviated their name to the Bishops, but had the stuffing knocked out of them when **Zenon de Fleur** died after being involved in a car crash and **Steve Lewins** left to form the Solid Senders with Wilko Johnson. The band split in 1979, reforming in 2005 for Ace Records 30th anniversary bash. **Mike Spenser** founded the Cannibals in 1976, who worked right up until 2008. **Johnny Guitar** was in both Dr Feelgood and the Inmates, but has moved back home to America where he works as a financial consultant.

Dr Feelgood
Whilst the Feelgood's are still going to this day, **Lee Brilleaux** died of cancer aged only 41 in April 1994. He was with the band until the end of his life, and in 1986 they signed to Stiff for a couple of albums, which was apt as Brilleaux's loan of £400 helped start the label. There are many memorial concerts, mainly at the Oysterfleet Hotel on Canvey with proceeds going to Southend Community Extended Nursing Team, who helped Lee to stay at home during the last months of his illness. **Wilko Johnson** formed the Solid Senders after leaving the Feelgoods in 1977 - they made one album. The Wilko Johnson Band has been a constant in his post-Feelgood career, even when he became a Blockhead with Ian Dury. Blockhead bassist **Norman Watt-Roy** subsequently joined Wilko's band in 1985. In January 2013, Wilko was diagnosed with late stage pancreatic cancer. He decided not to have treatment and threw himself into recording an album with Roger Daltry and a farewell tour of the UK and Japan. However, miraculous things can happen and in 2013, Wilko announced that, thanks to a second opinion and subsequent life-saving surgery, he was cancer-free. In 2015, Wilko and Julien Temple teamed for the documentary *The Ecstasy Of Wilko Johnson*, a film which explored Wilko's diagnosis of terminal cancer, and the unexpected reprieve that followed. he also published a memoir, *Don't You Leave Me Here* and continued to perform. Sadly, Wilko died on 21 November 2022.

Ducks Deluxe/Tyla Gang
Martin Belmont is much in demand as a sidesman as well as having cut two

solo albums. He spent two years as axeman for Carlene Carter, five with Nick Lowe and fifteen with the Johnny Nicky Band. Many people who watch live music in pubs will know him from his appearances with Hank Wangford and Los Pistoleros. The wheel has gone full circle for Belmont as he is also back in the reformed Ducks Deluxe - there is no escape! **Nick Garvey** released a solo album, *Blue Skies*, in 1982. He decided against joining the reformed Ducks Deluxe and bass duties went to Martin Belmont's long-time colleague Kevin Foster. After the Tyla Gang split up in 1978, **Sean Tyla** went solo and earned a gold disc in Germany for the single 'Breakfast In Marin'. He formed The Force with Deke Leonard in 1981, but quit the music business in 1983 to become a pig farmer, car salesman and cricket coach amongst other things. He rejoined the business in 2008 with a solo album *Back In The Saddle*. He reformed both Ducks Deluxe and the Tyla Gang with **Bruce Irvine, Mike Desmarais** and **Brian 'Kid' Turrington** and worked with Billy Bremner in the Trouble Boys. He died in May 2020.

Ian Dury
Dury's successful rock'n'roll career is well documented, but he also wrote the theme tune to the TV show the *Secret Diary of Adrian Mole Aged 13*, the musical *Apples and Pears* and appeared in several movies. He was also an ambassador for UNICEF after campaigning for AIDS awareness. He died of cancer in 2000.

Eddie and the Hot Rods
You can't keep a good band down. Eddie and the Hot Rods reformed for the new millennium and are still going, albeit without **Barrie Masters** who died in 2019.

Eggs Over Easy
After effectively starting Pub Rock, the Eggs moved back home to America - their last gig was at the Tally Ho in November 1971. They supported Yes in the States (ironic or what?) and kept at it until 1981. **Austin de Lone** persuaded Elvis Costello to reunite with Clover to reprise *My Aim Is True* for its 30th anniversary in 2007 for a fundraiser gig to raise money for research into Prader-Willi syndrome, a condition de Lone's son has. De Lone has also been a session player for Costello, Nick Lowe and others. **Jack O'Hara** is a recording engineer, while **Brien Hopkins** died in 2007.

Eric Goulden aka Wreckless Eric
Post Stiff, Goulden has been in several bands including the Captains Of Industry with ex-Blockhead Norman Watt-Roy, and appeared on support to the Damned in 2005. He wrote his autobiography *A Dysfunctional Success* for Jim Driver's Do Not Press publishing company. He now lives in America with American singer songwriter wife **Amy Rigby** with whom he records and tours

- they are well worth seeing if they play a town near you.

Jona Lewie
Lewie had a string of hit singles in the 1980s, including 'Stop The Cavalry' and 'You Will Always Find Me In The Kitchen At Parties'. Ex- Brinsley **Bob Andrews** and Blockhead **Norman Watt-Roy** were also on this Stiff Records album. In latter years, Lewie has taken an interest in the ukulele and contributed a couple of tunes to *Ukephoric: The London Ukulele Festival 2009*.

Kursaal Flyers
Will Birch has had an eclectic career since the demise of the Kursaal Flyers, as musician (with the Records), songwriter, producer, journalist and, latterly, author. His *No Sleep Till Canvey Island* provided inspiration for this book and his *Ian Dury: The Definitive Biography* has been a bestseller in both hardback and paperback. His latest book *Cruel To Be Kind: The Life and Music of Nick Lowe* was published in 2021. **Graeme Douglas'** career has been hampered by diabetes, but he is planning a new album. **Paul Shuttleworth** and **Vic Collins** have formed the Ugly Guys who perform great country rock. The Kursaals have reformed for brief tours, the last one being in 2001, so there is hope they may do so again.

Lene Lovich
Lovich found chart success in the late 1970s, but spent much of the 1980s raising a family with musical and life partner Les Chappell. She has made several records as well as appearing on Peter Hammill's *Fall Of The House Of Usher* and Hawkwind's *Take Me To Your Leader* album.

Mickey Jupp
Jupp has always ploughed a lonely furrow, but has made a number of albums for major labels and small independents. In 2009 he released *Never Too Old To Rock* with members of his old band Legend and continues to self-release albums via the Fans of Mickey Jupp Facebook page. Always respected, his songs have been covered by Delbert McClinton, the Judds and many others. Jupp has swapped the flatlands of Essex for a home in the mountains of the Lake District.

Andrew Jakeman aka Jake Riviera
After leaving Stiff, Riviera formed F-Beat and then Demon, which he has subsequently sold to Crimson productions in 1998. Whilst Costello jumped ship, Riviera continued to manage Nick Lowe for many years. Nick Lowe is currently managed by 2 Jakes Management, which, despite the name, has nothing to do with Riviera. His house on Eel Pie island burnt down in 2009 and he lost his record collection in the blaze. For someone that was so adept at publicity he avoids the public eye himself nowadays.

Dave Robinson
After Stiff Records, Robinson became president of Island Records. He then represented Rick Rubin, and ran Def Jam Records and American Recordings outside of North America, working with Johnny Cash amongst others. He also ran the Blue Note Club and Acid Jazz record label and was thus instrumental in the birth of Acid House and Drum and Bass. He is a consultant to many major record companies.

Graham Parker
The Rumour didn't so much split as fizzle out after 1980 and Parker has since found great success as a solo artist. He has also written three books. He reformed The Rumour in October 2010 and recorded two albums, *Three Chords Good* in 2012 and *Mystery Glue* in 2015.

Rockpile
Dave Edmunds spent the 1980s away from the spotlight producing, amongst others, the Stray Cats, the Every Brothers, and George Harrison. He also appeared with Paul McCartney in the film *Give My Regards To Broad Street* and toured with Ringo Starr in the 1990s. He toured Sweden in the summer of 2011 with Sean Tyla on support. An album release on 19 November 2013 called *...Again*, featured recordings from the 1990s, plus four new tracks, Edmunds' first for almost 20 years, with the title track released as a digital download single. In 2015, Edmunds released his first instrumental album *On Guitar... Dave Edmunds: Rags & Classics*, which featured instrumental covers of classic songs such as The Beach Boys' 'God Only Knows' and Elton John's 'Your Song'. The album was Edmunds' final album and after playing a final show in July 2017, he was reported to have retired from the music business. Edmunds lives in Monmouth, Wales. **Billy Bremner** has also been in demand, playing with the Pretenders, Shakin' Stevens, Carlene Carter and the Coal Porters as well as recording a solo album a decade! He has lived in LA and Nashville, but currently resides in Sweden. He continues to perform and record. **Terry Williams** has drummed for just about everybody from Dire Straits to Tina Turner as well as occupying Man's drum stool on several occasions. He also ran the Tawe Delta Blues Club in his hometown of Swansea. He too played with Sean Tyla. For **Nick Lowe** see Brinsley Schwarz, although we should say his first ever band included Sean Tyla with whom he was at school.

Discography

This section is for vinyl junkies only. This isn't an exhaustive discography and only features material released on vinyl from the period that the book covers.

Ace
Singles
A: How Long? B: Sniffin' About (Anchor ANC 1002),1974
A: I Ain't Gonna Stand For This No More B: Rock And Roll Runaway (Anchor ANC 1014),1975
A: No Future In Your Eyes B: I'm A Man (Anchor ANC 1024), 1975
A: You're All That I Need B: Crazy World (Anchor ANC 1036),1977
A: Found Out The Hard Way B: Why Did You Leave Me? (Anchor ANC 1040), 1977
Albums
Five-A-Side, Anchor, (Anchor ANCL-2001), 1974
Time For Another, (Anchor ANCL2013), 1975
No Strings, Anchor, (Anchor ANCL 2020),1977

The Action
Singles
A: Land Of 1000 Dances B: In My Lonely Room (Parlophone R 5354),1965
A: I'll Keep On Holding On B: Hey Sah-Lo-Ney (Parlophone R 5410),1966
A: Baby You've Got It B: Since I Lost My Baby (Parlophone R 5474),1966
A: Never Ever B: Twentyfourth Hour (Parlophone R 5572), 1967
A: Shadows And Reflections B: Something Has Hit Me (Parlophone R 5610),1967
A: I'll Keep On Holding On B: Wasn't It You? (Edsel E 5001), 1981
A: Since I Lost My Baby B1: Never Ever B2: Wasn't It You? (Edsel E 5002),1981
A: Shadows And Reflections B: Something Has Hit Me (Edsel E 5003),1982
A: Hey Sha-Lo-Ney B: Come On, Come With Me (Edsel E 5008), 1984

Brinsley Schwarz
Singles
A: Shining Brightly B: Hymn To Me (United Artists UP 35118), 1970
A: Country Girl B: Funk Angel (Liberty LBF 1541930), 1970
A: Country Girl B: Funk Angel (United Artists UP 35312),1972
A: Speedoo B: I Worry ('Bout You Baby) (United Artists UP 35588), 1973
A: I've Cried My Last Tear B: (It's Gonna Be A) Bring Down (United Artists UP 356421), 1974
A: (What's So Funny 'Bout) Peace, Love And Understanding B: Ever Since You're Gone (United Artists UP 35700), 1974
A: Everybody B: I Like You, I Don't Love You (United Artists UP 35768),1975
A: There's A Cloud In My Heart B: I Got The Real Thing (United Artists UP 35812),1975
A: Country Girl B1: Surrender To The Rhythm B2: Hooked On Love (United Artists UP 36409), 1978
A: (What's So Funny 'Bout) Peace Love And Understanding B: I've Cried My Last Tear (United Artists UP 36446),1978
Albums
Brinsley Schwarz (United Artists UAS 29111), 1970

Despite It All (Liberty LBG 83427), 1970
Silver Pistol (United Artists UAS 29217), 1972
Nervous On The Road (United Artists UAS 29374), 1972
Please Don't Ever Change (United Artists UAS 29489), 1973
Original Golden Greats (Compilation) (United Artists USP 101), 1974
The New Favourites Of Brinsley Schwarz (United Artists UAS 29641),1974
15 Thoughts Of Brinsley Schwarz (Compilation) (United Artists UAK 30177), 1978

Chilli Willi and the Red Hot Peppers
Singles
A: Breathe A Little B: Friday Song (Mooncrest, Moon 40), 1975
Albums
Kings of the Robot Rhythm (Revelation, Rev 002), 1972
Bongos Over Balham (Mooncrest, CREST 21), 1974

Elvis Costello
Singles
A: Less Than Zero B: Radio Sweetheart (Stiff Records, BUY 11), Mar 1977
A: Alison B: Welcome To The Working Week (Stiff Records, BUY 14), May 1977
A: Red Shoes B: Mystery Dance (Stiff Records, BUY 15),1977
A: Watching The Detectives (Elvis Costello And The Attractions) BI: Blame It On Cain (Live) B2: Mystery Dance (Live) (Stiff Records, BUY 20), 1977
A: Watching The Detectives B: Watching The Detectives (Edit) (Stiff Records BUY20DJ), 1977 Promo Only
A: (I Don't Want To Go To) Chelsea B: You Belong To Me (Radar ADA 3), 1978
A: Stranger In The House (Elvis Costello And The Attractions) B: Neat, Neat, Neat (Radar SAM 83), 1978
A: Pump It Up B: Big Tears (Radar ADA 10), 1978
A: Radio Radio B: Tiny Steps (Radar ADA 24),1978
A: Talking In The Dark B: Wednesday Week (Radar RG 1), 1978
Live At Hollywood High - A1: Accidents Will Happen (Live) A2: Alison (Live) B1: Watching The Detectives (Live) (Radar SAM 90), 1979
A: Oliver's Army B: My Funny Valentine (Radar ADA 31), 1979
A: Accidents Will Happen BI: Talking In The Dark B2: Wednesday Week (Radar ADA 35), 1979
Albums
My Aim Is True (Stiff Records, SEEZ 3), 1977
This Year's Model (Radar Records, RAD 3), 1978
Armed Forces (Radar Records, RAD 14), 1979

Dr Feelgood
Singles
A: Roxette B: (Get Your Kicks On) Route 66 (Live) (United Artists UP 35760), 1974
A: She Does It Right B: I Don't Mind (United Artists UP 35815), 1975
A: Back In The Night B: I'm A Man (Live) (United Artists UP 35857), 1975
A: Riot In Cell Block No 9 (Live) B: Johnny B Goode (Live) (United Artists FEEL 1), 1976
A: Roxette (Live) B: Keep It Out Of Sight (Live) (United Artists UP 361711), 1976
A: Sneakin' Suspicion B: Lights Out (United Artists UP 36255), 1977
A: She's A Windup B: Hi-Rise (United Artists UP 36304), 1977
A: Baby Jane B: Looking Back (United Artists UP 36332), 1977

A: Down At The Doctors B: Take A Tip (United Artists UP 36444), 1978
A: Milk And Alcohol B: Every Kind Of Vice (United Artists UP 36468), 1979
A: As Long As The Price Is Right B: Down At The (Other) Doctors (United Artists UP 36506), 1979
The Feelgoods Encore EP: A1: Riot In Cell Block No 9 (Live) A2: The Blues Had A Baby And They Named It Rock 'n' Roll (Live) B1: Lights Out (Live) B2: Great Balls Of Fire (Live) (United Artists FEEL 2), 1979
A: Put Him Out Of Your Mind B: Bend Your Ear (United Artists BP 306), 1979
Albums
Down By The Jetty (United Artists UAS 29727), 1975
Malpractice (United Artists UAS 29880), 1975
Stupidity (Live) (United Artists UAS 29990), 1976
Be Seeing You (United Artists UAS 30123), 1976
Sneakin Suspicion (United Artists UAS 30075), 1977
Private Practice (United Artists UAG 30184), 1978
Let It Roll (United Artists UAG 30269), 1979
As It Happens (United Artists UAK 30239), 1979

Ducks Deluxe
Singles
A: Coast To Coast B: Bring Back That Packard Car (RCA, RCA 2438),1973
A: Fireball B: Saratoga Suzie (RCA, LPBO 5019),1974
A: Love's Melody B: Two Time Twister (RCA, RCA 2477), 1974
A: I Fought The Law B: Cherry Pie (RCA, RCA 253), 1975
Jumpin' EP A1: I Fought The Law A2: Something's Going On B1: Jumpin' In The Fire B2: Here Comes The Night (Skydog EP-005), 1975
Albums
Ducks Deluxe (RCA LPSI 5008), 1974
Taxi To The Terminal Zone (RCA SF 8402), 1975
Don't Mind Rockin' Tonite (Compilation & Bonus tracks) (RCA NL 71153),1978

Ian Dury and The Blockheads
Singles
A: Sex & Drugs & Rock & Roll B: Razzle In My Pocket (Stiff BUY 17), 1977
A: Sweet Gene Vincent B: You're More Than Fair (Stiff BUY 23), 1977
A: Sex and Drugs and Rock & Roll B 1: Two Stiff Steep Hills B2: England's Glory (*NME* Give-a-way) (Stiff FREEBIE 1), 1977
A: What A Waste B: Wake Up And Make Love With Me (Stiff BUY 27), 1978
A: Hit Me With Your Rhythm Stick B: There Ain't Half Been Some Clever Bastards (Stiff BUY 38), 1978
A: Reasons to be Cheerful, Part 3 B: Common As Muck (Stiff BUY 50), 1979
Albums
New Boots and Panties!! - Ian Dury, (Stiff Records SEEZ 4), 1977
Do It Yourself - Ian Dury & The Blockheads, (Stiff Records, SEEZ 14), 1979

Eddie and the Hot Rods
Singles
A: Writing On The Wall B: Cruisin' (In The Lincoln) (Island WIP 6270),1976
A: Wooly Bully B: Horseplay (Weary Of The Schmaltz) (Island WIP 6306),1976
Live At The Marquee: A1: 96 Tears A2: Get Out Of Denver B1: Gloria B2: (I Can't Get No) Satisfaction (Island IEP 2),1976

A: Teenage Depression B: Shake Island (WIP 6354),1976
A: I Might Be Lying B: Ignore Them (Always Crashing In The Same Bar) (Island WIP 6388),1977
At The Sound Of Speed: A1: Hard Drivin' Man A2: Horseplay B1: Double Checkin' Woman B2: All I Need Is Money (Island IEP 5),1977
A: Do Anything You Wanna Do B: Schoolgirl Love (Island WIP 6401), 1977
A: Quit This Town B: Distortion May Be Expected (Island WIP 6411), 1977
A: Life On The Line B: Do Anything You Wanna Do (Live) (Island WIP 6438), 1978
A: Media Messiahs B: Horror Through Straightness (Island WIP 6464), 1979
A: The Power And The Glory B: Highlands One, Hopefuls Two (Island WIP 6474), 1979
Albums
Teenage Depression (Island ILPS-9457), 1976
Life on the Line (Island ILPS-9509), 1977
Thriller (Island ILPS-9563), 1979

Dave Edmunds
Singles
A: I Hear You Knocking B: Black Bill (MAM MAM 1), 1970
A: I'm Coming Home B: Country Roll (Regal Zonophone RZ 3032), 1971
A: Blue Monday B: I'll Get Along (Regal Zonophone RZ 3037),1971
A: Down, Down, Down B: It Aln't Easy (Regal Zonophone RZ 3059),1972
A: Baby I Love You B: Maybe (Rockfield ROC 1), 1972
A: Born To Be With You Dave Edmunds And Mickey Gee B: Pick Axe Rag (Rockfield ROC 2), 1973
A: Need A Shot Of Rhythm And Blues B: Let It Be Me (Rockfield ROC 4),1974
A: I Hear You Knocking B: Black Bill (MAM MAM 1), 1974
A: I Ain't Never B: Some Other Guy (Rockfield ROC 6), 1975
A: Here Comes The Weekend B: As Lovers Do (Swan Song SSK 19408),1976
A: Where Or When B: New York's A Lonely Town (Swan Song SSK 19409),1976
A: Ju Ju Man B: What Did I Do Last Night? (Swan Song SSK 19410),1977
A: I Knew The Bride B: Back To Schooldays (Swan Song SSK 19411), 1977
A: Deborah B: What Looks Best On You (Swan Song SSK 19413), 1978
A: Television B: Never Been In Love (Swan Song SSK 19414), 1978
A: A1 On The Jukebox B: It's My Own Business (Swan Song SSK 19417),1979
A: Girls Talk B: Bad Is Bad (Swan Song SSK 19418),1979
A: Queen Of Hearts B: Creature From The Black Lagoon (Swan Song SSK 19419),1979
A: Crawling From The Wreckage B: As Lovers Do (Swan Song SSK 19420),1979
Albums
Rockpile (Regal Zonophone RZ 3032), 1971
Subtle as a Flying Mallet (Rockfield RRL101), 1975
Get It (Swan Song, SSK 59404), 1977
Tracks on Wax 4 (Swan Song, SSK 59407),1978
Repeat When Necessary (Swan Song SSK 59409),1979

Wilko Johnson Solid Senders
Singles
A: Walking On The Edge B: Dr. Dupree (Virgin VS 214), 1978
Album
Solid Senders (Virgin V2105) (Initial copies came with a 6 track live LP - VDJ26)

Mickey Jupp & Legend
Singles
A: My Typewriter B: Nature's Radio (Stiff Records UPP 1), 1978 (7-inch promo)
Album
The Legend Of (Stiff Records GET 2), 1978 (Limited edition of 15,000)

Mickey Jupp
Singles
A: Old Rock 'n' Roller B: S.P.Y. (Stiff Records BUY 36), 1978
Album
Juppanese (Stiff Records SEEZ 10), 1978

Kilburn and the High Roads
Singles
A: Rough Kids B: Billy Bentley (Dawn, DNS 1090), 1974
A: Crippled With Nerves B: Huffety Puff (Dawn DNS 1102), 1975
Album
Handsome - Kilburn & the High Roads (Dawn DNLS 3065), 1975
Wotabunch! - Kilburn & the High Roads (Warner Brothers K56513), 1977

Kippington Lodge
Singles
A: Shy Boy B: Lady On A Bicycle (Parlophone R 5645), 1967
A: Rumours B: And She Cried (Parlophone R 5677), 1968
A: Tell Me A Story B: Understand A Woman (Parlophone R 5717), 1968
A: In My Life B: I Can See Her Face (Parlophone R 5776), 1969
A1: Rumours A2: Lady On A Bicycle B1: And She Cried B2: Shy Boy (EMI EMI 2894), 1978

Kursaal Flyers
Singles
A: Speedway B: Chocs Away (UK 2012001), 1975
A: Hit Records B: Brakeman (UK 116) 1975
A: Cruisin' For Love B: Slimmin' (For The Women) (UK 129), 1976
A: Little Does She Know B: Drinking Socially (CBS 4689), 1976
A: Radio Romance B: Girl Talk (CBS 4973), 1977
A: The Sky's Falling In On Our Love B: Revolver (CBS 5498), 1977
A: Television Generation B: Revolver (CBS 5771), 1977
Albums
Chocs Away (UK UKAL 1011), 1975
The Great Artiste (UK UKAL 1018), 1975
Golden Mile (CBS 81622), 1976
Five Live Kursaals (CBS 82253), 1977

Jona Lewie
Singles
A: The Baby's She's On The Street B: Denny Laine's Valet (Stiff Records BUY 30), 1978
A: God Bless Whoever Sent You B: Feeling Stupid (Stiff Records BUY 61), 1979
Album
On The Other Hand There's A Fist (Stiff Records SEEZ 8), 1978

Lew Lewis
Singles
A: Boogie On The Street B: Caravan Man (Stiff Records BUY 5), 1976
A: Out For A Lark B: You'd Better Watch Yourself (United Artists UA 36217), 1977
A: Lucky Seven B: Night Talk (LEW 1), 1978 (private pressing distributed by Stiff)
A: Lucky Seven B: Night Talk (Stiff Records LEW 1), 1978
Album
Save The Wail (Stiff Records SEEZ 16), 1979

Lene Lovich
Singles
A: I Think We're Alone Now B: Lucky Number (Stiff Records BUY 32), 1978
A: Lucky Number B: Home (Stiff Records BUY 42), 1978
A: Say When B: One Lonely Heart (Stiff Records BUY 46), 1979
A: Birdsong B: Trixi (Stiff Records BUY 53), 1979
A: Angels B: The Fly (Stiff Records BUY 63), 1979
Albums
Stateless (Stiff Records SEEZ 7), 1978
Flex (Stiff Records SEEZ 19), 1980

Nick Lowe
Singles
A: Keep It Out Ta Sight B: (I've Been Taking The) Truth Drug (Dynamite Records DYR 45007), 1976
A: So It Goes B: Heart Of The City (Stiff Records BUY 1), 1976
Bowi EP: A1: Born A Woman A2: Shake That Rat B1: Mary Provost B2: Endless Sleep (Stiff Records LAST 1), 1977
A: Halfway To Paradise B: I Don't Want The Night To End (Stiff Records BUY 21), 1977
A: I Love The Sound Of Breaking Glass B: They Called It Rock (Nick Lowe With Rockpile) (Radar ADA 1), 1978
A: Little Hitler B: Cruel To Be Kind (ADA 12), 1978
A: American Squirm B: (What's So Funny 'bout) Peace, Love And Understanding (Nick Lowe And His Sound) (Radar ADA 26), 1978
Albums
Jesus Of Cool (Radar Records RAD 1), 1978
Labour Of Lust (Radar Records RAD 21), 1979

Mighty Baby
Singles
A: Devil's Whisper B: Virgin Spring (Blue Horizon 2096 00327),1971
Albums
Mighty Baby (Head Records HDLS 6002), 1969
Jug Of Love (Blue Horizon 2931-001), 1971

The Motors
Singles
A: Dancing The Night Away B: Whiskey And Wine (Virgin VS 186), 1977
A: Be What You Gotta Be B: You Beat The Hell Outta Me (Virgin VS 194), 1977
A: Sensation B: The Day I Found A Fiver (Virgin VS 206), 1978
A: Airport B: Cold Love (Virgin VS 219), 1978

A: Forget About You B: Picturama (Virgin VS 222), 1978
A: Today B: Here Comes The Hustler (Virgin VS 236), 1978
Albums
The Motors (Virgin V2089)
Approved By The Motors (Virgin V2101)

Graham Parker And The Rumour
Singles
A: Silly Thing (Live) B: Kansas City (Live) (Phonogram GPS 1), 1976
A: Silly Thing B: I'm Gonna Use It Now (Vertigo 6059 135),1976
A: Soul Shoes B: White Honey (Vertigo 6059 147), 1976
A: Hotel Chambermaid B: Don't Ask Me Questions (Vertigo 6059 158),1976
A: Pourin' It All Out B: Help Me Shake It (Vertigo 6059 161), 1977
A: Hold Back The Night B: (Let Me Get) Sweet On You (Vertigo DINK 001), 1977
A1: Hold Back The Night A2: (Let Me Get) Sweet On You B1: White Honey (Live) B2: Soul Shoes (Live) (Vertigo PARK 001), 1977
A: New York Shuffle B: The Bleep (Vertigo 6059 185),1977
A: Hey Lord Don't Ask Me Questions B: Watch The Moon Come Down (Live) (Vertigo PARK 002), 1978
A: Protection B: I Want You Back (Alive) (Vertigo 6059 219), 1979
Albums
Live At Marble Arch (Vertigo GP1), 1976
Howlin' Wind (Vertigo 6360129), 1976
Heat Treatment (Vertigo 6360137), 1976
Stick To Me (Vertigo 9102 017), 1977
The Parkerilla (Vertigo 6641 797), 1978
Squeezing Out Sparks (Vertigo 6360 168), 1979

The Records
Singles
A: Starry Eyes B: Paint Her Face (The Record Company NB-2), 1978
A: Rock And Roll Love Letter B: Wives And Mothers Of Tomorrow (Virgin Records VS247), 1979
A: Teenarama B: Held Up High (Virgin Records VS250), 1979
A: Hearts In Her Eyes B: So Sorry (Virgin Records VS330), 1980
Albums
Shades In Bed with Bonus High Heels 12 EP (Virgin Records V2122),1979
Crashes (Virgin Records V2155), 1980

Rockpile
Singles
A: Wrong Way B: Now And Always (F-Beat XX 9), 1980
A: Teacher Teacher B: Fool Too Long (F-Beat XX 11), 1980
Albums
Seconds Of Pleasure initial copies with Nick Lowe And Dave Edmunds Sing The Everly Brothers EP (F-Beat XXLP 7) 1980 - A1: Take A Message To Mary A2: Crying In The Rain B1: Poor Jenny B2: When Will I Be Loved (F-Beat BEV 1)

The Rumour
Singles
A: Do Nothing Till You Hear From Me B: Somethin' Goin' On (Vertigo 6059 174), 1977
A: I'm So Glad B: This Town (Vertigo 6059 181), 1977
A: Frozen Years B: All Fall Down (Stiff Records RUM 1 - promo), 1979
A: Frozen Years B: All Fall Down (Stiff Records BUY 43), 1979
A: Emotional Traffic B: Hard Enough To Show (Stiff Records BUY 45), 1979
A: My Little Red Book B: Name And Number (Stiff Records BUY 71), 1980
A: I Don't Want The Night To End B: Pyramids (Stiff Records BUY 92), 1980
Albums
Max (Vertigo 6360149), 1977
Frogs, Sprouts, Clogs And Krauts (Stiff Records SEEZ 13), 1978
Purity Of Essence (Stiff Records SEEZ 27), 1980

Rachel Sweet
Singles
A: B.A.B.Y. B: Suspended Animation (Stiff Records BUY 39), 1978
A: I Go To Pieces B: Who Does Lisa Like? (Stiff Records BUY 44), 1979
A: Baby Let's Play House B: Wildwood Saloon (Stiff Records BUY 55),1979
Album
Fool Around (Stiff Records SEEZ 12), 1978

Tyla Gang
Singles
A: Styrofoam B: Texas Chainsaw Massacre (Stiff Records BUY 4), 1976
A: Dust On The Needle B: Pool Hall Punks (Beserkley BZZ 5), 1977
Sean's Demos EP: A1: Suicide Jockey A2: It's Only Rock And Roll (But It Gets Up Your Nose) B1: Mad Muchachos B2: Cannons Of The Boogie Night (Beserkley SEAN 1), 1977
A: Tropical Love B: Walking The Dog (Live) (Beserkley BZZ 15), 1978
Albums
Yachtless (Beserkley BSERK 11), 1977
Moonproof (Beserkley BSERK 16), 1978

Wreckless Eric
Singles
A: Whole Wide World B: Semaphore Signals (Stiff Records BUY 16), 1977
A: Reconnez Cherie B: Rags And Tatters (Stiff Records BUY 25), 1978
A: Take The Cash (K.A.S.H) B: Girlfriend (Stiff Records BUY 34), 1978
A: Crying, Waiting, Hoping B: I Wish It Would Rain (Stiff Records BUY 40), 1978
A: Hit And Miss Judy B: Let's Go To The Pictures (Stiff Records BUY 49), 1979
AI: Hit And Miss Judy A2: Let's Go To The Pictures B: I Need A Situation (Stiff Records S12 BUY 49) ,1979 (12-inch orange vinyl)
Albums
Wreckless Eric (Stiff Records SEEZ 6), 1978
Wreckless Eric (Stiff Records SEEZB 6), 1978 (10-inch brown vinyl)
The Wonderful World Of Wreckless Eric (Stiff Records SEEZ 9), 1978
Big Smash (Stiff Records SEEZ 21), 1980

Sources

Chapter 1
Melody Maker, April 20, 1974
Shindig! Annual Number 1
Melody Maker, August 1964
Melody Maker, July 1963
LWT Southbank Show, 1981.
Subculture the Meaning of Style, Dick Hebdige
Melody Maker, February 1963
Melody Maker, July 1963
Days In The Life, Jonathon Green
Mojo, February 2009
The Sue Label Story CD booklet
Bucket Full of Brains, issue 46
ZigZag, November 1974, Andy Childs, The Ballad of Chilli Willi and the Red Hot Peppers
International Times, August 1969
Ptolemaic Terrascope
Melody Maker, February 1969

Chapter 2
Hen's Teeth CD booklet
Melody Maker, April 1974
ZigZag, No. 55
Interview with the author
ZigZag No. ??, Pete Frame, Despite It All: The Brinsley Schwarz Aftermath
Interview with the author
Sounds, January 1973
Mojo, April 2009
No Sleep Till Canvey Island, Will Birch
Melody Maker, April 1974
Mojo, April 2009
Days In The Life, Jonathon Green
ZigZag, November 1975
Sounds, January 1973
Melody Maker, April 1974
PhishyinJamBandMusic, April 2009
Melody Maker, April 1974

Chapter 3
http://www.terrascope.co.uk/Features/LadbrokeGrove.htm
Days In The Life, Jonathon Green
Let It Rock, April 1974
Interview with the author
No Sleep Till Canvey Island, Will Birch
Jerry Gilbert, Sounds
Ptolemaic Terrascope,, November 1997
ZigZag, November 1975
ZigZag, No. 17, Pete Frame, Despite It All: The Brinsley Schwarz Aftermath
Let It Rock April 1974
Days In The Life, Jonathon Green
Interview with the author
NME April 1970
Melody Maker
Mojo April 2009
Reasons to be Cheerful: The Life and Work of Barney Bubbles, Paul Gorman

Chapter 4
International Times, August 1969
Ptolemaic Terrascope, 1995
Interview with the author
BBC paperwork 26 May 1970
Melody Maker, April 1974
ZigZag, November 1974, Andy Childs, The Ballad of Chilli Willi and the Red Hot Peppers

Chapter 5
NME, April 10 1970
Good 'n' Cheap CD booklet
NME, April 10 1970
Interview with the author
Melody Maker, October 3 1973
Melody Maker, 6 October 1973g
Mojo, April 2009
ZigZag 37, Vol. 4 No. 1

Lowe on Mark Radcliffe Show, BBC Radio 02, December 2003
Ian Hoare, source and date unknown
NME 30 March 1974
Sex & Drugs and Rock 'n Roll: The Life of Ian Dury, Richard Balls

Chapter 6
Sounds, 30 March 1974
Interview with the author
Sounds, 13 January 1973
Let It Rock October 1972
11 No Sleep Till Canvey Island, Will Birch
NME, 3 April 1971
Let It Rock, April 1973
No Sleep Till Canvey Island, Will Birch

Chapter 7
Interview with the author
Hawkhead Records biography
Let It Rock
Sounds, 26 November 1977
Interview with the author
Bongos Over Balham CD booklet
ZigZag, November 1974, Andy Childs, The Ballad of Chilli Willi and the Red Hot Peppers
Reasons to be Cheerful: The Life and Work of Barney Bubbles, Paul Gorman
Bongos Over Balham CD booklet

Chapter 8
Interview with the author
Steven Rosen interview with Paul and Linda McCartney July 6, 1973 Birmingham England
Sounds, 30 March 1974
NME, 14 July 1973
Mojo, April 2009
Sounds, 3 June 1978
Sounds, 30 March 1974

NME, 14 July 1973

Chapter 9
NME, 4 May 1974
Paul Morley, NME, 2 June 1979
Trouser Press, July 1978
Uncut, August 1998
Handsome CD booklet
Chris Welch, unpublished, Summer 1995
NME, 2 August 1975
NME, 2 June 1979
Sex & Drugs and Rock 'n Roll: The Life of Ian Dury, Richard Balls
Let It Rock, April 1973
No Sleep Till Canvey Island, Will Birch, page 149
Melody Maker, May 5 1973
NME, 1 September 1973
The Who: Maximum R&B, Richard Barnes
Negative Reaction, 1978

Chapter 10
Interview with the author
Shakin' Street, June 1974
Melody Maker, 6 October 1973
Interview with the author
Sounds, 1 January 1977
NME, 31 August 1974
ZigZag, April 1975, Andy Childs
ZigZag Talks To Willo Johnson of Dr. Feelgood,
Let It Rock, 1 June 1975
Blues Bag, No. 3, March 1990
NME, 15 November 1975
Tony Fletcher interview with Dave Edmunds
Let It Rock, May 1974
Sounds, 15 April 1977
Hawkhead Records press release
http://musicremedy.com/tlThe_101ers/album/Elgin_Avenue_Breakdown_Revisited-160 7.html

Let It Rock, July 1974
Down By The Jetty, The Dr Feelgood Story, Tony Moon

Chapter 11
Sex & Drugs and Rock 'n Roll: The Life of Ian Dury, Richard Balls
NME, 2 August 1975
Chris Welch, unpublished, Summer 1995
NME, 14 December 1974
Negative Reaction, February 1977
Trouser Press, July 1978
NME, 14 December 1974
NME, 2 August 1974
Negattve Reaction, 1978
ZigZag, number 47
Chris Welch, unpublished, Summer 1995
Handsome CD booklet
The England's Dreaming Tapes, Jon Savage
New Boots and Love Pants, BBC Radio
A Dysfunctional Success, Eric Goulden

Chapter 12
Sean Tyla press release
Interview with the author
ZigZag, number 39
Ptolemaic Terrascope, number 20, 1996
Bongos Over Balham, CD booklet
Chilli Willi and The Red Hot Peppers, CD booklet
Melody Maker, 10 August 1974
Reasons to be Cheerful: The Life and Work of Barney Bubbles, Paul Gorman

Chapter 13
The Face, August 1983
Let Them All Talk, Brian Hinton

Squatting archive: http://www.wussu.com/squatting/als09113.htm
The England's Dreaming Tapes, Jon Savage
Uncut, September 1999
Redemption Song: The Definitive Biography of Joe Strummer, Chris Salewicz
Melody Maker, 26 July 1975
Melody Maker, 1981
The Clash: Return of the Last Gang in Town: The Story of the Clash, Marcus Gray
Let It Rock, December 1975
Melody Maker, 6 July 1974
Ace Records: Labels Unlimited, David Stubbs
http://www.101ers.co.uk/stories.htm

Chapter 14
Let It Rock
Melody Maker, November 23 1974
NME, 15 January 1977
Melody Maker, 13 December 1975
Interview with the author
Sounds, 3 June 1978
Mojo, 2009
ZigZag, July 1975
Melody Maker, 22 March 1975

Chapter 15
NME, January 18 1975
Ptolemaic Terrascope Number 20, 1996
Reasons to be Cheerful: The Life and Work of Barney Bubbles, Paul Gorman
NME, January 18 1975
ZigZag, August 1975
Bongos Over Balham, CD booklet
Interview recorded 08/02119 79 for Industrial Wasteland

No Sleep Till Canvey Island, Will Birch

Chapter 16
Interview with the author
Sean Tyla press release
Q, August 1987
ZigZag, April 1975, Andy Childs
ZigZag Talks To Willo Johnson of Dr. Feelgood,
NME, June 14 1975
NME, 24 October 1975
Feelgood, page 15
NME, 25 October 1975

Chapter 17
Melody Maker, 9 October 1976
Melody Maker, 25 September 1976
Melody Maker, 1 March 1975
Eddie and the Hot Rods: Do Anything You Wanna Do, Steve Crancher
ZigZag, May 1976
NME, May 1975
Let It Rock, October 1975
Melody Maker, 19 October 1974
ZigZag, May 1976, Paul Kendal, Punk Rock Comes To Town
Melody Maker, 1976

Chapter 18
Interview with the author
ZigZag, January 1977, Andy Childs, Graham Parker
Sleeve notes 'Live at the Newlands Tavern' official bootleg CD
ZigZag, January 1977, Andy Childs, Graham Parker
NME, 30 July 1977
No Depression, July-August 2007
Melody Maker, 16 December 1978
NME, 1 May 1976

Chapter 19
Melody Maker, 26 July 1975
Ace Records: Labels Unlimited, David Stubbs
Record Mirror, 28 October 1978
Melody Maker, 1 March 1975
Sounds, January 1976
Melody Maker, 28 February 1981
The Clash: Return Of The Last Gang In Town
Melody Maker; 26 July 1975
http://northforksound.
blogspot.com/ searchllabellEddie2 OAnd 2 OThe2 OHot2 ORods

Chapter 20
Melody Maker, 27 December 1975
Melody Maker, 18 October 1975
ZigZag 57, 1975, Andy Childs, Dr. Feelgood On The Road
Melody Maker, 6 November 1976
Melody Maker, 18 October 1975
Trouser Press, July 1978
Chris Welch, unpublished, Summer 1995
NME, 27 December 1975
Channel 4 Television documentary
http://www.djhistory.com/features/chaz-jankel-2002 15
http://www.residentadvisor.netlfeature.aspx?9 28
Sounds, 25 February 1978

Chapter 21
Redemption Song: The Definitive Biography of Joe Strummer, Chris Salewicz
The Clash: Return of the Last Gang in Town: The Story of the Clash, Marcus Gray
Eddie and the Hot Rods: Do Anything You Wanna Do, Steve Crancher

When the Lights Went Out: Britain in the Seventies, Andy Beckett
Melody Maker, 28 February 1981
Mojo, April 2009
Melody Maker, 25 September 1976
In Session Tonight: Complete Radio 1 Recordings, Ken Garner
Interview with the author
Melody Maker, 30 October 1976

Chapter 22
NME, 17 April 1976
ZigZag, June 1976
Village Voice, Vol. XXI No. 11
BBC Radio Two, Stiff Records documentary
Interview with the author
If it ain'i Stiff, BBC 4 television documentary
Music Week, August 1976
BBC 2, The Late Show
Mojo, new wave special
Melody Maker, 14 August 1976
Melody Maker, 18 September 1976
Oil City Confidential DVD

Chapter 23
NME, 30 July 1977
Trouser Press, August 1978
NME, 14 August 1976
Melody Maker, 16 December 1978
Peter Grant: The Man Who Led Zeppelin, Peter Grant
Trouser Press, August 1978
NME, 30 July 1977
Creem, February 1981
http://www.geocities.com/mikegriffiths6/Billy_Bremner_Q_and_A.html
Mojo, November 2006
Sounds, September 1976
ZigZag, December 1976
Melody Maker, 18 December 1976
ZigZag, December 1976

Eddie and the Hot Rods: Do Anything You Wanna Do, Steve Crancher

Chapter 24
Mojo, May 1996
Complicated Shadows: The Life And Music Of Elvis Costello, Graeme Thomson
Cherry Red TV, interview with Charlie Gillett
Trouser Press, December 1977
My Aim Is True sleeve notes 7
NME, 27 August 1977
The Stiff Records Story, BBC Radio 2 documentary
Interview with the author
The England's Dreaming Tapes, Jon Savage
International Times, issue 4, number 15
NME, 6 November 1977
Mojo, new wave special
NME, 6 November 1976
NME, date unknown early 1977

Chapter 25
NME, 12 November 1977
NME, 27 September 1975
Tyla Gang press release
Trouser Press, December 1977
The Motors 1 sleeve notes
Melody Maker, 28 October 1978

Chapter 26
NME, 4 June 1977
NME, 3 June 1978
NME, 4 June 1977
Melody Maker, 30 October 1976
Down By The Jetty, The Dr Feelgood Story, Tony Moon
www.zanLco.uk/lnterviews
Q, August 1987
Melody Maker, 7 May 1977

NME, 8 October 1977
Sounds, 3 June 1978
NME, 17 September 1977

Chapter 27
My Aim Is True sleeve notes
Reasons to be Cheerful: The Life and Work of Barney Bubbles, Paul Gorman, page 88
thebigissuescotland.com
Interview with the author
Music Week, date unknown circa 1981-2
BBC Radio One Documentary, 1992
http://laist.com/2007 108/07/laist_interview_2S.php
Bass Player, June 1997
NME, 8 June 1977
http://www.spin.com/articles/spin-interview-elvis-costello
Melody Maker, August 6 1977
NME, 3 September 1977
Howling At The Moon: The True Story of the Mad Genius of the Music World, Walter Yetnikoff and David Ritz
The Stiff Records Story, BBC Television
Billboard, 15 October 1977
Sex & Drugs and Rock 'n Roll: The Life of Ian Dury, Richard Balls
Stiff The Story of a Record Label, Bert Muirhead

Chapter 28
Interview with the author
Nuggets magazine, June 1976
Sounds, 25 February 1978
Sounds 30 July 1977
NME, 30 July 1977
http://homepage.ntlworld.com/paul.gray / archives2 0&2 Ostories 1.htm

http://www.nuvo.netlhammer/intlgparker.html
No Depression, issue 58
Time, 9 July 1979
Eddie and the Hot Rods: Do Anything You Wanna Do, Steve Crancher
Trouser Press, April 1978
http://homepage.ntlworld.com/paul.gray / archives2 0&2 Osto¬ries2.htm
Tyla Gang press release

Chapter 29
Chris Welch, unpublished 1995
Ian Dury talks to Vinyl Mogul about New Boots And Panties, Demon Records, RANT1
Mojo, May 1996
NME, Dave Edmunds Gets Jilted by David Brown, date unknown
NME, 30 July 1977
Melody Maker. 15 October 1977
The Stiff Records Story, BBC Television
Mojo, October 1997
NME, 25 March 1978
Portland Mercury, 1 October 2009
Mojo, October 1997
Live Stiffs Live film
Trouser Press, August 1978
Sounds, 8 October 1977
NME, 8 October 1977

Chapter 30
BBC Radio documentary
Record Collector, September 1995
Billboard, 14 January 1978
Billboard, 25 March 1978
BBC Radio documentary
Bomp!, January 1979
Time, 26 December 1977
Sleeve notes This Year's Model CD

Chris Welch, unpublished, Summer 1995
Sex & Drugs and Rock 'n Roll: The Life of Ian Dury, Richard Balls
NME, 2 June 1979
Mojo new wave special 2008
Portland Mercury, 1 October 2009
NME, 18 March 1978
Trouser Press, May 1978
Jesus of Cool sleeve notes
Melody Maker, 16 December 1978
Musician, July 1981
Rip It Up (New Zealand), November 1988

Chapter 31
BBC Radio, The Stiff Records Story
Music Week, date unknown
Lene Lovich Radio Interview Album, Stiff Records LENE 1
Juppanese sleeve notes
Perfect Sound Forever, furious.corn/PERFECT llenelovich2 .html
BBC Radio, The Stiff Records Story
The Lewiston Daily Sun, 12 September 1979
Melody Maker, 28 October 1978
NME, 28 October 1978
Sounds, 1979
Billboard, 4 August 1979
National Public Radio, April 2006
Rhythm, October 1989
Trouser Press, May 1978
Musician March 1990
NME ,29 January 1979
Armed Forces sleeve notes
NME, 3 September 1977
BBC Radio Documentary
People, April 3 1979
Reasons to be Cheerful: The Life and Work of Barney Bubbles, Paul Gorman
Jesus Of Cool CD reissue booklet

The Welsh Connection, No. 20, April/May 1994
Trouser Press, Feburary 1981
Keith Phipps A.V. Club, July 31,2002
Creem, September 1982
Dave DiMartino, Creem, February 1981
Capital Radio, 22 October 1980
Musician, July 1981

Photo Credits

Page 123
Mighty Baby, Head Records publicity photo
Brinsley Schwarz, courtesy Ian Gomm

Page 124
Ducks Deluxe, RCA Records publicity photo
Dr Feelgood, courtesy Chris Needs

Page 125
Eddie and The Hot Rods, Island Records publicity photo
The Kursaal Flyers, unknown photographer

Page 126
Dave Edmunds, unknown photographer
Ian Dury, Dhphoto
Chilli Willi and The Red Hot Peppers, publicity photo
Lene Lovich, Richard Marchewka

Page 127
Elvis Costello, John Blaney
Graham Parker and The Rumour performing on stage at the Auckland Town Hall. Auckland Libraries Heritage Collections

Page 128
Nick Lowe, John Blaney
Wreckess Eric, Jona Lewie, Rachel Sweet, Lene Lovich and Mickey Jupp, Stiff Records publicity photo

Index

101ers, The   81, 82, 98-102, 133-135, 138, 141-144, 218

Ace   104-106, 108, 114, 147, 148, 180, 218, 220, 224
Action, The   15-20, 24, 38, 60, 104, 134, 224
Andrews, Bob   26, 28, 32, 34, 36-37, 40, 48, 52, 59, 63, 65, 79-80, 115, 122-123, 129, 201, 206, 219, 222
Armstrong, Roger   99, 100, 133-135, 141, 155, 161, 162, 176
Azoth   20

Bailey, Paul   60, 112, 122, 126
Be Stiff tour   204, 206, 208
Bees Make Honey   45, 47, 48, 57, 104, 218
Belmont, Martin   49, 56-59, 76, 80-81, 92-93, 97, 113, 122, 124, 129-130, 132, 180, 182-183, 200, 220, 221
Big Figure, The (John Martin)   77, 78, 84, 115, 124
Birch, Will   33, 78, 103, 108, 120, 125, 157, 222
Blackhill Enterprises   19, 38, 139, 148, 187, 189
Bodnar, Andrew   122, 129, 193, 201
Bon Temps Roulez   95, 96, 122, 129
Bremner, Billy   126, 154, 155, 169, 191, 210, 221, 223
Brilleaux, Lee (Lee Collinson)   14, 77, 78, 111, 114-115, 117, 124, 137, 147, 151, 167-169, 220
Brinsley Schwarz   21, 24, 32-37, 39-41, 46-49, 51-54, 56-57, 60, 63-64, 66, 68, 72, 74, 76, 79-80, 83-84, 95, 97-99, 106-108, 113, 114, 120, 122-123, 129, 130, 132, 148, 150, 152, 155, 219, 223-225
Bubbles, Barney (Colin Fulcher)   30, 36, 39, 59, 62, 95, 108, 110, 169, 172, 175-176, 202, 211, 218

Canvey Island   33, 77, 103, 116, 117, 119, 147, 169, 222
Carrack, Paul   104-105, 218, 219
Carroll, Ted   99-101, 133-135, 141, 149
Chandler, Chas   25, 43, 50
Chilli Willi and the Red Hot Peppers   39, 42, 59-60, 93, 95-96, 109, 110, 112, 126, 143, 175, 206, 219, 225
Chiswick Records   99, 133-134, 141-143, 149-150, 162, 176, 206

Clash, The 19, 67, 81, 101, 113, 143, 155-156, 168, 173, 182, 196, 207, 216, 217, 218
Clover 159, 171-172, 178, 221
Columbia Records 146, 159, 177-179, 197-202, 209, 214
Costello, Elvis 95, 97-98, 104, 127, 142, 143, 158-160, 171-178, 181, 184, 187, 189-193, 195-200, 202, 206-207, 209-212, 215, 216, 218-222, 225
Count Bishops, The 133-135, 155, 169, 220

Damned, The 67, 155, 162, 165, 174, 176, 178, 182, 187, 191, 214, 221
Davies, Dai 57, 78, 80, 92, 106, 114
Douglas, Graeme 103, 125, 181, 184, 222
Dr Feelgood 14, 77-78, 81-84, 92, 98, 99, 103, 104, 106, 109-112, 114-117, 120, 121, 124, 137-138, 143, 146-149, 151, 156, 158, 167-170, 177, 184, 196, 210, 220, 225
Ducks Deluxe 56-59, 61, 68, 71, 76, 78, 80-81, 92-93, 98, 113-114, 122, 124, 164-166, 219-221, 226
Dudanski, Richard 143, 218
Dury, Ian 68, 69, 86, 90, 101, 126, 138, 140, 178, 181, 189, 194, 198-199, 204, 206, 208-209, 213, 216, 220-222, 226

Eddie and the Hot Rods 117-121, 135, 136, 138, 141-142, 144, 155, 157, 181, 196, 199, 221
Edmunds, Dave 54, 79, 83-84, 92, 106, 126, 130, 150, 152, 154, 160, 169, 187, 190, 191, 201, 202, 216, 219, 223, 227, 230
Eggs Over Easy 25, 43-45, 48-50, 57, 221
Eichler, John 31, 37, 56, 79
Eire Apparent 26, 31, 32, 63, 64

Famepushers 31-33, 35, 36
Farren, Mick 25, 77, 115, 118, 134, 169
Fenwick, Chris 77, 109, 137, 138, 146
Flamin' Groovies 56, 58, 80, 165
Flip City 96-98, 158-160, 173

Garvey, Nick 58, 93, 124, 165, 221
Gillett, Charlie 50, 72, 73, 86, 130, 159, 171, 188, 206, 208
Gomm, Ian 41, 47, 48, 53, 57, 64, 80, 83, 92, 123, 179, 209, 213, 219
Goulding, Steve 122, 153, 169, 193, 201

Graham Parker and the Rumour   127, 130-132, 142, 153, 164, 174, 178, 180-184, 196, 203, 230
Gray, Paul   118, 125, 181

Hawkwind   27, 30, 51, 61, 118, 182, 211
Help Yourself   32, 34, 56-57, 164, 219
Higgs, Dave   117, 125, 184
Hollis, Ed   118

Jakeman, Andrew (see also Riviera, Jake)   103, 107, 109, 222
Jankel, Chaz   139
Johnson, Wilko   77, 120, 124, 174, 193, 220, 227
Jupp, Mickey   119, 128, 129, 205, 208, 222, 228

Kilburn and the High Roads   68-75, 77, 81, 82, 86-90, 138, 143, 159, 192, 228
Kippington Lodge   21-29, 31-32, 36, 37, 202, 228
Kokomo   95, 109, 111-112, 180
Kursaal Flyers   103-104, 107-108, 117, 125, 143, 156-157, 222, 228

Lauder, Andrew   34, 83, 137, 149, 178, 200
Lewie, Jona   205
Lewis, Huey   171
Lewis, Lew   118, 144, 162, 168, 229
Lithman, Phil   41, 59, 219
Lovich, Lene   126, 128, 129, 204-209, 222, 229
Lowe, Nick   13, 23-25, 27-28, 31-35, 40-41, 47, 50-51, 53-54, 59, 64, 66, 71, 83, 97, 106, 114, 123, 130-132, 134, 143, 146, 148-155, 160, 162, 169, 171-174, 177-178, 183, 187, 189-191, 193-198, 200-203, 205, 207, 209-211, 213-216, 219, 221-223, 229-230
Lydon, John   90, 142-143, 173

McCartney, Paul   49, 52, 63-65, 97, 216, 220, 223
McCullough, Henry   63-65, 168
McMaster, Andy   80, 93, 113, 124, 165-166
Maile, Vic   84-85, 137, 141
Marquee Club   17, 26, 45, 107, 144
Martin, George   17

Masters, Barrie 117-121, 125, 142, 145, 184, 221
Mayo, John 'Gypie' 169
Mighty Baby 30, 38-39, 41, 45, 59, 104, 123, 139, 229
Molton, Edward 30-33, 36-37, 39
Motors, The 93, 166, 182, 229-230

Nashville Rooms, The 121, 135, 142, 155, 174, 213
Naughty Rhythms Tour 109
Nelki, Gordon 73, 74, 188
Nesmith, Mike 94
Newton-Rohoman, David 71
Nieve, Steve 174, 211

O'Hara, Jack 43, 221
Ocean, Humphrey 74, 86
Old Grey Whistle Test 48, 66

Parker, Graham 15, 95, 122, 127, 129-132, 142, 143, 148, 153, 158-159, 164, 174, 178, 180-184, 196, 203, 210, 219, 223, 230
Pathway Studios 134, 141, 166, 169
Payne, Davey 71, 191, 192
Peel, John 45, 51, 73, 101, 144-145, 150, 161, 166, 173
Pink Fairies 61, 160, 162

Rankin, Billy 27, 31, 59, 65, 113, 123, 219
Radar Records 178, 200, 207, 209, 225, 229
Reed, Lou 81, 198-199
Revelation Records 59-61
Richardson, Barry 45, 47, 218
Riley, Paul 60-61, 129, 148, 152, 153, 169, 219
Riviera, Jake (see also Jakeman, Jake) 62, 146-152, 154, 160, 162, 165, 169, 171-178, 187, 189-193, 196-198, 200, 202, 209, 212, 216, 222
Robinson, Dave 25, 31-33, 35, 37, 40-41, 43-46, 51, 54, 65, 71, 78, 95, 101, 109, 110, 122, 138-139, 145, 147, 149, 152, 158, 161, 164, 187, 223
Rockfield Studios 53, 54, 76, 84, 92, 104, 106, 131, 152, 164, 165
Rockpile 154-155, 169, 190-191, 202-203, 205, 209, 210, 213-216, 223, 227, 229, 230
Roper, Tim 57, 113, 124

Roundhouse, The 51, 61, 156, 160, 169
Rumour, The 164, 182, 201, 223, 230, 231

Sex Pistols 81, 90, 133, 140, 142, 156, 162, 178, 196, 197, 212, 218
Shuttleworth, Paul 103, 125, 156, 222
Southend-on-Sea 78, 103, 117-120, 137, 205, 220
Stiff Records 19, 54, 62, 95-96, 134, 144, 148-150, 153, 159-163, 169, 171-174, 176-179, 181, 185, 187, 189, 193, 199-200, 204-209, 213, 222, 223, 225-226, 228-229, 231
Stiffs Greatest Stiffs – Live 190, 194-195, 201
Stone, Martin 18, 19, 38, 41, 59, 60, 123, 126, 143, 148, 160, 206, 219
Strummer, Joe 67, 81, 82, 101, 133, 143, 150, 156, 168, 172, 218
Swan Song 146, 153-154, 190, 191, 227
Sweet, Rachel 128, 129, 205, 207-209, 231

Tally Ho, The 44-45, 47, 49, 51, 57-58, 61, 64, 68, 72, 78, 217, 221
Treece, Richard 32, 56, 164
Thomas, Bruce 104, 174, 212
Thomas, Pete 61, 103, 122, 126, 169, 174, 191, 194, 195, 219
Timperley, Clive 99, 143, 218
Townshend, Pete 50, 52, 71, 74, 175
Top Of The Pops 40, 71, 92, 100, 108, 157, 177, 190

United Artists 34, 37, 47, 51, 56, 58, 83-84, 106-108, 110, 112, 144, 146, 148-149, 151, 162, 165, 200, 224-226, 229
Virgin Records 88, 89, 150, 159, 174, 182, 209, 230

Ward, Kingsley 53, 54, 92
Warwick, Stephen 30, 31
Watt-Roy, Norman 188, 192, 220-222
Welch, Chris 20, 70, 137, 198
Whaley, Ken 57
Williams, Terry 152, 154, 169, 210, 214, 223
Wings 63-65, 173, 216
Whiteman, Ian 18, 38, 123

Yes 23, 26-27, 36, 46, 49, 82, 106, 221

Zermati, Marc   81, 113, 155

www.ingramcontent.com/pod-product-compliance
Lightning Source LLC
Chambersburg PA
CBHW042129160426
43198CB00022B/2954